Taking Control of
Your Seizures

 **TREATMENTS** THAT WORK

Taking Control of Your Seizures

WORKBOOK

JOEL M. REITER
DONNA ANDREWS
CHARLOTTE REITER
W. CURT LAFRANCE, JR.

OXFORD
UNIVERSITY PRESS

OXFORD

UNIVERSITY PRESS

Oxford University Press is a department of the University of
Oxford. It furthers the University's objective of excellence in research,
scholarship, and education by publishing worldwide.

Oxford   New York
Auckland   Cape Town   Dar es Salaam   Hong Kong   Karachi
Kuala Lumpur   Madrid   Melbourne   Mexico City   Nairobi
New Delhi   Shanghai   Taipei   Toronto

With offices in
Argentina   Austria   Brazil   Chile   Czech Republic   France   Greece
Guatemala   Hungary   Italy   Japan   Poland   Portugal   Singapore
South Korea   Switzerland   Thailand   Turkey   Ukraine   Vietnam

Oxford is a registered trademark of Oxford University Press
in the UK and certain other countries.

Published in the United States of America by
Oxford University Press
198 Madison Avenue, New York, NY 10016

ISBN 978–0–19–933501–5

One of the most difficult problems confronting patients with various disorders and diseases is finding the best help available. Everyone is aware of friends or family who have sought treatment from a seemingly reputable practitioner, only to find out later from another doctor that the original diagnosis was wrong or that the treatments recommended were inappropriate, or perhaps even harmful. Most patients, or family members, address this problem by reading everything they can about their symptoms, seeking out information on the Internet, or aggressively "asking around" to tap knowledge from friends and acquaintances. Governments and healthcare policymakers are also aware that people in need do not always get the best treatments—something they refer to as *variability in healthcare practices*.

Now healthcare systems around the world are attempting to correct this variability by introducing *evidence-based practice*. This simply means that it is in everyone's interest that patients get the most up-to-date and effective care for a particular problem. Healthcare policymakers have also recognized that it is very useful to give consumers of healthcare as much information as possible, so that they can make intelligent decisions in a collaborative effort to improve physical health and mental health. This series, Treatments *ThatWork*, is designed to accomplish just that. Only the latest and most effective interventions for particular problems are described in user-friendly language. To be included in this series, each treatment program must pass the highest standards of evidence available, as determined by a scientific advisory board. Thus, when individuals suffering from these problems or their family members seek out an expert clinician who is familiar with these interventions and decides that they are appropriate, patients can have confidence that they are receiving the best care available. Of course, only your healthcare professional can decide on the right mix of treatments for you.

If you are one of the millions of people who have seizures, you may be looking for relief from the distress and limitations that can accompany your condition. This *Workbook* offers a comprehensive approach to improving seizure control and enhancing quality of life. Effective for both epileptic and nonepileptic seizures, this approach works best when a therapist or health professional is enlisted to work with you as a seizure counselor. This *Workbook* will provide guidance as you seek support and consult with your doctor about optimizing your drug therapy. You will observe and get to know your seizure triggers, learn to recognize your preseizure aura, and practice exercises that allow your brain to experience an awake relaxed state—a vital tool for reducing seizures. If you have nonepileptic seizures, your therapist should also use the companion *Treating Nonepileptic Seizures: Therapist Guide* in conjunction with this *Workbook* to guide you through treatment.

A unique aspect of the approach presented in this *Workbook* is that it offers insight into negative emotions, inner issues, and conflicts that affect your seizure control and well-being. As you progress through the *Workbook*, you are likely to notice a decrease in seizure frequency. The "taking control" process gives you the tools to manage your seizures, handle setbacks, and live a more fulfilling life.

David H. Barlow, Editor-in-Chief,
Treatments *ThatWork*
Boston, Massachusetts

Contents

Acknowledgments

The authors wish to express special thanks to Dr. Rosa Michaelis, who provided invaluable assistance in helping incorporate new Andrews/Reiter perspectives into this *Workbook*. She brought her wide-ranging intellect and compassion to the challenge of learning how to work with individuals with seizures and now leads the next generation of neurologists utilizing the "taking control" approach in Germany, Canada, and the United States.

Joel Reiter, Donna Andrews, and Charlotte Reiter wish to express their appreciation to W. Curt LaFrance, Jr., for initiating the open label study for nonepileptic seizures (NES) and conducting a randomized clinical trial at Rhode Island Hospital/Brown University and other centers on the effectiveness of this approach for patients with NES. We are grateful to him for giving patients with NES the opportunity to take control and we thank him for bringing his expertise on NES to this *Workbook*.

We greatly appreciate Max Hopkins, Dr. Albert Kastl, and Virginia Gadilauskas, long-standing board members of the Andrews/Reiter Epilepsy Research Program, for decades of wisdom and encouragement. We also wish to thank John and Ellen Park for sponsoring a conference on the Andrews/Reiter approach at the University of Toronto and for providing a venue for Dr. Rosa Michaelis' ongoing work with patients. Thanks to journalist Joshua Kors for exceptional reporting on his experience with the Andrews/Reiter approach. Thanks to Dr. Siegward Elsas for collaborating with Donna Andrews on a pilot project for patients with epilepsy at Oregon Health & Science University.

Andrea Flores Castillo skillfully converted illustrations into digital format. Barbara Harris and Phyllis Grannis transformed ideas into superb illustrations. Thank you!

We wish to acknowledge Dr. Christine Padesky for giving us permission to incorporate the Thought Record, an indispensable tool in self-examination, into the *Workbook*.

We are grateful to our patients and their families who bravely undertook the process described in the *Workbook*. By giving us their thoughtful and heartfelt feedback, they educated us about the impact of seizures on their lives and helped us fine-tune this approach. Thank you for teaching us how to be better counselors and doctors.

We cannot express enough thanks to Kate Scheinman, developmental editor at Oxford University Press, for her keen insight and graceful solutions to editorial challenges. We could not have completed this project without the vision and guidance of our superb editors Sarah Harrington and Andrea Zekus. We thank Craig Panner for connecting us with the OUP Treatments *ThatWork* group. To all the fine staff at OUP, we extend abundant thanks.

Taking Control of
Your Seizures

CHAPTER 1	Introduction for the Patient: Understanding Seizures

This patient *Workbook* is intended to guide you, your physician, and your seizure counselor through the process of taking control of your seizures. The approach outlined in this *Workbook* is unique in that it emphasizes a partnership between the patient, physician, and seizure counselor in which all of you work together toward effective management of your seizure disorder. The following explanation will familiarize you with some of the facts about seizures and the session-by-session process of "taking control."

What Is a Seizure?

Seizures are common and are characterized by recurring, time-limited episodes of changes in behavior, movement, and/or senses, with or without an alteration of consciousness, during which a person may or may not be aware of his or her surroundings. Seizures typically last from a few seconds to several minutes. In some people, seizures may also involve involuntary movements of the arms, legs, or face, strange feelings, or sensations, and at times bowel or bladder incontinence. Sometimes seizures have a known cause, such as a head injury, infection of the brain, or tumor. In these cases, the epileptic seizures are caused by abnormal brain cell function and are associated with epileptic activity on an electroencephalogram (EEG). Approximately half of the time, the cause of epileptic seizures is not known, described by the terms, "idiopathic" (genetic cause), or "cause unknown". Idiopathic seizures are frequently associated with EEG abnormalities.

Other seizures occur that are not associated with abnormal brain cell function, and when observed on video EEG, these events are not associated with epileptic activity on EEG. These events are referred to as nonepileptic seizures (NES). Either epileptic or nonepileptic seizures may be associated with stressors; with anxious, depressed, or repressed emotions; or with past traumatic experiences. When NES are associated with such stressors, they are called "psychogenic nonepileptic seizures."

Why Is It Important to Understand Your Seizure Disorder?

There are two main reasons that it is important to understand as much as possible about your seizures. The first reason is that often the fear of having a seizure does more damage than the seizures themselves. An individual with seizures may consider him- or herself an invalid who has a frightening, unpredictable disease unless he or she learns about the condition, including the fact that the vast majority of people with seizures are able to lead full and active lives.

The second reason for making the effort to understand your seizures is that this understanding is often the key to reducing the frequency of seizures and the ill effects that seizures may have on your life as a whole. Even if your seizures are eliminated by medications, knowing about your condition will help you cope positively and maintain good seizure control throughout your life.

If you are one of the many patients for whom medicines alone are not completely effective, your participation in this program is of special importance. The more you learn about the multitude of factors in your life that affect your health in general, and your seizures in particular, the more you will be able to contribute to the effectiveness of your treatment program.

What Kind of Seizure(s) Do You Have?

Most often, seizures begin for reasons that you and your family do not understand. For this reason, the onset of seizures can be a dramatic and frightening event. To help your physician identify the probable cause of your particular kind of seizures, your physician will take a detailed history (i.e., ask a series of questions about your past and present health status) and perform a physical examination. You will also be asked to undergo a series of medical tests, including an EEG or a video EEG and magnetic resonance imaging (MRI) brain scan, if you have not already had the test(s).

After this complete medical investigation, usually your physician will be able to tell you whether your seizures were caused by known damage to the brain (such as accident or illness). If your seizures are termed "idiopathic" or "cause unknown", this means that medical science does not understand the reason for your seizures and that your body and brain appear otherwise healthy.

What Are the Different Kinds of Seizures?

Seizures are divided among three categories:

- epileptic
- physiologic nonepileptic events (PNEE)
- psychogenic nonepileptic seizures (NES)

The simple distinctions are as follows:

- Epilepsy is caused by abnormal brain cell firing.
- PNEE is caused by a metabolic or medical issue, but it is not epilepsy.
- Psychogenic NES are caused by underlying psychological conflicts or stressors, and are many times associated with depression, anxiety, trauma, or personality issues.

There are several kinds of seizure presentations or semiologies.

Common types of seizures, including their current and old-fashioned names, are described below:

1. **Generalized tonic clonic or "Grand mal" seizures**: With no warning or minimal warning, such as dizziness or a full feeling in the stomach, a person loses consciousness, stiffens, and jerks.
2. **Absence or "Petit mal" seizures**: For a few seconds, the person loses contact and "spaces out." Onset for this type of seizure is usually prior to age 20.
3. **Complex partial or temporal lobe or focal dyscognitive seizures**: A person loses contact with his or her surroundings, and cannot communicate. Often there are movements such as smacking of the lips, wringing of the hands, jerking or tightening of an arm or leg. These seizures may be preceded by a warning known as a "pre-seizure aura".

4. **Myoclonic seizures**: Quick, lightning-like jerks of the limbs, head, or body, usually not associated with change in level of consciousness.
5. **"Drop attacks" or Atonic seizures**: A person loses awareness and quickly drops to the ground. Injuries may occur with the falls.

Nonepileptic seizures can resemble any of the seizure semiologies described above; however, when NES are observed on video EEG, no epileptic activity is observed. Nonepileptic seizures are not eplilepsy.

What Is the Physician's Role in Treating Seizures?

Dr job is to diagnose & treat

A physician—usually a neurologist or epileptologist—can help you by diagnosing the type of seizures you have and determining the probable cause of your seizures. Epileptic seizures are best treated by neurologists. Nonepileptic seizures are best treated by mental health professionals (psychiatrists, psychologists, therapists, or counselors) who are familiar with NES therapies. Your physician can also select and prescribe medications, as well as order periodic lab tests to help determine the amount of medicine you need to reduce the frequency of your seizures. Another important role of the physician is to clearly explain to you the beneficial reasons for taking medications, as well as the possible side effects, or to recommend stopping certain medications.

In addition, the approach outlined in this *Workbook* suggests a new role for the physician: that of assisting *you* to "take control" of aspects of your life, including your seizures and the effect that seizures have on your health and well-being. Usually this entails referring you to a trained seizure counselor, who will act as your guide as you proceed through the process of taking control, outlined in this *Workbook*.

What Is Your Role?

The standard medical approach to seizures assigns the patient a narrow role—that of taking medicines regularly as prescribed. While this is an important responsibility, our research shows that there are many additional factors besides drug therapy that determine whether seizure frequency is reduced and whether the patient learns to cope effectively with having seizures. For example, learning to recognize the sensation

1. I can recognise my symptoms

that precedes your seizures (pre-seizure aura) and identifying the major stresses in your life that affect seizure frequency are important steps in gaining control and learning to cope successfully.

> *No physician, counselor, family member or friend can do this work of self-observation and self-discovery for you. Only your efforts and active participation in this process will enable you to reach your optimum level of wellness, including seizure control. It is for this reason that you are the most important person in this process of taking control of your seizures. The goal of this process of taking control is to allow you to gain increasingly greater responsibility for your health, your seizures, and for finding fulfillment in your life.*

goal

What Is the Role of the Seizure Counselor?

Clinicians who utilize the methods of "taking control" of seizures that are outlined in this *Workbook* often will refer patients for weekly appointments with a seizure counselor. A seizure counselor is a person with a special interest and training in working with people with seizures. Your seizure counselor might be a psychiatrist or a neurologist (MD), a psychologist (PhD), a licensed counselor such as a marriage family therapist (MFT), a licensed social worker (LSW), a registered nurse (RN), or a nurse practitioner (NP) who has experience treating patients with seizures using this *Workbook*. While some physicians might prefer to see their patients themselves rather than referring to a seizure counselor, many do not because of the time required for this intensive treatment program—approximately 3–4 months of weekly one-hour sessions.

Because your seizure counselor will be working with you over a period of time on all aspects of your personal life, it is important that you find someone with whom you feel comfortable. You will need to have a seizure counselor who you can talk to—someone with whom you can share your thoughts, feelings, and life experiences. Although it takes time to get to know any counselor and develop a close therapeutic relationship, keep these criteria in mind as you participate in the process of selecting a seizure counselor. Ultimately, the experience you gain of working with your seizure counselor can be shared with others, such as family, friends, or others in your support network.

How Can You Find a Seizure Counselor if Your Physician Is Unable to Give You a Referral?

Ideally, your seizure counselor will be someone who is comfortable with patients with seizures, both epileptic and nonepileptic, and who has attended a training seminar on treatment for seizures. In that case, the counselor will have specific information about the treatment sessions, in addition to previous training and experience in counseling and/or patient education. If your physician is not familiar with any trained seizure counselors in your area, you or your physician may wish to write or telephone the closest Neuropsychiatry Department or Epilepsy Program for the names of available counselors in your area.

If you find that there are no trained seizure counselors in your area, you and your physician have a number of possible options. You may wish to contact one or more local counselors to see if they would be interested in working with you in this process. If so, perhaps they would agree to attend the next available training seminar offered on Treatment for Epileptic Seizures or NES. Professionals interested in receiving training for epilepsy or NES can contact the authors for training opportunities.

If this is not possible, you might be able to find a recommended counselor who is willing to use this *Workbook* as a guide for your sessions, without having specialized training in working with people with seizures. This counselor could then obtain ongoing consultation and guidance from your physician regarding medication and other aspects of seizure disorders with which he or she is unfamiliar.

Couldn't You Use This *Workbook* on Your Own to Learn as Much as Possible About How to "Take Control" of Your Own Seizures?

It is strongly recommended that you do not attempt to use this *Workbook* on your own, without the help of a physician or seizure counselor. The reason for this firm recommendation is that our experience shows that the greatest benefits from this "taking control" process have come through encountering the blind spots—the misconceptions and powerful gut reactions—that a counselor can work with you to help you uncover.

Some of the material in this *Workbook*, particularly the portions that deal with enhancing wellness and promoting a healthy lifestyle, is available in many self-help books, and it might be of benefit to you to read about and work with on your own. In addition, many patients and their families can benefit from learning more about seizures by reading the informational sections of this *Workbook*. But the true potential of this program—the possibility of changing your life—lies in the power of the counselor-patient relationship.

You will need the guidance of a trained counselor to help you through the painful moments, to support your growing independence and self-esteem, and to challenge your inner blocks to reaching your optimum potential. We urge you to take full advantage of the opportunity that this *Workbook* offers by seeking out a physician and counselor who will work with you in this process of taking control of your seizures and your life.

How Do the Patient, Physician, and Seizure Counselor Work Together in the Process of "Taking Control?"

The process of "taking control" of your seizures is a learning experience, similar to going to school or learning how to ride a bicycle. Your physician and seizure counselor will work with you to guide you through the process of learning positive ways to cope with your seizures. But like any other learning situation, your teacher can show you how to read or ride a bike but cannot do it for you. If you do not do your homework, you don't learn your lessons. If you do not practice your skills, you do not get better at them. In this process of "taking control," the responsibility for making the effort, and learning new skills and applying them—that responsibility is yours and yours alone.

If you can look at your seizures as something for you to learn about in order to cope most effectively with, you have made an important start. If you decide to work with this approach, this *Workbook* will serve as a resource for you, guiding you through the process of "taking control." This will include learning how your thoughts, moods, physical reactions, behaviors, and environment influence your life experiences (Figure 1.1), how these aspects affect your seizures, and how your doctor and possibly medicines can help you—and most of all, how you can help yourself to live comfortably free of or with your seizures.

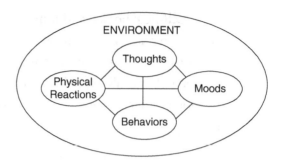

Figure 1.1

Five Aspects of Your Life Experiences
© 1986, Center for Cognitive Therapy, MindOverMood.com

What Results Can You Expect if You Undertake This "Taking Control" Program?

Most people who are motivated to undertake an in-depth program such as this one are among the many individuals with seizures that are not well controlled with medications. Others, whose seizures are fully controlled with medication, undertake this program because they want to minimize medication dosage and drug side effects and to improve the quality of their lives. Of those individuals who complete this program, many will be able to stop their seizures altogether, through a combination of medication, lifestyle changes, and psychological work. For others, because of the nature of their particular kind of seizures, eliminating all seizures will not be possible.

What *is* possible for everyone who decides to go ahead with this program is a great improvement in his or her ability to cope with having seizures. While not all kinds of seizures are totally "controllable" in the sense of eliminating them, everyone can learn to control how seizures affect his or her life. This means that you have the possibility of reducing the negative effects of having seizures, while enhancing the positive effects of increased self-esteem and level of wellness. Despite having a chronic illness, you can gain a sense of being "in control" of your seizures, of your life, and of your well-being.

How Do You Begin This Process of "Taking Control?"

Before you see your seizure counselor for your next visit, it is important that you do the following:

1. Complete the Seizure Log at the end of this chapter, document every day the number of seizures you have; and

2. Complete the first assignment worksheet exercise on distinguishing situations, moods, and thoughts at the end of this chapter. This exercise will help you and your seizure counselor discuss some of the important topics during your first session. ***Make sure to bring all paperwork (sessions, logs, assignments) with you to every session.***

Prior to your upcoming visit, complete the entire *Workbook* session, and write down any questions that arise. You will cover one session each visit. When you come for follow-up, you will discuss the content of this session that you completed beforehand. At the end of the appointment, you will receive instructions for the next chapter of the *Workbook* entitled, "Session 1: Making the Decision to Begin the Process of Taking Control," which outlines each step of the process, so that you will be aware of exactly what is involved. In the next session, you will prepare a list reasons that you want to "take control" and reasons that you may not. Most important, you need to come to your next appointment ready to answer the question: "Do I want to begin the process of taking control?"

Assignment

EXERCISE: *Distinguishing Situations, Moods, and Thoughts*

Worksheet 1.1 is an exercise to help you better distinguish your thoughts, moods, and situations. Write on the line at the right whether the item in the left column is a thought, mood (emotion), or situation (event). The first three items have been completed as examples.

Worksheet 1.1 Distinguishing Situations, Moods, and Thoughts

	Situation, Mood, or Thought?
1. Nervous	mood
2. At home	situation
3. I'm not going to be able to do this.	thought
4. Sad	Mood
5. Talking to a friend on the phone	Situation
6. Irritated	Mood
7. Driving in my car	Situation
8. I'm always going to feel this way.	thought
9. At work	Situation

10.	(I'm) going crazy.	thought
11.	Angry	Mood
12.	(I'm) no good.	thought
13.	4:00 P.M.	Situation
14.	Something terrible is going to happen.	thought
15.	Nothing ever goes right.	thought
16.	Discouraged	Mood
17.	I'll never get over this.	thought
18.	Sitting in a restaurant	Situation
19.	(I'm) out of control.	thought
20.	(I'm) a failure.	thought
21.	Talking on the phone to my mom	Situation
22.	She's being inconsiderate.	thought
23.	Depressed	Mood
24.	I'm a loser.	thought
25.	Guilty feeling about something in the past.	Mood
26.	At my son's house	Situation
27.	(I) believe I'm having a heart attack.	thought
28.	I've been taken advantage of.	thought
29.	Lying in bed trying to go to sleep	Situation
30.	This isn't going to work out.	thought
31.	Shame	Mood
32.	(I'm) going to lose everything I've got.	thought
33.	Panic	Mood

From Dennis Greenberger and Christine A. Padesky, *Mind Over Mood*, The Guilford Press, © 1995.
© 1986, Center for Cognitive Therapy, MindOverMood.com

Following are answers to Worksheet 1.1. Check your responses and write the correct answer by your original one. Review the pertinent sections of this chapter to clarify any differences between your answers and the ones given.

1. Nervous .... Mood

2. At home .... Situation

3. I'm not going to be able to do this. .... Thought

4. Sad .... Mood

5. Talking to a friend on the phone .... Situation

6. Irritated .... Mood

7. Driving in my car .... Situation

8. I'm always going to feel this way. .... Thought

9. At work .... Situation

10. I'm going crazy. .... Thought

11. Angry .... Mood

12. I'm no good. .... Thought

13. 4:00 p.m. .... Situation

14. Something terrible is going to happen. .... Thought

15. Nothing ever goes right. .... Thought

16. Discouraged .... Mood

17. I'll never get over this. .... Thought

18. Sitting in a restaurant .... Situation

19. I'm out of control. .... Thought

20. I'm a failure. .... Thought

21. Talking on the phone to my mom .... Situation

22. She's being inconsiderate. .... Thought

23. Depressed .... Mood

24. I'm a loser. .... Thought

25. Guilty feeling about something in the past. .... Mood

26. At my son's house .... Situation

27. I believe I'm having a heart attack. .... Thought

28. I've been taken advantage of. .... Thought

29. Lying in bed trying to go to sleep .... Situation

30. This isn't going to work out. .... Thought

31. Shame .... Mood

32. I'm going to lose everything I've got. .... Thought

33. Panic .... Mood

If you had difficulty distinguishing among situations, moods, and thoughts, review them with your counselor, as it is important to distinguish these parts of your experience in order to make changes in your life. By separating these components from each other, you will be better able to make changes that are important to you.

A Note About This *Workbook*: Origins, Research, and Usage

This workbook was initially published as *Taking Control of Your Epilepsy: A Workbook for Patients and Professionals* by Joel Reiter, MD, Donna Andrews, PhD, and Charlotte Janis, FNP. The current *Workbook* incorporates modifications for nonepileptic seizures (NES) by W. Curt LaFrance, Jr., MD, MPH and includes updates by Dr. Reiter and Dr. Andrews.

Using the modified *Workbook*, results from two treatment studies (an open-label treatment trial for patients with NES (LaFrance et al., 2009) and a multi-site pilot randomized clinical trial (LaFrance et al., 2014) reveal a significant reduction in NES *and* improvement in depression and anxiety symptoms, along with improved quality of life. In a pilot study (Elsas et al., 2011) and a retrospective study (Michaelis et al., 2012) using this approach for patients with epileptic seizures, half demonstrated a significant reduction in seizures and all reported better quality of life.

This *Workbook* provides a systematic treatment approach for patients with epileptic seizures and for patients with NES. The *Workbook* has also been used successfully for treating patients with other somatoform disorders.

For patients, *Taking Control of Your Seizures* provides a validated, session-by-session approach for helping you take control of your seizures and your life. At the same time, it provides essential information for your treating professionals (which might include physicians, psychologists, therapists, social workers, nurses, and others) to guide you through the "taking control" process. You will need to purchase your own *Workbook* and use it to complete the weekly reading and assignments. You will then review this material in appointments with your seizure counselor.

For patients with NES, your seizure counselor will use the companion *Treating Nonepileptic Seizures Therapist Guide* to conduct weekly sessions. Seizure counselors who desire training and other interested professionals may contact Dr. LaFrance at Rhode Island Hospital, 593 Eddy Street, Providence, Rhode Island, USA, 02903. Phone 401-444-3534. Fax 401-444-3298.

The authors have integrated feedback from clinicians who have administered this treatment, and from patients who have completed the *Workbook* with their seizure counselors. Continuing input from patients and professionals is welcomed and encouraged.

References

LaFrance WC Jr, Miller IW, Ryan CE, Blum AS, Solomon DA, Kelley JE, Keitner GI. Cognitive behavioral therapy for psychogenic nonepileptic seizures. *Epilepsy and Behavior* 2009;14(4):591–596.

LaFrance WC Jr, Baird GL, Barry JJ, Blum AS, FrankWebb A, Keitner GI, Machan JT, Miller I, Szaflarski JP … Multicenter pilot treatment trial for psychogenic nonepileptic seizures: a randomized clinical trial. *JAMA Psychiatry* 2014;71(9):997–1005.

Elsas SM, Gregory WL, White G, Navarro G, Salinsky MC, Andrews DJ. Aura interruption: the Andrews/Reiter behavioral intervention may reduce seizures and improve quality of life—a pilot trial. *Epilepsy and Behavior* 2011 Dec;22(4):765–772.

Michaelis R, Schonfeld W, Elsas SM. Trigger self-control and seizure arrest in the Andrews/Reiter behavioral approach to epilepsy: a retrospective analysis of seizure frequency. *Epilepsy and Behavior* 2012 Mar;23(3):266–271.

SEIZURE LOG   For the Week of _7 31 / 22 to 8 / 6 / 22_   Init:_____
ID:_____
Instructions: Please fill in the diary at the end of each day to record the number and descriptions   Week: _____
listed. This information will be reviewed with your physician at each appointment.   Type:_____

SUNDAY _7_ / _31_ / _22_ (day 1)
Number of Seizures:_____
Time(s) of day:_____
Duration (sec or min):_____
Description:_____
Location(s):_____
Severity (1: mild, 2: mod, 3: severe):_____
Trigger(s):_____
Precursor(s):_____
Improved with:_____
Impact on your day:_____
Impact on others:_____

MONDAY _8_ / _1_ / _22_ (day 2)
Number of Seizures:_____
Time(s) of day:_____
Duration:_____
Description:_____
Location(s):_____
Severity (1: mild, 2: mod, 3: severe):_____
Trigger(s):_____
Precursor(s):_____
Improved with:_____
Impact on your day:_____
Impact on others:_____

TUESDAY _8_ / _2_ / _22_ (day 3)
Number of Seizures:_____
Time(s) of day:_____
Duration:_____
Description:_____
Location(s):_____
Severity (1: mild, 2: mod, 3: severe):_____
Trigger(s):_____
Precursor(s):_____
Improved with:_____
Impact on your day:_____
Impact on others:_____

WEDNESDAY _8_ / _3_ / _22_ (day 4)
Number of Seizures:_____
Time(s) of day:_____
Duration:_____
Description:_____
Location(s):_____
Severity (1: mild, 2: mod, 3: severe):_____
Trigger(s):_____
Precursor(s):_____
Improved with:_____
Impact on your day:_____
Impact on others:_____

Total: _Ø_____   Rater: _____

THURSDAY _8_ / _4_ / _22_ (day 5)
Number of Seizures:_____
Time(s) of day:_____
Duration:_____
Description:_____
Location(s):_____
Severity (1: mild, 2: mod, 3: severe):_____
Trigger(s):_____
Precursor(s):_____
Improved with:_____
Impact on your day:_____
Impact on others:_____

FRIDAY _8_ / _5_ / _22_ (day 6)
Number of Seizures:_____
Time(s) of day:_____
Duration:_____
Description:_____
Location(s):_____
Severity (1: mild, 2: mod, 3: severe):_____
Trigger(s):_____
Precursor(s):_____
Improved with:_____
Impact on your day:_____
Impact on others:_____

SATURDAY _8_ / _6_ / _22_ (day 7)
Number of Seizures:_____
Time(s) of day:_____
Duration:_____
Description:_____
Location(s):_____
Severity (1: mild, 2: mod, 3: severe):_____
Trigger(s):_____
Precursor(s):_____
Improved with:_____
Impact on your day:_____
Impact on others:_____

Use **the space below or on back** to describe any significant information not covered in this record:
_____
_____
_____
_____
_____

Were you successful in stopping any seizures this week:
yes ☐   no ☐

Please mark which seizures you stopped with an asterisk (*).

SEIZURE LOG   For the Week of 8 / 7 , 22 to 9 , 13 , 22   Init:_____

Instructions: Please fill in the diary at the end of each day to record the number and descriptions   ID:_____

listed. This information will be reviewed with your physician at each appointment.   Week:_____

   Type:_____

SUNDAY 8 / 7 / 22 (day 1)
Number of Seizures:_____1_____
Time(s) of day:_____morining_____
Duration (sec or min):___3min_____
Description:_Convulsions_____
Location(s):___at work_____
Severity (1: mild, 2: mod, 3: severe):___1___
Trigger(s): didn't understand job
Precursor(s): headache
Improved with: take anxiety pill
Impact on your day: had to go home
Impact on others:_____

THURSDAY __/__/__ (day 5)
Number of Seizures:_____
Time(s) of day:_____
Duration:_____
Description:_____
Location(s):_____
Severity (1: mild, 2: mod, 3: severe):_____
Trigger(s):_____
Precursor(s):_____
Improved with:_____
Impact on your day:_____
Impact on others:_____

MONDAY __/__/__ (day 2)
Number of Seizures:_____
Time(s) of day:_____
Duration:_____
Description:_____
Location(s):_____
Severity (1: mild, 2: mod, 3: severe):_____
Trigger(s):_____
Precursor(s):_____
Improved with:_____
Impact on your day:_____
Impact on others:_____

FRIDAY __/__/__ (day 6)
Number of Seizures:_____
Time(s) of day:_____
Duration:_____
Description:_____
Location(s):_____
Severity (1: mild, 2: mod, 3: severe):_____
Trigger(s):_____
Precursor(s):_____
Improved with:_____
Impact on your day:_____
Impact on others:_____

TUESDAY __/__/__ (day 3)
Number of Seizures:_____
Time(s) of day:_____
Duration:_____
Description:_____
Location(s):_____
Severity (1: mild, 2: mod, 3: severe):_____
Trigger(s):_____
Precursor(s):_____
Improved with:_____
Impact on your day:_____
Impact on others:_____

SATURDAY __/__/__ (day 7)
Number of Seizures:_____
Time(s) of day:_____
Duration:_____
Description:_____
Location(s):_____
Severity (1: mild, 2: mod, 3: severe):_____
Trigger(s):_____
Precursor(s):_____
Improved with:_____
Impact on your day:_____
Impact on others:_____

WEDNESDAY __/__/__ (day 4)
Number of Seizures:_____
Time(s) of day:_____
Duration:_____
Description:_____
Location(s):_____
Severity (1: mild, 2: mod, 3: severe):_____
Trigger(s):_____
Precursor(s):_____
Improved with:_____
Impact on your day:_____
Impact on others:_____

Total: _____   **Rater:** _____

Use **the space below or on back** to describe any significant information not covered in this record:

_____
_____
_____
_____
_____
_____

Were you successful in stopping any seizures this week:
yes ☑   no ☐

Please mark which seizures you stopped with an asterisk (*).

CHAPTER 2

Session 1: Making the Decision to Begin the Process of Taking Control

Unlike other medical conditions, such as high blood pressure or diabetes, where the symptoms may not be noticeable, the symptoms of seizures are obvious and are often alarming to oneself and other people. For some people with seizures, the idea that their brains (and sometimes their bladders) may be temporarily "out of control" is particularly difficult to accept. As a result, many people with seizures, especially those for whom medications are only partly effective, feel that their lives are helplessly "out of control."

Taking control of your seizures means, first and foremost, learning to take control of your life, whether or not your seizures are under control. You will need to learn how *your* life, with all its ups and downs, interacts with your seizures in particular and your health in general. Many people with seizures develop a pattern of blaming problems in their lives on their seizures. While seizures can certainly be a tough problem to cope with, the attitude that you are helpless because your seizures are the cause of all your difficulties will prevent you from having the kind of life you would choose for yourself.

The question is whether you allow your disorder to control you, or whether you choose to develop as a person—able to take control of your life and well-being. This is what is meant by "making the decision to take control."

What Exactly Is Involved in Working on the "Taking Control" Sessions Outlined in This *Workbook* With a Seizure Counselor?

The most effective way to give you a picture of what this process involves is to briefly review the sessions outlined in this *Workbook*. While you may attempt to use this on your own, you will get the most benefit by working with a counselor who has experience in helping people who have seizures. Therefore each of these sessions is designed to be covered in one or more visits with a seizure counselor. Between appointments, you will be asked to make observations about relevant aspects of your life, to write about assigned topics in your journal, and to keep a Seizure Log in which you record the occurrence of seizures. At times you will be asked to practice a given exercise dealing with self-observation or relaxation on a daily basis. In addition, each week you will be reading the next chapter, or "session," and writing pertinent information in your *Workbook* in preparation for your next appointment with your seizure counselor.

The sessions of this *Workbook* are designed to be covered sequentially, but you will find that each of them covers valuable concepts that you may wish to come back to, again and again. In 30 years of working intensively with over 2,600 individuals with seizures, the authors have found the content offered in these sessions to be essential to enable the majority of patients to take control of their seizures and their lives.

Introduction for the Patient: Understanding Seizures (Chapter 1)

Upon agreement to enroll in this treatment, you received an introduction to the program. The introduction describes the difference between different seizure types, including epileptic seizures and nonepileptic seizures, the importance of understanding your seizures, and the use of the *Workbook* in this treatment.

Session 1: Making the Decision to Begin the Process of Taking Control (Chapter 2)

In this session, you will look in depth at what this approach has to offer and will explore your own motivating factors and obstacles to taking control of your seizures. In this session, you will make the decision whether or not to begin this work with a seizure counselor.

Session 2: Getting Support (Chapter 3)

Many people who begin this process lack the supportive relationships they need and often feel isolated and lonely. This session offers skills to help you avoid isolation, improve communication, and develop positive relationships with others.

Session 3: Deciding About Your Drug Therapy (Chapter 4)

This session will be scheduled to include you and your seizure counselor, in collaboration with your prescribing physician. This session encourages you to discuss and decide jointly what level of medication will be most beneficial for you while undertaking this "taking control" program. While too little medication may result in more frequent seizures (followed by periods when it is difficult to communicate or to think clearly), too much medication may leave you drowsy, confused, or unable to remember what you read or discussed at your last counseling appointment. Session 3 is your opportunity for a "team conference" to determine the most beneficial drug regimen for you and to clear up any questions you may have about your anticonvulsant drug therapy.

Session 4: Learning to Observe Your Triggers (Chapter 5)

Triggers are factors that often bring about, or "trigger," seizures. Common examples are situations that lead to an emotional state of excitement or frustration, skipping medications, or overusing alcohol or drugs. In Session 4, you will begin to identify and observe your own triggers, in order to eventually enable you to reduce the frequency of your seizures.

Session 5: Channeling Negative Emotions Into Productive Outlets (Chapter 6)

The triggers you observed in Session 4 usually lead to seizures because they first produce a negative emotion, such as fear, anger, or hurt. Session 5 provides skills for dealing positively with negative states, including expression to yourself and others, self-acceptance, and seeing your negative state as a demand for action.

Session 6: Relaxation Training: Experiencing the Sensation of the Brain Changing Itself (Chapter 7)

This session offers a large variety of different methods and skills that people find effective for reducing tension and achieving relaxation. These

Hunter to come to this

get rid of seizures
work | drive | make money

body pain
headache

methods can potentially offer you greater control over your seizures, as well as enhance your physical and psychological health.

Session 7: Identifying Your Pre-Seizure Aura (Chapter 8)

The pre-seizure aura consists of a symptom or sensation that precedes a seizure. Learning to identify your aura is important because you will be able to utilize this pre-seizure warning to take control. Recognizing your aura may help you to prevent seizures, or to avoid injury or embarrassment because you are aware that a seizure is about to take place.

Session 8: Dealing With External Life Stresses (Chapter 9)

"Dealing with life stresses" means both gaining awareness of the factors of your life that are stressful for you—and taking responsibility for relieving those that are within your control. With long-term efforts, this process can have a dramatic impact on reducing your seizure frequency and increasing well-being.

Session 9: Dealing With Internal Issues and Conflicts (Chapter 10)

The feelings, conflicts, and issues that are part of a person's inner being affect overall health as much or more than external stresses do. Examples are feelings of inadequacy, constantly blaming others for one's difficulties, and chronic states of anxiety or depression. Becoming aware of these issues and learning to deal with them are the focus of in-depth therapy, which some individuals who reach Session 9 decide to undertake with their seizure counselor or another trained therapist.

Session 10: Enhancing Personal Wellness (Chapter 11)

Wellness includes all the lifestyle choices that affect your bodily health, and extends beyond the physical into the realm of emotion, spirit, and meaning. This session allows you to move toward reaching your optimum level of wellness, by reviewing your past successes in coping with seizures and assisting you to make new goals for ongoing self-care. This session also addresses common lifestyle factors that can contribute to an increased occurrence of seizures, such as sleep issues, nutritional aspects, and sensitivity to sensory stressors.

Session 11: Other Symptoms Associated With Seizures (Chapter 12)

"Other seizure symptoms" include altered states such as *déjà vu*, out-of-body experiences, memory problems and scattered thinking, as well as behavioral symptoms such as a slowing of activity or sudden outbursts of anger. The goal of Session 11 is to recognize, accept, and cope positively with your "other seizure symptoms."

Taking Control: An Ongoing Process (Chapter 13)

At this point, most people want to ask: "Where do I go from here?" The choice is yours; the answer lies within you. Now it is up to you to determine how you want to continue this ongoing process of taking control. You play an important part in your continued growth—the choice of whether to live your life to the fullest, and the choice to make a path that leads you to where you want to go. YOU CAN DO IT!

How Do I Know What the Process of Taking Control Will Be Like for Me?

The process of taking control is different for each person who makes the decision to undertake it. Each person starts this process with his or her own unique inner resources and potential, and will be dealing with his or her own personality, health status, relationships, and set of life circumstances. Because each individual is so different, no one can tell you exactly what you will experience or what will be required in order for you to reach the point where you will feel in control of your seizures and your life.

To help clarify the descriptions of the various sessions outlined in this workbook, examples are provided throughout the text, which describe how one person may have experienced that particular step in the "taking control" process. These examples are based on real case studies of individuals who participated in this program, but details have been changed to protect the identity of the patient. (In keeping with the standard of confidentiality maintained by all healthcare professionals, your physician and seizure counselor will keep all verbal conversations and medical records confidential, to be released only with your signed consent.)

The following examples are provided to help give you a realistic idea of what the process of "taking control" entails. (The examples and case studies in this *Workbook* do not tell the stories of specific patients, but are written to encapsulate experiences common to many people who have seizures.)

TAKING CONTROL: AN EXAMPLE

Mike began having seizures at age 19 while he was in college. Several times a week, he would notice an unpleasant smell and then have a generalized tonic-clonic seizure ("grand mal" seizure). After he was put on anticonvulsant medications, he continued to have complex partial seizures with a brief loss of consciousness. Because of his seizures, he stopped college and moved back with his parents. For the next five years, he did not work or go to school and continued to have seizures despite three or four medications. He was seen by several experts at large university medical centers, who recommended increasing his anticonvulsant medicines.

Each time his medications were increased, Mike felt more drugged, while his seizure frequency stayed about the same. He wanted to be on less medication because he felt tired all the time and it was hard to think clearly. He didn't like living at home—he found it hard to deal with his strict father and overprotective, loving mother. He wanted to drive, to work, to go to school, to date girls, and eventually to marry and have a family—but he kept having at least one seizure a week. In his mind, having seizures meant he could not do any of the things he wanted to do with his life.

It was at this point that Mike started to work with a seizure counselor, at the suggestion of his neurologist. He learned about his pre-seizure aura (the unpleasant smell), triggers to his seizures, and relaxation methods. During this time, he continued to live at home, spending his time watching TV and listening to music. He had no job and he was not going to school; he kept to himself and rarely got together with friends. Mike seemed motivated not to have seizures, but he continued to have as many as before—and those seizures were totally controlling his life.

Because Mike was motivated, his seizure counselor told him that taking control of his life could give him a chance to reduce the frequency of his seizures. With the support of his seizure counselor, Mike decided he was ready to learn about his feelings and to get moving in his life. For the first time, he began to write about his emotional reactions in his journal, and to talk openly about his feelings with his seizure counselor. He got a job as a volunteer—earning no money, but at least his employer accepted the fact that sometimes he had seizures at work and was informed on what to do if that happened. He worked regularly at this job and started taking classes at a local college. He continued to have seizures, but less often.

Then he decided not to let his seizures prevent him from having an active social life. He began to go out with friends he met at college. After several months of seeing each other regularly, he developed a close relationship with a girlfriend. When he began to share with her some of his feelings about having seizures and his experience of working with his seizure counselor, he found her to be understanding and supportive. Mutual sharing deepened their relationship and allowed trust to grow between them. Despite the fact that his seizures continued, he had become so competent at his volunteer job that he was offered a paying job at the same office where he had been a volunteer. Now that he could afford it, he got a place of his own. Several months later, he and his girlfriend got married.

Over the next year, Mike learned to recognize tensions in his life that created the type of feelings that preceded his seizures. He was able to talk about his feelings before the tensions got out of hand. He also got in the habit of taking brisk, long walks several times a week. He looked and felt more relaxed. His seizures came under control—while still taking two medications—and after two years without seizures, he finally got a driver's license.

In Mike's case, he took control of his life, not his seizures. He learned that he could take responsibility for having a full life, even with seizures. He was fortunate that his seizures did eventually stop, because it is not possible for every person with seizures to eliminate all seizures. But even if he had continued to have seizures, one could say that he had made the decision and completed the process of "taking control" of his seizures and his life.

Taking Control: What It Means For Six Different People With Seizures

Taking control depends on the type of seizures each person has and how having seizures is affecting that person's life. Here are examples from six people who have experienced seizures.

J. S.: Taking control is accepting that she has seizures and learning to sit down before she has a seizure, thus preventing injuries that might otherwise result from falling.

M. N.: Taking control is going to school and traveling around the world with an orchestra.

L. P.: Taking control is learning to understand why she is angry and anxious and learning to redefine her relationship with her mother and husband.

A. R.: Taking control is taking medicines regularly, not skipping doses, and realizing that medicines are his friends since they prevent generalized seizures.

S. H.: Taking control is getting the courage to begin a new career as a teacher.

D. F.: Taking control is learning to live independently and to find fulfillment in her art.

Each session has a "GOAT" to help structure your work and session time.

Goal

Throughout this *Workbook*, each session will contain a goal that summarizes your work for that particular session. The goal of the first session is to make the decision to begin the process of taking control.

Obstacles

For every session, you and your seizure counselor will discuss some of the obstacles that other people have had to overcome in order to achieve that session's goal. This discussion of obstacles helps to acknowledge that the step you are trying to take is not easy. In fact, it is normal and OK to feel unsure and ambivalent about going ahead with the process of "taking control." The following list includes some of the most frequent obstacles that people with seizures experience as they make the decision to begin the process of taking control.

Select (circle) the one(s) that you think apply to you, if applicable:

- Not wanting responsibility (preferring to be taken care of by family members and to have one's doctor take all the responsibility for seizure control)
- Fear of failure
- Wanting to avoid going out into the world
- Wanting to continue being the center of attention (because of seizures, inability to drive, etc.)
- Wishing to maintain control over one's family (Some families treat members with seizures as special or fragile, allowing the individual with seizures to have his or her way much of the time.)
- Afraid of losing help from family and friends.

You will have the opportunity to explore your own obstacles in depth before deciding whether you want to go ahead with making the decision to take control.

OBSTACLES: AN EXAMPLE

When Maggie was first seen at age 14 by a neurologist, she communicated like an 8- or 9-year-old child. She had experienced complex partial seizures from early childhood. Her generalized tonic-clonic seizures were controlled with two antiepileptic medications, but she continued to have up to 12 complex partial seizures every day. At school she stayed to herself and felt odd and left out. At home she spent most of her time acting angry and surly with her father.

During visits with her doctor, she showed no interest in discussing her seizure medications; all discussion about the medications took place between her physician and her father. While they talked about her situation, she sat looking angry and occasionally said a few unpleasant words to her father. She made it clear that she was very unhappy—and in her mind, her seizures and her father were to blame.

At her physician's suggestion, Maggie started to work with a seizure counselor. In her first sessions, she began to express some of her anger more openly. She was able to see how much she blamed her father and her seizures for everything she did not like about her life. As time went on, she began to reach out and develop friendships at school—to plan some social activities after school and on weekends that she really enjoyed. The first step to taking control for Maggie was to stop blaming, and to start taking some responsibility for making her life better.

Tools

Each session will offer you a new "tool" toward taking control. These tools include a variety of methods for self-observation, self-awareness, and changing patterns of behavior. As you practice these methods in the office setting or at home, you will find some that are particularly beneficial for you and which you may choose to incorporate into your lifestyle.

This *Workbook* will ask you to prepare for a particular discussion or activity *in the week preceding* your next appointment. You will be expected to fill in all *Workbook* sections as you read the text, as well as to complete the assignments at the end of the previous chapter.

The "tool" for helping you to make a decision about whether you want to undertake intensive work with a seizure counselor will be a discussion of all your positive and negative feelings about beginning this process of "taking control." Before coming in for your next office visit, make a list of your own obstacles, as well as the reasons that you are motivated to go ahead and make the decision to begin the process of taking control.

obsticles
• Seizures are controlling my life
• emotions take control of mental health

Use the following space in your *Workbook* to write down your pros and cons, in preparation for the discussion you will have with your physician and/or seizure counselor at your next office visit.

Worksheet: Motivating Factors and Obstacles

MOTIVATING FACTORS

Why I want to take control

- get rid of them
- want to work
- Drive
- feeling better
- living independent
- w/o worry

OBSTACLES

Why I don't want to take control

- too hard
- too much
- Take a lot of time to see results.

Tool: In-Office Discussion

The tool for accomplishing the goal of Session 1 will be a discussion of the motivating factors and obstacles you have listed above. This will give you an opportunity to become more aware of your own feelings, and to begin a process of honest communication between you, your physician, and your seizure counselor.

At the end of this discussion, your physician or counselor will ask you to make a decision about whether or not you want to begin this process of taking control. If your answer is "Yes," you may then wish to discuss arrangements for your regular counseling sessions and to bring up any questions about the program you have decided to undertake. If your answer is "No," you will have the option of continuing to see your physician for seizure medications and necessary lab tests, but you will be choosing not to undertake the intensive program for taking control of your seizures outlined in this *Workbook*.

For some people who recognize the challenges presented in a program such as this one, the decision about whether to undertake it will not be an easy one. Many people experience a kind of inner "war" for and against going ahead with such a major life decision. It will be extremely helpful to talk with the seizure counselor about your pros and cons—which are the motivating factors and the obstacles that you listed above. Then you can make an informed decision, based *not* on what your doctor or your family might want, but based on what you want for yourself at this particular time in your life.

DO I WANT TO BEGIN THIS PROCESS OF TAKING CONTROL?

Yes ✓ No_____   Signature *Alexis Hinks*   Date 8/23/22

Assignments

Complete these assignments for your appointment with your physician or seizure counselor to discuss Session 1. Reading these assignments carefully in advance will enable you to clarify any questions you have at this time, including acquiring a journal or working on the assignments. During the appointment you can discuss your decision about whether or not to undertake this program and any questions about the following assignments:

Seizure Log

The Seizure Log is a daily record of seizure activity, which you will record on the forms provided in this *Workbook* on the pages at the end of every chapter. You will be asked to keep careful records of your seizure frequency on these Seizure Logs throughout the entire "taking control" process, as well as during the months following your completion of this program.

The purpose of the Seizure Log is to provide you, your seizure counselor, and your physician with an accurate record of how often your seizures occur. In this way, you will be able to see your progress and to learn what methods are effective in helping you decrease the frequency of your seizures. Because these Seizure Logs are a learning tool in this process of "taking control," it is essential that you fill them out accurately, on a daily basis.

Each Seizure Log form provides space to record one full week of seizure activity, from Sunday to Saturday. Although most people see their seizure counselor for weekly appointments, two blank Seizure Log forms are provided after each session in order to allow for two weeks of records. Should more than two weeks elapse between counseling sessions, you may wish to make copies of the Seizure Log forms or to record seizures in your journal.

Beginning with this week, record the following information on the Seizure Log form provided in your workbook:

- **Number of seizures**: At the end of each day, record how many seizures you had that day (including "0" if you had none that day).
- **Time(s) of day**: Write what time of the day the seizure(s) occurred.
- **Duration**: Record approximately how long the seizure lasted (seconds/minutes). You may want to consult a family member or another person who witnessed the seizure about how long the seizure lasted.
- **Description**: Record what symptoms you experienced with the seizure, before, during, and after the event. If you were unaware of the event, how did others describe it? Again, consult anyone who witnessed the seizure for assistance in describing what happened to you when you had the seizure.
- **Location(s)**: Record where you were when the seizure occurred. Be as specific as you can.
- **Severity (1: mild, 2: moderate, 3: severe)**: Use the numbers for the following terms (mild, moderate, severe) to rate the severity of the seizure.
- **Trigger(s)**: Record what occurred *right before your seizure.* Any action, emotion, thought, or experience can be listed as a trigger. Be as specific as possible. For instance, instead of just writing "stress," record the specific stressful event, emotion, or thought.
- **Precursor(s)**: Record *what was happening during the day.* Any event, situation, or mood in the time leading up to the seizure can be a precursor. You can think of this as the "climate" for the day.
- **Improved with**: Record how you recovered from your seizure. What made the seizure stop?
- **Impact on your day**: Record how the seizure affected the rest of your day.
- **Impact on others**: Record how the seizure, or your recovery, affected those around you, including witnesses, or other family or friends.

Before starting to record on your Seizure Logs, clarify any questions you may have with your seizure counselor.

Journal-Keeping

Journal-keeping is an important part of this "taking control" program. Writing in your journal will constitute a valuable portion of your weekly assignments as you progress through the sessions in this *Workbook*. After you have made the decision to begin the process of taking control, you will need to obtain or purchase a notebook (such as a spiral-bound notebook) or a blank bound book of your own choosing to use as your own personal journal.

What Is the Purpose of Keeping a Journal, and How Will It Help You?

A journal is a way to get more connected with yourself. Writing on a regular basis in your journal will help you to notice and express your thoughts and feelings—to get in touch with your hopes, your fears and desires, your joy and your anger. Your journal is a safe, personal space to write about yourself and your life, your experiences, your progress, your aspirations, your loves, hates, times of happiness, and times of loneliness and sorrow. It is a sanctuary where you can answer the question: "How do I really feel about this?"

Making a strong connection with your own feelings and reactions is an integral part of your work with your seizure counselor. However, your journal is a private place to explore your inner self. You are not required to show anything you have written in your journal to another person, whether that be your friends, physicians, or family members, *unless you yourself decide you want to read a particular section to someone whom you trust*. You might choose to do this in seeking understanding and support for your feelings, or to ask your seizure counselor to help you gain insight into your own emotional responses. The weekly journal-keeping assignments that are given in this workbook—as well as the daily entries you may make about your life and reactions—remain your personal province.

Once you develop the habit of writing regularly in your journal, it will become a reliable resource for self-discovery. It will provide you with the opportunity to ask yourself questions, to let go of feelings, to explore preoccupations and powerful emotional responses. It will allow you to observe and understand your behavior and motivations. In particular, you will gain insight into how your life experiences affect your seizures and overall well-being. It will provide reminders of the things that you are learning as you participate in this process. If you work at writing in your journal daily, it will become an increasingly valuable tool for taking control of your seizures and your life.

For those who are already journaling, keep it up. For those who have never journaled and may not know how to get started, just write the day's date and write a couple of sentences. You will soon get the hang of it. In addition to making daily entries in your journal about personal events and emotional responses, you will be given a specific topic on which to write.

This week's topic is to *write a detailed description in your journal of what you did and felt before, during, and after a seizure.* If you do not experience a seizure this week, complete this assignment after you have your next seizure.

Identify a Support Person Before Your Next Session

A support person is someone whom you choose to help give you support throughout this process of "taking control." Your support person can be a family member, friend, or spouse. Choose someone whom you trust and know well, and who will be available to you on a regular basis over the next 3–6 months.

Note: Occasionally, a person with seizures does not have anyone he or she feels comfortable identifying as a support person. In these instances, talk with the seizure counselor about options for identifying a support person.

SEIZURE LOG   For the Week of 8 / 15 / 22 to 8 / 19 / 22

Instructions: Please fill in the diary at the end of each day to record the number and descriptions listed. This information will be reviewed with your physician at each appointment.

Init:_____
ID:_____
Week:_____
Type:_____

SUNDAY __/__/__ (day 1)
Number of Seizures:_____
Time(s) of day:_____
Duration (sec or min):_____
Description:_____
Location(s):_____
Severity (1: mild, 2: mod, 3: severe):_____
Trigger(s):_____
Precursor(s):_____
Improved with:_____
Impact on your day:_____
Impact on others:_____

MONDAY __/__/__ (day 2)
Number of Seizures:_____
Time(s) of day:_____
Duration:_____
Description:_____
Location(s):_____
Severity (1: mild, 2: mod, 3: severe):_____
Trigger(s):_____
Precursor(s):_____
Improved with:_____
Impact on your day:_____
Impact on others:_____

TUESDAY __/__/__ (day 3)
Number of Seizures:_____
Time(s) of day:_____
Duration:_____
Description:_____
Location(s):_____
Severity (1: mild, 2: mod, 3: severe):_____
Trigger(s):_____
Precursor(s):_____
Improved with:_____
Impact on your day:_____
Impact on others:_____

WEDNESDAY __/__/__ (day 4)
Number of Seizures:_____
Time(s) of day:_____
Duration:_____
Description:_____
Location(s):_____
Severity (1: mild, 2: mod, 3: severe):_____
Trigger(s):_____
Precursor(s):_____
Improved with:_____
Impact on your day:_____
Impact on others:_____

Total:_____   Rater:_____

THURSDAY __/__/__ (day 5)
Number of Seizures:_____
Time(s) of day:_____
Duration:_____
Description:_____
Location(s):_____
Severity (1: mild, 2: mod, 3: severe):_____
Trigger(s):_____
Precursor(s):_____
Improved with:_____
Impact on your day:_____
Impact on others:_____

FRIDAY 8 / 18 / 22 (day 6)
Number of Seizures: 3
Time(s) of day: morning / night
Duration:_____
Description: during stressed out
Location(s): on Ray   at home
Severity (1: mild, 2: mod, 3: severe): 3
Trigger(s): upset / stress
Precursor(s): no
Improved with: Colanapin med
Impact on your day: made me tired
Impact on others: Boyfriend upset.

SATURDAY __/__/__ (day 7)
Number of Seizures:_____
Time(s) of day:_____
Duration:_____
Description:_____
Location(s):_____
Severity (1: mild, 2: mod, 3: severe):_____
Trigger(s):_____
Precursor(s):_____
Improved with:_____
Impact on your day:_____
Impact on others:_____

Use **the space below or on back** to describe any significant information not covered in this record:

_____
_____
_____
_____
_____
_____

Were you successful in stopping any seizures this week:
yes ☐   no ☐

Please mark which seizures you stopped with an asterisk (*).

<u>**SEIZURE LOG**</u> **For the Week of** ____/____/____ **to** ____/____/____

Instructions: Please fill in the diary at the end of each day to record the number and descriptions listed. This information will be reviewed with your physician at each appointment.

Init:_____
ID:_____
Week: _____
Type:_____

SUNDAY 8.20.27 __/__/__ (day 1)
Number of Seizures:_____
Time(s) of day:_____
Duration (sec or min):_____
Description:_____
Location(s):_____
Severity (1: mild, 2: mod, 3: severe):_____
Trigger(s):_____
Precursor(s):_____
Improved with:_____
Impact on your day:_____
Impact on others:_____

MONDAY 8.27.22 __/__/__ (day 2)
Number of Seizures:_____
Time(s) of day:_____
Duration:_____
Description:_____
Location(s):_____
Severity (1: mild, 2: mod, 3: severe):_____
Trigger(s):_____
Precursor(s):_____
Improved with:_____
Impact on your day:_____
Impact on others:_____

TUESDAY 8.3.22 __/__/__ (day 3)
Number of Seizures:_____
Time(s) of day:_____
Duration:_____
Description:_____
Location(s):_____
Severity (1: mild, 2: mod, 3: severe):_____
Trigger(s):_____
Precursor(s):_____
Improved with:_____
Impact on your day:_____
Impact on others:_____

WEDNESDAY 8.24.22 __/__/__ (day 4)
Number of Seizures:_____
Time(s) of day:_____
Duration:_____
Description:_____
Location(s):_____
Severity (1: mild, 2: mod, 3: severe):_____
Trigger(s):_____
Precursor(s):_____
Improved with:_____
Impact on your day:_____
Impact on others:_____

Total:_____   **Rater: _____**

THURSDAY 8.25.22 __/__/__ (day 5)
Number of Seizures:_____
Time(s) of day:_____
Duration:_____
Description:_____
Location(s):_____
Severity (1: mild, 2: mod, 3: severe): _____
Trigger(s):_____
Precursor(s):_____
Improved with:_____
Impact on your day:_____
Impact on others:_____

FRIDAY 8.24.22 __/__/__ (day 6)
Number of Seizures:_____
Time(s) of day:_____
Duration:_____
Description:_____
Location(s):_____
Severity (1: mild, 2: mod, 3: severe): _____
Trigger(s):_____
Precursor(s):_____
Improved with:_____
Impact on your day:_____
Impact on others:_____

SATURDAY 8.27.22 __/__/__ (day 7)
Number of Seizures:_____
Time(s) of day:_____
Duration:_____
Description:_____
Location(s):_____
Severity (1: mild, 2: mod, 3: severe): _____
Trigger(s):_____
Precursor(s):_____
Improved with:_____
Impact on your day:_____
Impact on others:_____

Use **the space below or on back** to describe any <u>significant information not covered in this record:</u>

_____
_____
_____
_____
_____
_____
_____

Were you successful in stopping any seizures this week:
yes ☐   no ☐

Please mark which seizures you stopped with an asterisk (*).

CHAPTER 3 ▶ Session 2: Getting Support

Now that you have made the decision to begin, the next step is learning about sources of support, and how to get support from other people as you go through the process of taking control. "Getting support" means asking for help and encouragement when you need it and expressing your feelings openly to the people you feel close to. It means developing relationships with family members and friends in which you feel accepted and supported in your efforts to take control of your life. Because relationships are mutual, this means accepting others and offering support to them in return. Write in the name of the person you came up with at the end of the last session, whom you designated as your support person: ___MOM_____.

This world can be a lonely place for anyone, with or without seizures. Just think about the number of people you know who do not have seizures, yet who seem to feel alone and unloved. How many people do you know who have gotten divorced, or who have problems getting along with their spouses, parents, or children? What about the many people who constantly squabble with their coworkers or who just do not have any friends?

Loneliness is a widespread problem in our society, and people with seizures often experience profound loneliness. Seizures are *not* the cause of loneliness or social isolation, but they can certainly contribute to it. This happens both because other people may be frightened or put off by seizures, and because people with seizures themselves may be uncomfortable about how others may react and therefore avoid socializing. Some individuals with seizures also find that the few close relationships they have are full of anger and resentment both from within or from others, in part because of the frustration that can result from dealing with the seizure disorder itself.

If you feel rejected and angry with people you want to be close to, you are missing important support for coping with seizures. And you are lacking this same needed support if you do not have close friends with whom you can talk openly. In fact, research studies have actually shown that "friends are good medicine"—that people who frequently contact supportive friends have higher levels of physical and mental health than people without much contact with friends:

Social support is getting a lot of attention these days because of the new evidence that shows its profound impact on our mental and physical well-being. Most of us have experienced the positive influence friends and family have on resolving our mental anxieties and depressions. Now the new research shows that there is also a correlation between the quality of our relationships and our physical well-being. …

In a large scale study of approximately 7000 California adults between the ages of 30 and 59 (conducted by Lisa Berkman and Leonard Syme of U.C. Berkeley's School of Public Health), a strong correlation between social "connectedness" and length of life was documented. Social support also seemed to account for protection against certain diseases like heart disease, cancer, cerebral vascular accidents, and circulatory diseases. … While social isolation appears to be a predisposing condition for health deterioration, the result of integrating friends into our lives is enhanced well-being. Another word for it is wellness.[1]

Session 2 deals with learning skills that will help you avoid loneliness and get positive support from others. Because isolation and difficulty getting along with other people often result from poor communication, this session emphasizes the skills you need for communicating effectively with others. Developing these communication skills will give you the opportunity to improve relationships with many people in your life, including your family, friends, physician, and seizure counselor. In the long run, the work you do to improve your communication skills will help you gain the support you need, which in turn will help you feel valued and respected by other people.

---

[1]Pacificon Productions, *Friends Can Be Good Medicine* (Sacramento, CA: California Department of Mental Health, 1981).

Goal

The goal for this session is to get the support you need for the process of "taking control."

Obstacles

Select the statements below that may be obstacles for you.

- Blaming your family or your doctor.
- Feeling hurt or rejected by others.
- Seeing family and friends as responsible for taking care of you.
- Poor memory, which interferes with social interactions.
- Not feeling able to ask for emotional support.
- Feeling angry and frustrated about past efforts to communicate.
- Seeing seizures as a stigma that isolates you from other people.
- The attitude that asking for support is a sign of weakness.
- Allowing yourself to be treated as a child or "helpless" adult.
- Fear of approaching other people socially—and of putting yourself in social situations where you will meet other people.
- Other (not listed): _____

Tools

Tool #1: Improving Communication Skills

As a tool for improving communication skills, you will be working with a model of communication that has been utilized successfully by many people, including top managers and psychologists. This model divides communication styles into three categories: passive, aggressive, and assertive.

Passive communication occurs when a person avoids expressing personal needs directly and often leads to situations where that person feels resentful.

Example of Passive Communication

WIFE: *"Excuse me, do you think you could help me carry out the garbage now?"*
HUSBAND: *"I'm busy watching TV."*
WIFE: *"Oh, all right. I'll just do it by myself."*

As you can see from this example, this wife, who communicated passively, did not get the help she wanted from her husband. While carrying out the garbage, how do you think she will be feeling? Angry, hurt, resentful, blaming her husband for being lazy, while outwardly working hard to do the chore alone. The passive communicator then expresses these feelings, sometimes nonverbally as pouting or resentful avoidance and sometimes with an angry outburst when a series of these situations have built up. The result is poor communication, unspoken resentment, and unsupportive relationships with the people most needed for support.

Aggressive communication is characterized by verbal attacks that blame or threaten other people in order to get what is wanted. Aggressive communication often leads to situations where the other person feels pushed around and in turn avoids or rejects the aggressive person.

Example of Aggressive Communication

WIFE: *"You're always sitting around watching TV when it's time to carry out the garbage. Come on, you better help me do it right now."*
HUSBAND: *"Leave me alone! I'm busy watching TV."*
WIFE: *"You lazy slob, you never do any of the work around here! If you don't get up this minute, I'm going to dump the garbage all over your stupid TV!"*

The aggressive communicator (in this case, the wife) began with an accusation (a "you" message) and the situation went from bad to worse. This type of accusing, demanding statement is quite common between people and almost always leads to a situation where nobody wins. The person who initiates the conversation will not get the help that he or she wants. Instead, the other person will get angry, will feel threatened, and will probably avoid the other person or attack in response. Aggressive communication also has the disadvantage that it leads to subsequent interactions that also result in mutual attack—resulting in a relationship with diminished possibilities for warmth and support.

Assertive communication involves expressing feelings honestly and standing up for oneself over issues that are personally important. It includes respect for the other person's feelings and opinions, while at the same time respecting oneself and one's own needs. Assertive communication conveys the feeling that you care about the other person and the relationship enough to try to express what you want as clearly as possible.

Example of Assertive Communication

Wife: *"I would like you to help me carry out the garbage."*

Husband: *"I'm watching TV."*

Wife: *"I know you don't like to be interrupted, but this is the only time I can do it before I go out. It makes me angry that you're not available to help when it takes two people to do the job."*

Husband: *"OK, how about if you get the small can now, and I'll get Jerry to help me carry out the heavy one after you leave?"*

Wife: *"Fine, I appreciate your help."*

In this example, the assertive communicator (again, the wife) used clear "I" messages, such as "I would like you to help me" and "I feel angry when. . .". These messages strongly convey both the communicator's need for help and the angry feelings that resulted when the other person was unwilling to do what was asked. There was also a statement, "I know you don't like to be interrupted," which acknowledged the other person's feelings. The assertive communicator stood up for her own needs and feelings, and also indicated a willingness to modify the original request in order to take into account her husband's wishes.

The result was that the assertive communicator got what she wanted: to get the job done through joint participation and responsibility for the chore. In addition, trust was enhanced between the two people because they were able to solve an interpersonal problem in a way that neither person felt blamed or taken advantage of. This kind of assertive communication, which may be used in talking about household chores and responsibilities or about more personal needs for recognition or affection, is useful in building the kind of relationships that meet our basic human needs for caring and support.

Now, fill in the following section of your Workbook, before continuing with your reading. Throughout this *Workbook,* you will encounter sections like the one that follows, which ask you to fill in some information about *your own experiences* or observations about the subject at hand. These sections are included for two specific reasons:

1. To make the text much more practical and real by asking you to write in your own relevant information, and
2. To provide useful personal material that will become a basis for discussion of that step with your seizure counselor.

While there will not be time to talk about **every** entry you make in your *Workbook* with your seizure counselor, many sections will be utilized as a starting point for productive discussion. Other entries will be a source of personal growth and insight. In order to get the most out of your experience of using this *Workbook, make a point of filling in all Workbook sections before coming to your next appointment.* Indicate with a red pen or star (*) any sections that you particularly want to talk about with your seizure counselor. If you have difficulty completing a section in the *Workbook,* let your counselor know at your next session. Remember that *it is up to you* to make the effort and get the most out this process of "taking control" of your seizures.

Worksheet: Passive, Aggressive, and Assertive Communication

Write in examples of your own style of passive, aggressive, and assertive communication, and what results from these examples in the space provided below.

Write an example of *Passive Communication*:

passive communication
occurs when a person avoids expressing
personal needs directly and often leads
to situations where that person
feels resentful.

How did it affect you and the other person?

I affect me in the other person
becase I got so mad at a
situation I took out on that
person. that other person was
sad.

Write an example of *Aggressive Communication*:

Aggressive communication is characterized
by verbal attacks that blame or
threathen other people in order
to get what they want

How did it affect you and the other person?

I yelled at my mom because I didnt want to do the dishes So then my mom yelled at me back and got Stressed out.

Write an example of *Assertive Communication*:

Assertive communication involves expressing feelings honestly and Standing up for oneself over issues that are personally important.

How did it affect you and the other person?

Assertive Communication I also Stand up for my issues.

To review and summarize, one could say that there are three main styles of communication.

- In passive communication, you respect the needs of the other person, while your own needs are not respected.
- In aggressive communication, you respect your needs while disrespecting the other person.
- In assertive communication, you respect your needs and the needs of the other person.

Passive communication and aggressive communication are unhealthy styles that may contribute to relational difficulties and can tear apart relationships. Assertive communication can be helpful to you and those with whom you interact and can build relationships. A key tool in getting support in the process of taking control of your seizures is avoiding unhealthy communication and practicing assertive communication.

Improving Relationships with Yourself and Others

1. **Be your own best friend**. The most important way to prevent a feeling of loneliness and to attract friends into your life is: Be your own best friend. If you are feeling lonely, you may experience that finding friends is very difficult, particularly when there are areas in your life that cause you to feel dissatisfied with yourself or your life's circumstances. The most effective way to avoid feeling lonely and to attract like-minded friends into your life is to be your own best friend! Becoming your own best friend can be a long journey, and future sessions in this *Workbook* will assist you in practicing the art of self-acceptance and self-confidence. While this session focuses on communication with others in order to ensure that you bring your needs to their attention in a respectful manner, you can also start to pay attention to your inner dialogue. Make sure that your inner dialogue is assertive; that is, remind yourself of your own needs and expectations in a self-respectful manner.

2. **Change your attitude toward criticism**. Assertive communication allows you to share critical thoughts with your fellow human beings in a respectful manner. Some people find this very hard to do because they are still afraid of hurting someone with the critical content of their words. In order to increase your comfort with the delivery of assertive criticism, it may be helpful to explore the real meaning of criticism in relation to how you have begun the process of change. Just a little while ago, you made the decision to take control of your seizures, and you were fully aware that this process would require you to undertake a critical examination of yourself and your life in order to detect the things that you will have to change. Some of those areas you might identify yourself; others might be pointed out by your social support person or your seizure counselor to help you with this effort of taking control of your life and your seizures. Are those things that they point out criticisms as well? Yes, they are. They are criticisms with the single purpose of helping you achieve what you have decided you want to achieve for yourself. Since the sharing of criticism is a somewhat uncomfortable task for most people, it might be regarded as a form of caring in which another person undergoes discomfort in order to increase your awareness of an area that you will have to work

on for your own sake. *Therefore you need to remember: If you point out a critical observation to another person in an assertive manner, it means that you care about your relationship with that person very much.* You accept personal temporary unpleasantness to facilitate a sustainable ongoing relationship.

3. **Accepting criticism**. Have you ever reacted to a critical remark with being miffed? Making excuses? Justifying your behavior? You are not alone. Accepting criticism can be harder than criticizing other people. But if you do not listen to a valid and properly phrased criticism in order to protect your "faultless" self-image, you really deprive yourself of a wonderful opportunity to learn and improve. Clear acceptance of a mistake or a flawed trait of character without retreating to guilt, blame, or defensiveness will allow you to learn from well-intended constructive criticism.

Tool #2: Goal-Setting

Goal-setting is another useful tool that will help you to gain supportive relationships, as well as to accomplish any other positive lifestyle changes you may choose for yourself throughout this "taking control" process. Learning to set small, realistic goals that you can succeed at each week will give you the sense of accomplishment you need to feel good about your efforts. The overall goal of each session is generally a major goal, such as this week's goal, "to get the support you need for the process of taking control." For most people, achieving this goal will take time; you may not come back each week and tell your counselor that the goal is fully accomplished.

On the other hand, you can develop your skills in setting short-term goals that will help you to reach major goals, such as the one for Session 2. Most people have experienced frustration sometime in the past with setting goals for themselves that are too difficult to accomplish, leading to disappointment and a sense of failure. That setup for failure is what we want to avoid as you learn to work with this tool of goal-setting with your seizure counselor. In order to improve your chances of success, choose goals that have the following characteristics:

1. **Small is beautiful**. Small goals are goals that you can really meet. They give you a well-deserved feeling of personal satisfaction from your accomplishment. And lots of small, successfully accomplished goals lead to big changes in your life, as well as increased confidence and self-esteem.

2. **Realistic is essential**. In planning your weekly goals, ask yourself: "Will I really be able to do this?" Do not depend on circumstances being good, on running into the right person, or on finding extra time. Choose something that you can do despite all the demands of your life. Then ask again: "Will I really be able to do this, even if I have a rough week?" If your answer is "yes," then you have chosen a realistic goal for yourself.

3. **Action-oriented goals are doable, whereas feeling-oriented goals are not**. Very often, you will not be able to meet a goal that deals with your emotions, such as "to feel relaxed when I have dinner with my parents this week." But you *can* choose to do some action that you have complete control over, such as deciding that after having dinner with your parents this coming week, you will write in your journal about how you felt. Or you will call your best friend and talk about your reactions. These are action-oriented goals that can help you cope with feelings, get support, and be successful in completing the goals you set for yourself.

4. **Avoid thinking in *shoulds/coulds***. Try to phrase things positively when you formulate your goals. Choosing to phrase your goal positively, rather than negatively, is another tool that can help you to focus your energy on what it is you want to do, rather than what you do not want to do.

    -   Example of a wording that lacks self-confidence: "I should try to find time to go to a dance class this upcoming week."
    -   Positive example: "I will make time to go to a dance class this week."

Have you ever decided that you wanted to eat fewer cookies? Formulating a goal like "I will not eat cookies" is a classic setup for failure. Why is that? Because you end up focusing all your energy on what *not* to do, which means it will end up being on your mind all the time.

-   Positive example: "I'll take some apple slices or nuts to eat, which make me healthier."
-   Negative example: "I do not want to stay up too late on weekdays."
-   Positive example: "I will go to bed on time."

This week, one of your assignments will be to choose __ONE__ small, realistic, action-oriented goal related to Session 2. Please take a look at the following suggestions to get ideas about the kinds of goals you might choose to help improve your relationships and get support. As you read through these goals, remember that you will only be selecting *one* for this week. One goal is doable; more than one might get lost in the shuffle. You are welcome to choose other goals in the following weeks. Setting yourself one goal at a time will enable you to learn to use the tool of successful goal-setting as a way to make gradual, positive changes in your life.

Improving Relationships

___ Arrange to see a friend in a setting where you can talk openly.

___ Tell a friend or family member about your decision to begin the process of taking control of your seizures.

___ Let a family member know that you appreciate his or her support.

___ Call someone just to talk.

___ Tell a friend how much you enjoy getting together.

___ Talk to a family member or friend about something that's on your mind.

___ Other:

_____

Making Friends

___ Enroll in an ongoing class or activity where you will meet other people.

___ Go to an event or place where you will meet others.

___ Ask someone you do not know very well to accompany you for a meal or other social event.

___ Arrange a get-together with someone you have lost touch with but would like for a friend.

___ Join a support group for individuals who have seizures.

___ Invite neighbors, coworkers, or classmates over to your home.

___ Other:

_____

Improving Communication Skills

___Observe and record in your journal three instances where you communicated with someone this week. Write down whether your communication was passive, aggressive, or assertive for each case.

___Ask for something you want using assertive communication techniques.

___Talk to someone assertively about something that made you angry.

___Talk to someone assertively about something you did that made the other person angry.

___Other:

_____

If You Are Single (and do not want to be)

___Ask out someone to whom you are attracted.

___Go to a place where people meet and socialize.

___Exchange phone numbers with someone with whom you feel comfortable.

___Call a friend just to talk.

___Invite a group of people to come over to your home, or to go out, including someone in whom you are particularly interested.

___Other:

_____

Tool #3: Nonverbal Communication—Observe and Experiment With the Relationship Between Posture and Self-Esteem

Your physical posture, gestures, and facial expressions are all part of your nonverbal communication. Psychologists have found that nonverbal communication plays a huge role when it comes to other people's reactions toward you. Your counselor can help you to explore the connection between your physical posture and expressions in order to help you increase your awareness of the interaction between the way you think, the way you feel, the way you represent yourself in your life, and the way other people react to you. Discuss with your counselor the ways that you tend to express yourself, nonverbally.

At each session, you and your seizure counselor will turn to this point in the text of each chapter entitled "In-Office Discussion." Please read these sections and make notes in your *Workbook* prior to your appointment, as preparation for the in-office discussion with your seizure counselor.

Obstacles to Getting Support

Looking at the obstacles to Session 2 listed above, which ones apply to you, presently?

Accepting criztm

What are your feelings about approaching this question of social support with your seizure counselor and support person today?

I feel good about myself

Complete the Following Questions:

After you have completed all of the questions below, choose a few of them to discuss with your seizure counselor in today's appointment. Before coming to your appointment, make some notes in the space provided below. Use this space to jot down your own responses and concerns, both as you read through the material on your own and later when you talk about these questions in the office. (From now on, whenever you see blank space in the *Workbook*, take it as an open invitation to write down your own experiences and questions.)

To make the best use of your session, make a star (*) beside the question(s) that you most want to talk about with your counselor and support person. Allow sufficient time to talk about at least one question from Topic #1 and one from Topic #2.

Topic #1: Your Experience of Having Seizures

Worksheet: Your Experience of Having Seizures

1. How you feel about having seizures in front of other people.

I feel ambressed

2. Factors that you and your support person have noticed that seem to bring on seizures. (These are the feelings and events that are termed "triggers," which you will be learning to observe in Session 4.)

what triggers is past term

3. Sensations you have that precede seizures, that is, your "aura." (These sensations may be hard to describe, but it is worth a try. If you are able to start noticing any change in feeling or sensation before you have a seizure, it will help you when you reach "Session 7: Identifying Your Pre-seizure Aura.")

My Aura my seruzer

4. How your seizures look to another person, for example, your support person.

They look like Covens

5. Are your experiences similar to or different from those of other people who have seizures?
(Your physician or seizure counselor can help answer this question.)

driffent

6. Any other observations, questions, or concerns that you or your support person wants to bring up.

_NO_

Topic #2: Communication Skills and Barriers

Worksheet: Communication With Your Seizure Counselor

Now is the time to get some nitty-gritty experience in communication with two other people in your life: your support person and your seizure counselor. You may wish to discuss one or more of the following topics:

1. Some recent examples where you felt communication between the two of you was particularly good and/or especially bad or difficult.

I think me and my consluer can agree to stop the Serzer but we cant agree on being off meds.

2. Something your seizure counselor or support person said that you did not like.

Nothing

3. In what ways you feel you need help and support for the process of "taking control." (For example, are there any particular aspects that you feel your counselor or support person does not understand that you would like to talk about in the session?)

I need help with my commication Skills better and takeing control of my sersc

Assignments *(to Complete Prior to Your Next Session)*

Seizure Log

Keep a detailed seizure log throughout the upcoming week, as explained in the Assignment section of Session 1. Two seizure log forms are provided at the end of this and all sessions.

Journal-Keeping

Your journal topic assignment is to talk with your support person sometime during the week about something that is bothering you. Examples might be how you feel about having seizures, feelings about taking anticonvulsant medicines, or some other aspect of your life. Write in your journal how this conversation went. Did you feel cared for and understood? What areas did you feel were not understood? Did you feel you got or did not get the support you needed? Were you able to express support and understanding of the other person's feelings and perceptions?

In addition to this journal assignment, continue to make frequent entries in your journal about your reactions to life events.

Goal-Setting for Session 2

In the space below, record the goal you selected for this week from Tool #2 Goal List, above. Pick a goal that you think will help you get more support from family members and/or friends. You can ask your seizure counselor for assistance with the choice if needed. Indicate the goal you have selected with a check mark. In the space provided below, write specific details as to how you did or did not accomplish it, the date you met your goal, and any comments about how it went.

Only one goal is recommended for this week. You may choose to work on an additional goal from this list next week and for any of the following weeks that you choose to do so. The purpose of goal-setting is to give you a specific task each week that you can accomplish successfully. Any one of these goals will help your progress with "Session 2: Getting Support," and will therefore help you toward your long-term goal of taking control.

After you have selected your goal, write down in your own words specifically what you plan to do to meet this goal during this coming week. For example, "Before Friday, I plan to talk to my brother about his returning the tool he borrowed a month ago," using assertive techniques. I'll say something like: "It makes me angry when you say you're going to return something you borrowed from me, and you don't do it. I don't feel like lending things to you anymore, and it makes for bad feelings between us—which I don't want to have happen. If you are finished with it, can I have the tool I loaned you?" The more specific you are, the easier it will be to meet your goal during the week.

Worksheet: Goals for This Week

My goal for the week ending (give date) _____ is:

My goal is to get a Jorunel
and write how I feel
in it.

_____

_____

_____

_____

_____

Sometime during the week that you are planning to meet this goal, write in the following information to show your counselor at your next session.

On _____ (give date), I tried to meet this goal with the following results:

I try to meet this goal
last time

_____

_____

_____

_____

_____

I consider that I did____/did not____meet the goal that I set for myself this week.

Preparing for Your Next Appointment

- After completing this session and discussing it with your seizure counselor, you will read and complete "Session 3: Deciding About Your Drug Therapy" in preparation for your next appointment.
- Contact your prescribing doctor to let him or her know you will be discussing your medications with your seizure counselor and making important decisions regarding the medications that he or she prescribes for you. Let your prescribing doctor know that he or she can contact your seizure counselor with any comments or information.

Resources for Further Reading

Berkman, L. F., & Syme, S. L. Social networks, host resistance, and mortality. *American Journal of Epidemiology*, 1979;109(2):186–204.

Bower, S. A., & Bower, G. H. *Asserting Yourself*. Boston: Da Capo Press, 2004.

Carter, L., & Minirth, F. B. *The Anger Workbook*. Nashville, TN: T. Nelson, 2012.

Chapman, Gary D. *The 5 Love Languages*. Chicago: Northfield Publishing, 2009.

Cloud, Henry, & Townsend, John. *Boundaries*. Grand Rapids, MI: Zondervan Publishing, 1992.

Davis, M., Eshelman, E. J. L., & McKay, M. *The Relaxation and Stress Reduction Workbook*, 6th ed. Richmond, CA: New Harbinger Publications, 2008.

Dobson, James C. *Love Must Be Tough: New Hope for Families in Crisis*. Dallas, TX: Word, 1996.

Hemfelt, R., Minirth, F., & Meier, P. *Love Is a Choice*. Nashville, TN: T. Nelson, 1989.

Jaffe, D., & Scott, C. "Chapter 4: Creating Support Systems and Networking," in *From Burnout to Balance: A Workbook for Peak Performance and Self-Renewal*. New York: McGraw-Hill Paperbacks, 1984.

Pacificon Productions. *Friends Can Be Good Medicine.* Sacramento, CA: California Department of Mental Health, 1981.

Parrott, Les, & Parrott, Leslie. *Love Talk: Speak Each Other's Language Like You Never Have Before.* Grand Rapids, MI: Zondervan, 2004.

Smalley, G., & Trent, J. T. *The Language of Love.* Wheaton, IL: Tyndale House Publishers, 1998.

Resources for Finding a Seizure Support Group and Seizure Information

Epilepsy Foundation, 8301 Professional Place, Landover, MD 20785, (800) 332–1000. www.epilepsy.com

Nonepileptic Seizures Blog, blog.nonepilepticseizures.com

American Epilepsy Society. www.aesnet.org/

SEIZURE LOG   **For the Week of** ____/____/____ **to** ____/____/____

Instructions: Please fill in the diary at the end of each day to record the number and descriptions listed. This information will be reviewed with your physician at each appointment.

Init:_____
ID:_____
Week: _____
Type:_____

SUNDAY ___/___/___ (day 1)
Number of Seizures:_____
Time(s) of day:_____
Duration (sec or min):_____
Description:_____
Location(s):_____
Severity (1: mild, 2: mod, 3: severe):_____
Trigger(s):_____
Precursor(s):_____
Improved with:_____
Impact on your day:_____
Impact on others:_____

MONDAY ___/___/___ (day 2)
Number of Seizures:_____
Time(s) of day:_____
Duration:_____
Description:_____
Location(s):_____
Severity (1: mild, 2: mod, 3: severe):_____
Trigger(s):_____
Precursor(s):_____
Improved with:_____
Impact on your day:_____
Impact on others:_____

TUESDAY ___/___/___ (day 3)
Number of Seizures:_____
Time(s) of day:_____
Duration:_____
Description:_____
Location(s):_____
Severity (1: mild, 2: mod, 3: severe):_____
Trigger(s):_____
Precursor(s):_____
Improved with:_____
Impact on your day:_____
Impact on others:_____

WEDNESDAY ___/___/___ (day 4)
Number of Seizures:_____
Time(s) of day:_____
Duration:_____
Description:_____
Location(s):_____
Severity (1: mild, 2: mod, 3: severe):_____
Trigger(s):_____
Precursor(s):_____
Improved with:_____
Impact on your day:_____
Impact on others:_____

Total: _____   **Rater:**_____

THURSDAY ___/___/___ (day 5)
Number of Seizures:_____
Time(s) of day:_____
Duration:_____
Description:_____
Location(s):_____
Severity (1: mild, 2: mod, 3: severe): _____
Trigger(s):_____
Precursor(s):_____
Improved with:_____
Impact on your day:_____
Impact on others:_____

FRIDAY ___/___/___ (day 6)
Number of Seizures:_____
Time(s) of day:_____
Duration:_____
Description:_____
Location(s):_____
Severity (1: mild, 2: mod, 3: severe): _____
Trigger(s):_____
Precursor(s):_____
Improved with:_____
Impact on your day:_____
Impact on others:_____

SATURDAY ___/___/___ (day 7)
Number of Seizures:_____
Time(s) of day:_____
Duration:_____
Description:_____
Location(s):_____
Severity (1: mild, 2: mod, 3: severe): _____
Trigger(s):_____
Precursor(s):_____
Improved with:_____
Impact on your day:_____
Impact on others:_____

Use **the space below or on back** to describe any significant information not covered in this record:

_____
_____
_____
_____
_____
_____
_____

Were you successful in stopping any seizures this week:
yes ☐   no ☐

Please mark which seizures you stopped with an asterisk (*).

SEIZURE LOG   For the Week of ____/____/____ to ____/____/___   Init:_____
Instructions: Please fill in the diary at the end of each day to record the number and descriptions   ID:_____
listed. This information will be reviewed with your physician at each appointment.   Week: _____
          Type:_____

SUNDAY __/__/__ (day 1)
Number of Seizures:_____
Time(s) of day:_____
Duration (sec or min):_____
Description:_____
Location(s):_____
Severity (1: mild, 2: mod, 3: severe):_____
Trigger(s):_____
Precursor(s):_____
Improved with:_____
Impact on your day:_____
Impact on others:_____

MONDAY __/__/__ (day 2)
Number of Seizures:_____
Time(s) of day:_____
Duration:_____
Description:_____
Location(s):_____
Severity (1: mild, 2: mod, 3: severe):_____
Trigger(s):_____
Precursor(s):_____
Improved with:_____
Impact on your day:_____
Impact on others:_____

TUESDAY __/__/__ (day 3)
Number of Seizures:_____
Time(s) of day:_____
Duration:_____
Description:_____
Location(s):_____
Severity (1: mild, 2: mod, 3: severe):_____
Trigger(s):_____
Precursor(s):_____
Improved with:_____
Impact on your day:_____
Impact on others:_____

WEDNESDAY __/__/__ (day 4)
Number of Seizures:_____
Time(s) of day:_____
Duration:_____
Description:_____
Location(s):_____
Severity (1: mild, 2: mod, 3: severe):_____
Trigger(s):_____
Precursor(s):_____
Improved with:_____
Impact on your day:_____
Impact on others:_____

Total:_____   Rater:_____

THURSDAY __/__/__ (day 5)
Number of Seizures:_____
Time(s) of day:_____
Duration:_____
Description:_____
Location(s):_____
Severity (1: mild, 2: mod, 3: severe): _____
Trigger(s):_____
Precursor(s):_____
Improved with:_____
Impact on your day:_____
Impact on others:_____

FRIDAY __/__/__ (day 6)
Number of Seizures:_____
Time(s) of day:_____
Duration:_____
Description:_____
Location(s):_____
Severity (1: mild, 2: mod, 3: severe): _____
Trigger(s):_____
Precursor(s):_____
Improved with:_____
Impact on your day:_____
Impact on others:_____

SATURDAY __/__/__ (day 7)
Number of Seizures:_____
Time(s) of day:_____
Duration:_____
Description:_____
Location(s):_____
Severity (1: mild, 2: mod, 3: severe): _____
Trigger(s):_____
Precursor(s):_____
Improved with:_____
Impact on your day:_____
Impact on others:_____

Use **the space below or on back** to describe any significant
information not covered in this record:

_____
_____
_____
_____
_____

Were you successful in stopping any seizures this week:
yes ☐   no ☐

Please mark which seizures you stopped with an
asterisk (*).

CHAPTER 4 — Session 3: Deciding About Your Drug Therapy

The purpose of Session 3 is to allow you and your prescribing physician to make decisions about the best way for you to use your medications at this time. Here are some questions to be considered during the upcoming session:

- Will changes in your medication usage improve your seizure control or your intellectual and memory abilities?
- Are medication side effects interfering with your ability to participate in the "taking control" process detailed in this workbook?
- Will adjustment of medications decrease your seizure frequency and severity, thereby allowing you to participate in the "taking control" process more fully?

Central nervous system (CNS) active medications are drugs that act in the brain and include *anticonvulsants/antiepileptic drugs (AEDs)*, used for epilepsy; *antidepressants*, used for depression; and *anxiolytics*, used for anxiety. Other CNS medication classes exist, but this session will focus on these three classes. Anticonvulsants reduce the number and severity of epileptic seizures for a majority of people with epilepsy, but they do not treat nonepileptic seizures. Eighty percent of generalized tonic-clonic ("grand mal") epileptic seizures are controlled by AEDs, but less than 50% of complex partial epileptic seizures are controlled by AEDs. *In contrast, research shows that AEDs may make nonepileptic seizures worse.*

Antidepressants/anxiolytic medications help relieve symptoms of depression and anxiety and are effective in up to 70% of patients with depression or anxiety. CNS medications can also cause disturbing side effects, interfering with memory, cognitive abilities, alertness, personality, or mood. Session 3 encourages you, your seizure counselor, and your prescribing physician to discuss and decide jointly what degree of medication treatment is most beneficial for you while undertaking this "taking control" program.

Many people starting this treatment program, particularly those with uncontrolled seizures, are taking such high doses of medications that they are experiencing drug side effects, such as memory loss and disruption of the ability to think clearly or read. For these individuals, it may be necessary to lower medication doses to enable the person to have sufficient mental clarity and psychological insight to use this *Workbook*, even if seizure frequency increases slightly as a result. On the other hand, individuals who are not on antiseizure drugs because they are opposed to taking any medication may need to consider low-dose CNS medications in order to reduce seizure frequency sufficiently to allow participation.

> *Complete the following checklist now in preparation for discussion with your seizure counselor and your prescribing physician.*

The following checklist is provided as a basis for later discussion about your CNS drug therapy with your prescribing physician. Before reading further in this chapter and gaining more information about CNS medications, it would be helpful for you to complete this checklist now. Your answers will be the focus of the In-Office Discussion at your appointment with your seizure counselor and prescribing physician.

Worksheet: Your Seizures and Treatments

	Yes	No	Sometimes
My prescribing doctor listens to me when I talk about seizure medications.	Yes		
I understand my drug choices.	Yes		
My seizures are better controlled on present medicine than ever before.			Sometimes

Or

	Yes	No	Sometimes
My seizures were better controlled on other medicine.		NO	
I feel tired most of the time.	Yes		
I have problems with my memory.	Yes		
I have sharp mood swings.			Sometimes
People say I seem worse since I have been on my current seizure medication.		NO	

Or

	Yes	No	Sometimes
People say I seem better since I have been on my current seizure medication.	Yes		
I am able to concentrate when I read the assigned chapters in this *Workbook*.	Yes		

Your answers to this checklist will help you and your doctor to answer the central question of this session: Is my seizure medication correct for me now, or does it need to be changed to help with proceeding with Sessions 4 through the end of this *Workbook*? Before discussing this question with your prescribing physician, you will need more information about CNS medications. The goal is for you to be an active participant in your medication decisions. To facilitate this goal, this chapter will now provide you with the information you need to have a basic understanding of central nervous system (including AED/anticonvulsant/antidepressant/anxiolytic) drug therapy.

There are a variety of different *anticonvulsant (antiepileptic) drugs*, including diphenylhydantoin (Dilantin or Phenytek), phenobarbital, carbamazepine (Tegretol, Carbatrol, Equetro), eslicarbazepine (Aptiom), oxcarbazepine (Trileptal or Oxtellar XR), valproic acid (Depakene or Stavzor), divalproex sodium (Depakote), ethosuximide (Zarontin), ezogabine (Potiga), felbamate (Felbatol), primidone (Mysoline), gabapentin (Neurontin), pregabalin (Lyrica), lamotrigine (Lamictal), levetiracetam (Keppra), topiramate (Topamax, Trokendi XR, Qudexy XR), tiagabine (Gabitril), vigabatrin (Sabril), lacosamide (Vimpat), rufinamide (Banzel), perampanel (Fycompa), and zonisamide (Zonegran), which are classified as "anticonvulsants" because they help to reduce seizure activity. Certain benzodiazepines that work on GABA receptors are also used as antiseizure medications, including diazepam (Valium or Diastat), clonazepam (Klonopin), chlorazepate (Tranxene), lorazepam (Ativan), and clobazam (Onfi, Frisium, or Urbanol). Other medications that can be used for epileptic seizures include acetazolamide (Diamox). ***Select any of the above noted medications you have taken or write any not listed to the side.***

As a general explanation, anticonvulsants work by inhibiting (reducing) excitation (activity) of nerve cells in the brain. By inhibiting the electrical activity of the brain, they act to decrease both the frequency and severity of epileptic seizures.

Normal brain activity consists of two basic processes of "excitation" and "inhibition." Brain cells (called neurons) communicate with each other all the time, telling each other to fire (excitation) or to be quiet (inhibition), as shown in Figure 4.1. With epileptic seizures, the balance between excitation and inhibition is upset in a particular part of the brain. Too much excitation occurs, so too many neurons fire at the same time. This overexcitation causes an epileptic seizure. *In contrast to epileptic seizures, with nonepileptic seizures (NES), the abnormal neuronal firing found in epilepsy is not present.*

Many anticonvulsant drugs work in epileptic seizures to increase inhibition in the damaged area of the brain, theoretically preventing excessive excitation, as illustrated in Figure 4.2. On the other hand, if they cause too much inhibition of normal brain processes, side effects occur. Figure 4.3 illustrates this principle.

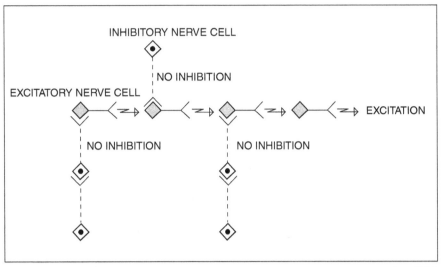

Figure 4.1

Brain Cell Firing in Epileptic Seizures

Anticonvulsant drug effects may be specific to a specific *epileptic* seizure. For example, phenytoin, carbamazepine, and oxcarbazepine help control generalized and complex partial and other focal epileptic seizures, but not absence epileptic ("petit mal") seizures. Valproic acid and lamotrigine are effective for absence and generalized epileptic seizures. Ethosuximide helps only with absence epileptic seizures. As you can see from Tables 4.1 and 4.2, the drug information charts (where you can note your medications) later in this chapter, the epilepsy type needs to be matched with the appropriate medication. *No anticonvulsant has been shown to effectively treat nonepileptic seizures.*

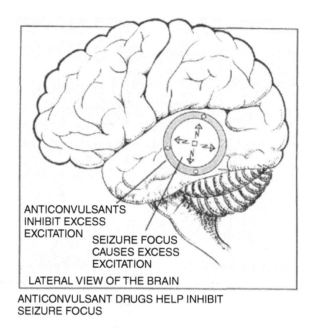

ANTICONVULSANTS INHIBIT EXCESS EXCITATION

SEIZURE FOCUS CAUSES EXCESS EXCITATION

LATERAL VIEW OF THE BRAIN

ANTICONVULSANT DRUGS HELP INHIBIT SEIZURE FOCUS

Figure 4.2

Anticonvulsant Medication Inhibition in Epileptic Seizures

In contrast to epilepsy, NES has a different mechanism on the body, brain, and behavior. Epilepsy is reflected in the brain with abnormal neuronal firing. *Abnormal neuronal firing does not occur in NES*; rather, brain networks are thought to be disrupted. The suspected brain network abnormalities do not "cause" NES, but may be a brain activity signal in some patients with NES in response to stressors and conflicts.

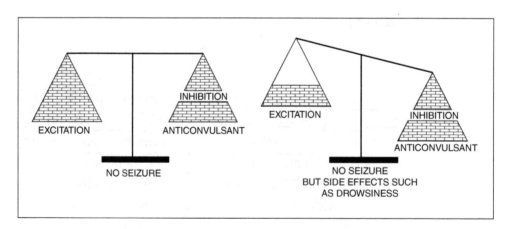

EXCITATION   INHIBITION ANTICONVULSANT   NO SEIZURE

EXCITATION   INHIBITION ANTICONVULSANT   NO SEIZURE BUT SIDE EFFECTS SUCH AS DROWSINESS

Figure 4.3

Epileptic Seizure Control With Anticonvulsants

Table 4.1 Anticonvulsant (Antiepileptic) Drug Information Chart

Medication	Medication Type	Dosage Range	Adverse Events/Side Effects*	Your Notes:
Acetazolamide (Diamox)	Anticonvulsant	Adult: 250–1000 mg/day Child: 10–30 mg/kg/day	Electrolyte, skin, liver, blood abnormalities, kidney stones, tingling	
Carbamazepine (Tegretol, Carbatrol)	Anticonvulsant/ Mood stabilizer	Adult: 400–1800 mg/day Child: 10–30 mg/kg/day	Double vision, mental confusion, electrolyte and blood abnormalities	
Clonazepam (Klonopin)	Anticonvulsant/ Anxiolytic	Adult: 0.5–5 mg/day Child: .1–.2 mg/kg/day	Drowsiness, imbalance, dependency	
Diazepam (Valium, Diastat)	Anticonvulsant/ Anxiolytic	Adult: 2–40 mg/day Child: 0.12–0.8 mg/kg/day	Dependency, heart/lung depression, blood disorders, mood changes	
Diphenylhydantoin (Dilantin)	Anticonvulsant	Adult: 200–600 mg/day Child: 5–10 mg/kg/day	Imbalance, double vision, confusion	
Ethosuximide (Zarontin)	Anticonvulsant	Adult: 500–1500 mg/day Child: 15–30 mg/kg/day	Nausea, loss of appetite, drowsiness	
Ezogabine (Potiga)	Anticonvulsant	Adult: 200–400 mg/day	Nausea, dizziness, drowsiness, confusion, blurred vision	
Felbamate (Felbatol)	Anticonvulsant	Adult: 2400–3600 mg/day Child: 15–45 mg/kg/day	Blood disorders, liver failure, headache, gastrointestinal upset, fatigue	
Gabapentin (Neurontin)	Anticonvulsant	Adult: 300–3600 mg/day Child: 25–40 mg/kg/day	Drowsiness, dizziness, nausea, tremor, hostility	
Lacosamide (Vimpat)	Anticonvulsant	Adult: 100–400 mg/day	Heart rhythm changes, dizziness, headache, double vision	

(continued)

Table 4.1 Continued

Medication	Medication Type	Dosage Range	Adverse Events/Side Effects*	Your Notes:
Lamotrigine (Lamictal)	Anticonvulsant/Mood stabilizer	Adult: 200–400 mg/day Child: 1–10 mg/kg/day	Rash, skin and blood disorders, dizziness, headache, mood changes	
Levetiracetam (Keppra)	Anticonvulsant	Adult: 500–1500 mg/day Child: 60 mg/kg/day	Kidney stones, mood changes, drowsiness, anxiety	
Lorazepam (Ativan)	Anticonvulsant/ Anxiolytic	Adult: 0.5–5 mg/day Child: 0.02–0.05 mg/kg/day	Dependency, lung depression, mood changes, blood/liver disorders	
Oxcarbazepine (Trileptal, Oxtellar XR)	Anticonvulsant/Mood stabilizer	Adult: 600–2400 mg/day Child: 60 mg/kg/day	Electrolyte and blood abnormalities, double vision, headache, fatigue	
Perampanel (Fycompa)	Anticonvulsant	Adult: 8–12 mg/day Child: 4–12 mg/day	Dependency, behavior changes, dizziness, somnolence	
Phenobarbital	Anticonvulsant	Adult: 30–180 mg/day Child: 2–6 mg/kg/day	Drowsiness, confusion, agitation, nervousness	
Pregabalin (Lyrica)	Anticonvulsant	Adult: 150–600 mg/day	Blood abnormalities, skin reactions, dizziness, blurred vision	
Primidone (Mysoline)	Anticonvulsant	Adult: 250–1500 mg/day Child: 15–30 mg/kg/day	Drowsiness, memory loss Children: hyperactivity	
Rufinamide (Banzel)	Anticonvulsant	Adult: 400–3200 mg/day Child: 10–45 mg/kg/day	Heart rhythm and blood abnormalities, seizures, somnolence, headaches	

Sodium valproate (Depakene, Depakote)	Anticonvulsant/Mood stabilizer	Adult: 600–3000 mg/day Child: 20–50 mg/kg/day	Weight gain, increased levels of other anticonvulsants drugs; when used during pregnancy: can cause birth defects in fetus & cognitive delay in child
Tiagabine (Gabitril)	Anticonvulsant	Adult: 32–56 mg/day Child: 32–56 mg/day	Rash, CNS depression, gastro-intestinal symptoms, confusion
Topiramate (Topamax, Trokendi XR, Qudexy XR)	Anticonvulsant	Adult: 50–200 mg/day Child: 5–9 mg/kg/day	Weight loss, electrolyte imbalance, kidney stones, language difficulty
Vigabatrin (Sabril)	Anticonvulsant	Adult: 500–3000 mg/day Child: 50–150 mg/kg/day	Vision loss, anemia, headache, fatigue, brain abnormalities, weight gain
Zonisamide (Zonegran)	Anticonvulsant	Adult: 100–600 mg/day >16 y.o.: 100–600 mg/day	Skin abnormalities, pancreatitis, mood changes, seizures, kidney stones
Other:	Anticonvulsant	Adult: Child:	

(*, The medication and side effect list is not exhaustive)

Table 4.2 Other CNS Active Drug Information Chart

Medication	Medication Type	Dosage Range	Adverse Events/Side Effects*	Your Notes:
Amitriptyline (Elavil)	Antidepressant	Adult: 75–150 mg/day	Drowsiness, visual disturbance, weakness	
Bupropion (Wellbutrin, Budeprion)	Antidepressant	Adult: 150–300 mg/day	Agitation, nausea, insomnia seizures (4 cases per 1000 people)	
Citalopram (Celexa)	Antidepressant/Anxiolytic	Adult: 20–60 mg/day	Nausea, dry mouth, insomnia, increased sweating	
Clomipramine (Anafranil)	Antidepressant/Anxiolytic	Adult: 25–250 mg/day	Drowsiness, dizziness, dry mouth, constipation	
Clonazepam (Klonopin)	Anticonvulsant/Anxiolytic	Adult: 0.5–5 mg/day Child: .1–.2 mg/kg/day	Drowsiness, imbalance, dependency	
Duloxetine (Cymbalta)	Antidepressant/Anti-anxiety/ pain	Adult: 30–60 mg/day	Mood changes, seizures, blood and skin abnormalities, nausea	
Desipramine (Norpramin)	Antidepressant	Adult: 100–200 mg/day	Sleepiness, dry mouth, constipation	
Diazepam (Valium, Diastat)	Anticonvulsant/Anxiolytic	Adult: 2–40 mg/day Child: 0.12–0.8 mg/kd/day	Dependency, heart/lung depression, blood disorders, mood changes,	
Doxepin (Sinequan/Adapin)	Antidepressant	Adult: 75–150 mg/day	Drowsiness, dizziness, dry mouth, constipation	
Duloxetine (Cymbalta)	Antidepressant	Adult: 40–60 mg/day	Nausea, dry mouth, constipation, insomnia, dizziness, fatigue	

Drug	Classification	Dosage	Side Effects
Escitalopram (Lexapro)	Antidepressant/Anxiolytic	Adult: 10–20 mg/day	Headache, tremor, agitation, nausea, suicidality
Fluoxetine (Prozac)	Antidepressant/Anxiolytic	Adult: 20–60 mg/day	Headache, tremor, agitation, difficulty concentrating
Fluvoxamine (Luvox)	Anxiolytic	Adult: 50–300 mg/day Child: 25–200 mg/day	Headache, tremor, agitation, nausea, suicidality
Imipramine (Tofranil)	Antidepressant	Adult: 75–200 mg/day	Drowsiness, dizziness, dry mouth, constipation
Lacosamide (Vimpat)	Anticonvulsant	Adult: 100–400 mg/day	Heart rhythm changes, dizziness, headache, double vision
Lamotrigine (Lamictal)	Anticonvulsant/Mood stabilizer	Adult: 200–400 mg/day Child: 1–5 mg/kg/day	Rash, skin and blood disorders, dizziness, headache, mood changes
Lorazepam (Ativan)	Anticonvulsant/Anxiolytic	Adult: 0.5–5 mg/day Child: 0.02–0.05 mg/kg/day	Dependency, lung depression, mood changes, blood/liver disorders
Mirtazapine (Remeron)	Antidepressant	Adult: 15–45 mg/day	Drowsiness, nausea, weight gain, increased appetite
Nortriptyline (Pamelor, Aventyl)	Antidepressant	Adult: 75–100 mg/day	Drowsiness, dizziness, dry mouth, constipation
Oxcarbazepine (Trileptal)	Anticonvulsant/Mood stabilizer	Adult: 600–2400 mg/day Child: 60 mg/kg/day	Electrolyte and blood abnormalities, double vision, headache, fatigue
Paroxetine (Paxil)	Antidepressant/Anxiolytic	Adult: 20–50 mg/day	Headache, agitation, tremor, nausea, suicidality, mania

(continued)

Table 4.2 Continued

Medication	Medication Type	Dosage Range	Adverse Events/Side Effects*	Your Notes:
Phenelzine (Nardil)	Antidepressant	Adult: 45–90 mg/day	Low blood pressure, insomnia, sexual dysfunction, many drug interactions	
Sertraline (Zoloft)	Antidepressant/Anxiolytic	Adult: 25–200 mg/day Child: 25–200 mg/day	Headache, tremor, agitation, nausea, suicidality, mania	
Sodium valproate (Depakene, Depakote)	Anticonvulsant/Mood stabilizer	Adult: 600–3000 mg/day Child: 20–50 mg/kg/day	Weight gain, tremor, increased levels of other anticonvulsant drugs; when used during pregnancy: can cause birth defects in fetus and cognitive delay in child	
Tranylcypromine (Parnate)	Antidepressant	Adult: 30–60 mg/day	Low blood pressure, insomnia, sexual dysfunction, many drug interactions	
Trazodone (Desyrel)	Antidepressant	Adult: 150–400 mg/day	Dizziness, drowsiness, headache, insomnia	
Other:		Adult: Child:		

(*, The medication and side effect list is not exhaustive)

- It is helpful to know that most people with epileptic seizures need to take an anticonvulsant drug. Many times, the person with epilepsy will need to take medication every day for the rest of his or her life. A few individuals who experience seizures only at times of intense stress or during periods of substance abuse can control seizures without using medication.

- It is useful to know that anticonvulsant drugs are not 100% effective in preventing epileptic seizures. (If they were, there would not be a need for a *Workbook* like this one, or for the process of seizure counseling!) Some people who take anticonvulsant medication never have another seizure as long as they take their medicine regularly. Others—at least 20% of people with generalized epileptic seizures—continue to have some seizures on one or several anticonvulsant drugs.

- Different people react differently to anticonvulsant drugs. You might have good results with a medication that is not effective in controlling someone else's seizures. You might have a side effect from a drug that another person would not, and vice versa. There will be more discussion later in this chapter about how you can minimize the negative side effects of drugs by communicating openly with your prescribing physician.

- When you take an anticonvulsant drug, your body gets used to having it in your bloodstream. Your brain becomes sensitized to the effects of the drug. If you stop seizure medicine suddenly, your brain may react with severe withdrawal symptoms, such as continuous severe epileptic seizures (status epilepticus), which can be life-threatening. Therefore, anticonvulsant drugs should be withdrawn slowly by tapering the dose. However, even if a seizure medicine is reduced slowly, your brain can sense the withdrawal. When you finally stop the last small dosage, your brain may sense the total absence of that particular chemical and produce a single seizure. A single withdrawal seizure is not reason to restart a particular medication. But if recurrent seizures occur after completely stopping a medication, restarting that drug or a similar one should be strongly considered.

- Because anticonvulsant drugs do not treat/reduce nonepileptic seizures, for those with nonepileptic seizures and not epilepsy, tapering off AEDs can be done safely.

For individuals with NES and not epilepsy who are taking anticonvulsant drugs for other indications (for example, migraine prevention or mood stabilization in bipolar disorder), the medication may be continued for the indication but *not* for treating NES.

How Do Other CNS Active Medications Work to Reduce Other Symptoms?

There are also a variety of other drugs, *antidepressants and anxiolytics (anti-anxiety)*, which may help with depression and anxiety disorders that occur with epileptic and nonepileptic seizures. These drugs include citalopram (Celexa), fluoxetine (Prozac), fluvoxamine (Luvox), paroxetine (Paxil), sertraline (Zoloft), and escitalopram (Lexapro), which are classified as SSRIs, or selective serotonin reuptake inhibitors, because they help increase the levels of serotonin in the brain. Another class of drugs, mixed mechanism antidepressants, includes bupropion (Wellbutrin), mirtazapine (Remeron), trazodone (Desyrel), nefazodone (Serzone), venlafaxine (Effexor), desvenlafaxine (Pristiq), and duloxetine (Cymbalta). These drugs are called "mixed mechanism" because they work by both inhibiting and exciting different nerve cells in the brain. Tricyclic antidepressants include amitriptyline (Elavil), clomipramine (Anafranil), desipramine (Norpramin), doxepin (Sinequan or Adapin), imipramine (Tofranil), notriptyline (Pamelor or Aventyl), protriptyline (Vivactil), and trimipramine (Surmontil). Tricyclic antidepressants (TCAs) work by raising levels of norepinephrine in the brain. Another class of antidepressants, monoamine oxidase inhibitors (MAOIs), work by raising levels of different neurotrasmitters in the brain. These drugs include isocarboxazid (Marplan), phenelzine (Nardil), and tranylcypromine (Parnate). Some AEDs are used as mood stabilizers or to prevent migraines, or to treat chronic pain conditions, along with TCAs. The benzodiazepines are also used for anxiety, and were described above. Some medications that work on the adrenergic system used for heart conditions, such as beta-blockers or alpha-blockers, including prazosin (Minipress), also treat anxiety and symptoms of post-traumatic stress disorder (PTSD), which commonly occur in patients with NES.

Basic Concepts to Help You Understand Your CNS Medication Therapy

There are some basic concepts about how drugs work that will help you to understand the explanations about medications that you will find in this *Workbook*, as well as in other sources of information on drugs. It is suggested that you first read through the following glossary of terms to familiarize yourself with the different concepts. Then refer to the glossary again when you read later material about the features of the particular anticonvulsant drugs that you are taking.

Glossary of Terms Relating To Medications

Blood levels: a blood test to measure the amount of a drug (concentration) in the blood stream (serum). Helps to determine whether the dosage of medication is correct. Often measured as milligrams per milliliter (mg/ml).

Brand name: the proprietary name of a drug (e.g., Dilantin, Tegretol, Celexa, Tylenol).

Dosage: the amount (usually in mg, or milligrams), frequency (how many times a day), and number of doses of a particular medication, as prescribed by the physician for each individual patient.

Drug allergy: acquired hypersensitivity to a substance (allergen), manifested most frequently as a skin rash or wheezing. With anticonvulsant drugs, the usual sign of drug allergy is a skin rash.

Generic name: the chemical (non-proprietary) name of a drug (e.g., diphenylhydantoin, carbamazepine, citalopram, acetaminophen).

Serum half-life: the time required by the body to inactivate (metabolize) half the amount of a medication taken in, as measured in the serum (liquid portion of the blood, which is also known as plasma). This is an important consideration in determining the proper amount and frequency of the drug to be taken.

Side effects: the action or effect of a drug other than the desired response. Commonly this is an undesirable effect such as dizziness, drowsiness, imbalance, difficulty concentrating, or memory disturbance.

Signs of toxicity: signs that a drug is harmful to the body, for example, abnormal blood count or liver function tests, and lethargy or imbalance that is observed by another person.

Therapeutic range: the range of concentrations of a given drug in the serum (plasma) required to achieve a satisfactory pharmacologic response without serious toxicity. Upper limits are often defined by onset of side effects. Lower limits are defined by onset of a therapeutic response.

You may be taking an anticonvulsant, or you may have had the antiepileptic medication discontinued if your video EEG revealed nonepileptic seizures. Tables 4.1 and 4.2 list the major CNS active medications used for seizures and migraine prevention, as well as mood stabilizers for bipolar disorder, depression, and anxiety, and provide you with basic information about each drug. The medication and side effect list is not exhaustive, and new medications are being released every year. Refer frequently to the glossary above to clarify the different categories listed in the tables. It is also a good idea to jot down any questions you might have about your own medications as you study these tables. A space is provided in the *Workbook* for you to list your questions, so that you will be able to discuss them with your physician at your next visit.

Although every effort has been made to make these tables accurate and up to date, remember that drug information does change from year to year. Ask your prescribing physician or pharmacist to clarify any medication questions you have.

Questions About Your Medications

Worksheet: Questions About Your Medications for Your Prescriber

After reading over Tables 4.1 and 4.2, mark the medications on the Tables that you take now and have taken in the past, and below, write down any questions or observations you have about your CNS active medications. You will be discussing these questions with both your prescribing physician and your seizure counselor.

Neurontin, Lrica
_____

_____

_____

_____

_____

In Tables 4.1 and 4.2, Why Is It That Some Medications Have to Be Taken Three Times a Day, and Others Are Only Given Once a Day?

How often you take a particular drug is determined by a laboratory measurement: the actual length of time that the specific drug remains active and effective in the body. Drugs are metabolized (broken down) by the liver and are eliminated from the body by the kidneys at different speeds. When a drug is eliminated quickly, it is said to have a short half-life—which was defined earlier as the time it takes to eliminate half of the ingested quantity of the drug from the body. When a drug is metabolized and eliminated slowly, it has a long half-life (see Figure 4.4).

It therefore follows that if a medication has a short half-life, it has to be taken several times during the day to maintain a steady and effective blood level. But if it has a long half-life, it can be taken once a day because the drug will remain in the body and continue to be active for a full 24-hour period. Phenobarbital has a long half-life (96 hours), and that explains why the entire day's dose can be taken at bedtime. Carbamazepine has a shorter half-life (12 hours), which means that, in order to maintain a steady blood level, the day's dose has to be divided into 2 or 3 parts, to be taken every 8–12 hours.

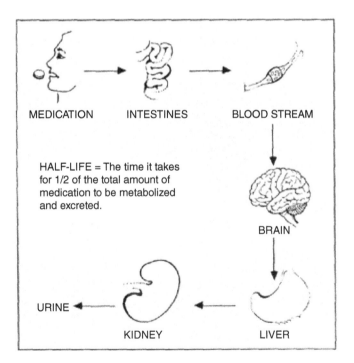

Figure 4.4

Drug Metabolism

How Do You Know if You Are Experiencing a Drug Allergy?

An allergy to many drugs first shows up as a rash that may look like measles and/or raised red itchy blotches called hives. If an allergy is going to develop, it usually occurs within several days to one month from starting a new drug. If you develop any unexplained rash within the first month of taking a new medication, notify your physician immediately. He or she will probably want to investigate your rash, and if an allergy is suspected, the drug will be stopped.

You Are Taking Your Pills as Prescribed, So Why Does Your Doctor Keep Ordering Blood Tests to Measure the Amount of Anticonvulsant Drugs in Your System? Is Your Doctor Trying to Check Up on You?

No, your prescribing physician is not ordering these blood levels just to check whether you are really taking your medicines. These blood tests tell your physician whether the dosage prescribed is giving you an effective amount of anticonvulsant drug. Your doctor looks at your lab results to see whether your blood level falls within "therapeutic range"—the range within which the drug is known to safely reduce seizure frequency and severity.

These blood tests are necessary because of the fact that each person responds to a given drug differently. As was explained earlier in this session, drug responses vary from one person to the next. It is necessary for your doctor to measure blood levels of your medicines to fine-tune the amount of drug you are taking to minimize side effects and to be sure you are receiving an effective dose.

On the other hand, it is certainly true that forgetting doses or not taking your pills intentionally will affect your blood level results. If you've been lax about taking your medicines and do not tell your doctor, he or she may mistakenly increase your dosage when all that was needed was for you to find a way to remember to take your pills regularly. Honest communication will help you and your physician get the most information out of your blood level results.

Why Does Your Doctor Order Other Kinds of Blood Tests—Such as a Complete Blood Count or a Liver Enzyme Test?

The best way your doctor can assure that you do not damage your liver or bone marrow with anticonvulsant drugs is by ordering blood tests that measure the health of any affected organs on a regular basis. Most of the anticonvulsant drugs are capable of becoming toxic (poisonous) to one or more body organs in a small number of people, particularly if dosages are high for a long period of time.

If a drug is known to cause a decreased blood count or liver problems in a small percentage of people using it, blood tests are obtained regularly for the first 6 to 12 months after you start the drug. Blood tests can then be checked one to three times per year if no problem has developed.

Although most people don't relish the prospect of going to the lab for yet another test, these blood tests are important insurance both for you and your physician. If any problems are detected with these blood tests, your physician can immediately change your dosage or medication to prevent any organ damage. Each time you get a good lab result, you can be assured that your anticonvulsant drug therapy is safe and effective.

The following lab tests are often ordered for people on anticonvulsant drug therapy.

CBC (Complete Blood Count): measures bone marrow function by counting all the different cells that are produced in the bone marrow and found in the blood, such as white blood cells and red blood cells.

Platelet Count: measures the number of platelets in the blood, which are the little cells responsible for normal blood clotting. Because platelets are produced by the bone marrow, this test compliments the CBC in checking bone marrow function.

AST (SGOT): one of the enzymes normally found in the liver. When liver cells are damaged, this enzyme is released into the bloodstream; therefore an elevated AST means there is some kind of liver damage.

Liver function studies: may include AST, ALT, GGT, alkaline phosphatase, serum bilirubin, and fibrinogen levels. All of these tests measure the overall health of the liver.

Urinalysis: this is a series of tests done on a sample of your urine. It is a good overall checkup to detect the possibility of kidney damage.

Side Effects

What You Should Do if You Think You Are Experiencing Drug Side Effects

It is your responsibility to notice side effects such as drowsiness, fatigue, imbalance, memory problems, or sharp mood swings and to let your prescribing physician know that you are having them. When you discuss such side effects with your doctor, be as accurate as you can about how often you experience the side effect, and how noticeable it is for you. Side effects that do not occur very often and do not bother you very much (such as feeling occasional drowsiness) may well be safe to ignore—but that is for you and your doctor to decide, after fully discussing your symptoms. More serious side effects may mean either that you are on too high a dose or that you do not respond well to that particular drug.

How Does Your Doctor Tell Whether Your Side Effects Indicate That Your Drug Dosages Are Too High?

As was mentioned before, blood levels of your medications are a reliable way of checking on your dosage. There is a **therapeutic range**, different for each drug, which indicates that you are receiving an effective dosage. This range establishes the lowest dose at which the medication is effective and the highest dose beyond which unsafe side effects are likely to develop.

Some individuals have seizures that can be controlled at the lowest dose, while others need to be in the higher range in order to obtain seizure control. Some people have seizures that aren't controllable with a particular medication, even at a higher therapeutic dose; these individuals may develop unpleasant side effects when the dosage of medication is increased further. A few people will develop side effects even when the blood level of medication is in a mid-therapeutic range.

For example, the therapeutic range for phenytoin (Dilantin) is 6–20 micrograms per milliliter (mcg/ml). Many people have generalized tonic-clonic ("grand mal") seizures that are controlled at a level of phenytoin of 6 mcg/ml; some have epileptic seizures controlled with a level of 16 mcg/ml. Others have seizures that are uncontrolled even at a level of 22 mcg/ml, at which point they have side effects of imbalance or drowsiness. For others, a phenytoin (Dilantin) level of 14 mcg/ml might result in control of seizures but also some serious side effects.

The purpose of these explanations is to help you to understand how your doctor might go about the process of determining the best course of action with regard to any drug side effects that you experience. *This Workbook is certainly not provided to encourage you to make your own decisions about side effects, medications, and drug dosages.* It is hoped that you will gain some understanding of how complicated the process of fine-tuning anticonvulsant drug therapy can be—and of how important it is to establish a cooperative partnership with your doctor.

Summary of What to Do About Drug Side Effects

1. Read over the possible side effects known to occur with the medications you are taking. (Refer to Tables 4.1 and 4.2 and to the drug facts supplied when you received the medications for this information.)
2. Notice any side effects that you experience. Note, for example, how often, how severe or bothersome, or how long the symptom lasts.
3. Promptly notify your prescribing physician about your side effects, describing the details you noted in 2. Be honest about how much medication you are actually taking (less than prescribed, more than prescribed, other drugs that you take).
4. Discuss with your prescribing physician what he or she plans to do regarding your drug side effects. Are they of minor or major concern? Are blood tests necessary? Will a change in medication or in dosage be necessary?
5. Once your tests are completed and your doctor has made a recommendation about what to do, ask any questions you may have about the recommendation—and then reach a joint decision about your medication that you will follow.

Why Can't There Just Be One Right Dose, Like There Is for Antibiotics?

The reason that anticonvulsant drug therapy can be so complicated is that, unlike many other drugs, the response to anticonvulsant medication is **specific for each person.** This makes anticonvulsants very different from antibiotic medications because antibiotics have pretty much the same effect on people of more or less equal body weight, as long as they are infected with bacteria that are killed by that particular medication. Anticonvulsants affect the brain, which is far more complex than the bacteria that are destroyed by antibiotics!

If you can remember that anticonvulsants affect each person differently—because each person's brain has a different epileptic seizure focus and responds individually to drugs—then it will help you to understand why your medication needs may be different from other people with similar seizure disorders.

Take the example of the anticonvulsant drug phenytoin. Phenytoin has a therapeutic range of 6–20 micrograms per milliliter (mcg/ml) of blood. All of the following people take phenytoin, but by reading these examples, you can see how differently each person responds to the same drug.

- *Person A has generalized tonic-clonic epileptic seizures controlled with a phenytoin level of 8 mcg/ml on 300 mg per day. Imbalance and double vision occur with a level of 18, on 400 mg per day. Person A needs a phenytoin dose in a low therapeutic range.*
- *Person B has generalized tonic-clonic epileptic seizures not controlled at a level of 8 mcg/ml on 400 mg of phenytoin per day. After increasing the dose to 500 mg per day, Person B has no seizures, a blood level of 15 mcg/ml, and no side effects.*
- *Person C has generalized nonepileptic seizures not controlled at a phenytoin level of 8 mcg/ml on 350 mg per day or at 18 mcg/ml on 500 mg per day. Raising the dosage creates side effects of problems with coordination and walking, and the seizures worsen. Person C considers tapering off the phenytoin during counseling.*

Why Does Your Doctor Decide Your Medications So Much on the Basis of Trial and Error? Shouldn't These Decisions Be More 'Scientific'?

Because the response to anticonvulsant medication is specific to each person, trial and error is often required to determine the best drug therapy program for you. There is no other scientific way to find out what drug dosage or combination will give *you* maximum seizure control with minimal side effects, without trying some different dosages and drug combinations to see how you respond.

Generally, you can expect that your prescribing physician will start you on a low dose of one medication and will gradually increase the dosage if necessary until seizure control is achieved. If you still have seizures or develop unpleasant side effects, your prescribing physician may change to a different drug: for example, from phenytoin to carbamazepine or from citalopram to sertraline.

Many neurologists believe it is best to use only one drug at a time. Yet some people have seizures that are not controlled at a tolerable dosage of one drug. For these people it may be more effective to use lower doses of two drugs together for refractory epileptic seizures. Some combinations include valproic acid and lamotrigine (this combination is not to be used if there is a possibility of pregnancy) or carbamazepine and levetiracetam.

When a second medication is added, it may also require gradual dose adjustments over time, depending on your response. During the period that your physician is working on finding the optimum medication program for you, he or she may check blood levels of your medicines more frequently than usual in order to find the dosage that is most effective for you. Then, once an optimum drug therapy program has been established, you can expect the blood tests and dosage changes to be less frequent.

It is hoped that this explanation will give you the idea that when it comes to anticonvulsant drugs, some trial and error is necessary for the practice of good health care. This process is indeed more scientific than it seems because it is based on the latest information available about recommended doses for each drug, your lab data, and your own reported response to your medications. This explanation also highlights the importance of good communication with your doctor about how often you are actually taking your prescribed medicines, your seizure frequency, any side effects you notice, and how well you feel overall on the medicines you are taking.

The following example shows how trial and error is often necessary in order to get optimum benefits from drug therapy:

> *Person D has generalized tonic-clonic and complex partial epileptic seizures. His generalized epileptic seizures are controlled at 400 mg of phenytoin per day and a blood level of 10 mcg/ml. But Person D still has 2–3 complex partial seizures per day, so his doctor increases his phenytoin to 450 mg per day. As a result, his seizures decrease to 2–3 complex partial seizures per week, but he feels off balance and tired. His blood level of phenytoin is now 22 mcg/ml, which is higher than the maximum recommended blood level of 20. This explains why he is having major side effects.*
>
> *Even though the seizures were in better control, the side effects were too great, so the phenytoin was reduced, and lamotrigine 100 mg twice daily was added. At this point, Person D had no side effects and had decreased his seizure frequency to 1–2 complex partial seizures per week. His blood level of phenytoin was 12 mcg/ml, within the safe therapeutic range. In this example the doctor and patient maximized the effectiveness of medications while minimizing side effects, through a gradual process of trying different dosages and medications.*

If Your Doctor Has Tried Numerous Drug Combinations and Still Cannot Find One That Stopped Your Seizures and You Do Not Have Side Effects

About 20%–30% of people with generalized tonic-clonic epileptic seizures, and more than 50% of those with complex partial epileptic seizures, continue to have seizures on optimum drug therapy, even after thorough trials on different combinations. Some of these people may have experienced total seizure control on medications, only to develop severe side effects or to show evidence of toxicity that required the medication to be stopped or decreased. Others continue to have some seizures no matter what drugs they take because they have a kind of seizure that just can not be fully controlled with drugs.

In all of these situations, ***primary emphasis in using anticonvulsant medicines should be placed on the quality of an individual's life***, not on the person's number of seizures. Sometimes it is better to tolerate a few seizures than to have the side effects that occur on the higher doses of medicine that are required to obtain total control of seizures. Where is the benefit to having no seizures whatsoever if a person is too drowsy to do much but lie in bed all day? If seizure control means you are so off balance from medicines that you fall down from this side effect of medication, what good is the seizure control?

Like any medical treatment, the benefits of anticonvulsant drug therapy have to be weighed against the risks and negative effects of the therapy in each individual case. Remember that the goal is to improve the overall quality of a person's life, and to decrease the deleterious effects that having a seizure disorder has on an individual's health and well-being.

The following case study helps to illustrate the idea of basing medication decisions on quality of life, as experienced by the individual involved:

A. T. had complex partial seizures for 15 years. After trials on a variety of different medicines, it was found that A. T.'s seizures were controlled best with carbamazepine. But A. T. told his doctor that carbamazepine caused memory problems, severe enough that he sometimes lost track of what he was doing. When his doctor tried him on phenytoin, lamotrigine, and then valproate, his memory improved but he had more frequent seizures. A. T. was frustrated because he had fewer seizures on carbamazepine, but he could not remember things and his life was more impaired.

Complex Partial (Focal Dyscognitive) Seizures and Medications

It has already been mentioned several times that about 50% of complex partial epileptic seizures are controlled totally with anticonvulsant medications. Indeed, Dr. A. Richens, in his 1982 comprehensive *A Textbook of Epilepsy*, posed the question with regard to treatment of complex partial epileptic seizures: "What is the evidence that two drugs are better than one, and three better than two in patients with difficult seizures?" Since then, studies have shown that taking more than 2 AEDs in combination does not improve seizure control.

Since total control of complex partial **epileptic** seizures is so elusive, it is particularly important that individuals with this form of seizures learn other ways to reduce seizure frequency and severity and cope with effects of their seizures. A majority of these individuals also experience generalized tonic-clonic ("grand mal") epileptic seizures that are more effectively controlled with medications. Therefore, it is especially important to balance positive and negative effects of medications in these individuals so that they can participate fully in Sessions 4 through the end of this *Workbook*.

The following example illustrates the need to balance seizure control with ability to participate in the sessions of this *Workbook*:

> *S. G. has complex partial epileptic seizures 4–5 times per week, and at times of stress up to 4–5 times per day. Use of carbamazepine 300 mg three times daily resulted in reduction of seizures to 2–3 per week with a therapeutic blood level of 7 mcg/ml (therapeutic range 3–10 mcg/ml). Carbamazepine dosage was slowly increased to 400 mg three times daily with a resultant blood level of 10 mcg/ml and reduction of seizures to 1 per week. But S. G. had problems concentrating, reading, and remembering things. S. G. and her physician decided to reduce carbamazepine to 300 mg three times daily and to begin work from Session 4 to the end of this Workbook.*

Does Taking Anticonvulsant Drugs Affect Your Nutritional Requirements?

No, generally not. Most individuals who eat three healthy meals per day will not have nutritional problems because of anticonvulsant drugs. "Healthy" means a diet that includes plenty of fresh vegetables, fresh fruits, and whole grains, as well as some sources of protein such as dairy products, beans and seeds, fish, poultry, and/or lean meat. There is no reason to take vitamin or mineral supplements unless a person is unable to eat a varied, wholesome diet due to financial or other circumstances, or is pregnant. (Even so, it is usually less expensive and more beneficial to purchase fresh carrots, apples, lettuce, etc., than to buy vitamin preparations.)

One exception where anticonvulsants can cause nutritional problems concerns children and pregnant women who take AEDs. Several AEDs interfere with calcium metabolism, and patients on phenytoin, valproate, and phenobarbital should take supplemental vitamin D and calcium on prescription from their physician. Of concern for pregnant women is the fact that phenytoin, valproate, carbamazepine, and phenobarbital can cause mid-line developmental birth defects, which can be reduced to some extent by taking folic acid supplements. The special considerations concerning pregnancy and anticonvulsants are discussed more fully below.

If You Have Seizures and Would Like to Have a Baby, Should You Continue Taking Your Anticonvulsant Medicine While Pregnant?

The risks of each anticonvulsant medication to the developing fetus must be weighed against the risks of an individual woman's seizures to both herself and her developing child. To as great an extent as possible, medications should be minimized, and those with greater relative safety utilized. The first 8–12 weeks of pregnancy pose the greatest threat to fetal damage from anticonvulsant drugs. ***No drug is absolutely safe***.

This subject is of sufficient importance that it should be discussed by each prospective mother with her family doctor, obstetrician, and neurologist ***before she plans to get pregnant***. If you are already pregnant, it is too late to start planning anticonvulsant drug changes since fetal development has already passed through critical stages where birth defects may occur. Also, stopping an anticonvulsant drug or changing from one to another can lead to an increase in seizures, which is potentially damaging to the mother or fetus.

It is the responsibility of each woman to learn about the risks that seizures may pose to her or her child *before* she plans a pregnancy, and the extent to which it is necessary for her to use antiseizure medications. Seizure risks are related to the severity of seizures and the resulting complications. Frequent generalized epileptic seizures result in diminished blood flow and oxygen availability to the fetus and should be prevented by use of anticonvulsant medications. Seizures that result in frequent falls can also damage the developing baby and if possible should be treated to reduce them by taking medications.

On the other hand, brief partial seizures may be of no harm to the mother or fetus and need not be prevented by using potentially harmful medications. It may be wise to restrict driving during pregnancy and instead to tolerate infrequent non-harmful partial seizures. For most women with seizures, a compromise will be necessary, and continuing use of medication indicated. In these instances, the risk of birth defects is estimated to be 3% or less, and a majority of these defects are relatively minor. (The incidence of birth defects with valproate taken during the first 12 weeks of pregnancy has been estimated to be as high as 7%–10%.) Registries of the relative safety of anticonvulsants drugs taken during pregnancy are updated frequently. Therefore, a woman with seizures should discuss the issue of anticonvulsant medication therapy with her obstetrician and neurologist *before* planning to become pregnant.

When a woman has frequent or severe generalized tonic-clonic epileptic seizures, controlled only with therapeutic levels of an anticonvulsant medication, she should know that blood levels often are significantly reduced during the second and third trimesters of pregnancy. Blood tests should be obtained several times during these stages of pregnancy to ensure a therapeutic effect.

How Does Alcohol Affect a Person With Seizures? Will Drinking Alcohol Make Your Anticonvulsant Medicines More or Less Effective?

Alcohol can increase seizure frequency and severity when used in excess. More than one or two alcoholic drinks per day are ***not*** recommended for individuals with seizures. In addition, anyone who is habituated to alcohol (usually anyone who drinks 2 or more alcoholic drinks every day) may have seizures when he or she withdraws from alcohol.

Alcohol and most anticonvulsants interact to accentuate the effect of alcohol; this means that it takes less alcohol to make an individual on anticonvulsant drugs "drunk." This happens because alcohol and most anticonvulsants have a sedative action that combines to have a stronger effect than either alcohol or regular anticonvulsant would have alone. For this reason, people taking anticonvulsant drugs need to watch their alcohol intake carefully to avoid becoming overly drunk or sedated. Obviously, it is extremely important that you do not drive a car after drinking alcohol. If you have a seizure disorder and can do without alcohol, it is probably better to avoid drinking.

How Will Stimulant Drugs Affect You if You Are Taking Anticonvulsant Medications?

Strong stimulant drugs, such as amphetamines and cocaine, can aggravate seizures and reduce the effectiveness of anticonvulsant drugs. This means that if you take these stimulants, you can expect to have more frequent seizures that are likely to be more severe. Stimulants cause an excessive arousal level of the brain—which increases the possibility of disorganized electrical activity, leading to seizures. It is recommended that you avoid the stronger stimulants such as amphetamines (speed, Dexedrine, etc.) and cocaine completely. Prescribed CNS stimulants when taken as prescribed *have not* been shown to worsen controlled epileptic seizures. The same is assumed for nonepileptic seizures.

On the other hand, caffeine is a less powerful stimulant that most people can take safely in small amounts. But large amounts of caffeine can function the same way as a strong stimulant drug, thereby increasing problems with seizures. Caffeinated beverages include coffee, black teas, and colas; it is suggested that you limit your total intake of these drinks to 2 cups per day. Other sources of caffeine include chocolate and drug preparations (such as Anacin, Fiorinal, and No-Doz), so be moderate in your chocolate intake and read drug labels carefully to avoid compounds that contain caffeine. If you are in the habit of consuming lots of caffeinated beverages every day, substituting herbal teas, decaffeinated coffee, and caffeine-free cola may actually improve the effectiveness of your anticonvulsant medicines.

What About Marijuana, for People on Anticonvulsants?

Marijuana use and intoxication can interfere with work or school performance and may be physically hazardous in situations such as driving. Because marijuana and the psychoactive properties of cannabis (caused by delta-9-tetrahydrocannabinol, or THC) affect the brain, using marijuana can render the positive effects of prescribed medications less effective. While some individuals report that smoking marijuana, particularly at night, reduces the frequency of seizures or the required dosage of anticonvulsant medications, chronic cannabis use has been shown to result in higher rates of psychosis and cognitive decline. Larger amounts of marijuana can aggravate seizures and reduce the effectiveness of anticonvulsant medications. Marijuana intoxication, or getting "high," can include a feeling of euphoria and perceptual disturbances; however, the high may also include short-term memory impairment, impaired judgment, and lethargy. Longer-term complications of chronic use of marijuana can be loss of motivation, social withdrawal, anxiety, and paranoia. The other health risks associated with long-term marijuana use are similar to those of smoking cigarettes, including lung damage (infections and emphysema) and cancer. If you are using marijuana, consider having a discussion with your seizure counselor and prescribing physician(s) to weigh the risks of marijuana against the short-term, felt benefit. As with drinking alcohol, if you do choose to use marijuana, it is extremely important not to drive a car after taking even small amounts because of the dangers of the combined sedative action of marijuana and anticonvulsants.

The availability of marijuana from state-sanctioned dispensaries, so-called medical marijuana, and more recent legislation in several states to allow recreational use of marijuana have allowed marijuana to be legally used for both medical and recreational purposes according to the laws of individual states. (The US government still prohibits legal use of marijuana but has chosen not to prosecute marijuana use in states that have legalized its use.) This led parents of a 5-year-old girl in Colorado with myoclonic seizures of infancy known as Dravet's syndrome to place her on a strain of marijuana high in cannabidiol (CBD), a non-psychoactive component of marijuana. They reported an immediate reduction of seizure frequency from several hundred per week to a few per month. The widespread publication of this in news sources kindled increased request for the use of marijuana for seizures. However, the increased availability of marijuana to the general public has not been mirrored by access to marijuana and cannabinoids by epilepsy researchers. To date there have been no double-blind studies of marijuana or selected cannabinoids in the treatment of epileptic seizures or NES and, therefore, no scientific proof of effectiveness. Dr. Orrin Devinksy, an internationally recognized epilepsy researcher, has put the issue into perspective as follows: "scientific studies have yet to bear out the hopes of these desperate families. The truth is we lack evidence not only for the efficacy of marijuana, but also for its safety. This concern is especially relevant in children, for whom there is good evidence that marijuana use can increase the risk of serious psychiatric disorders and long-term cognitive problems." In response to these concerns, the FDA has given approval to conduct a clinical trial that will study the safety and tolerability of CBD in children with epilepsy. There is a pressing need for more scientific studies to provide answers about the pluses and minuses of marijuana for epileptic seizures both in children and adults.

Are There Any Other Drug Interactions That You Should Be Aware of—For Example, if Another Doctor Prescribes a Medication While You Are Taking Anticonvulsant Medicines?

Anticonvulsant drugs may increase the rate at which the liver metabolizes other medications. They may also cause decreased absorption of other drugs from the gastrointestinal tract. Specific interactions may include reduction of antibiotic absorption, necessitating higher doses of antibiotic, reduced effect of oral contraceptives, reduced effectiveness of steroid agents and nonsteroidal anti-inflammatory drugs, and reduction of serum folic acid and calcium. Your prescribing physician should be aware of possible drug interactions if you are taking anticonvulsant medications. A specific interaction to be aware of is that macrolide antibiotics (including erythromycin, clarithromycin, or Biaxin, azithromycin, or 'Z-pak') quickly raise carbamazepine levels into a dangerous range. Because information about drug interactions is updated frequently, it is best to check with your doctor or pharmacist about possible drug interactions before starting any new medication.

What If You Forget to Take Your Anticonvulsant Medication?

Most people forget to take regularly prescribed medication occasionally. It is best to have a system to help you remember when you've taken your medication. A weekly medication box (see Figure 4.5) or a daily medication box is a helpful reminder.

Your doctor can help by minimizing the number of times each day you take a dose of a particular medication. As noted previously, different medications are metabolized at different speeds, and this determines the number of times each day you must take a medication. For example, phenytoin (Dilantin) and phenobarbital can be taken as a once a day

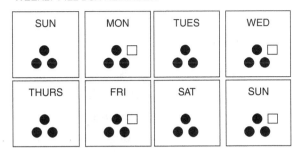

WEEKLY PILL BOX REMINDER

● = TAKE THIS MEDICATION ONE TABLET 3 TIMES EACH DAY

☐ = TAKE THIS MEDICATION ONE TABLET EVERY OTHER DAY

Figure 4.5

Weekly Pill Box Reminder

dosage, carbamazepine and ethosuximide (Zarontin) can be taken two or three times per day, and valproate (Depakote), lamogitrine (Lamictal), and levetiracetam (Keppra) can be taken twice a day. Extended-release formulations can be taken once or twice a day.

If a medicine is prescribed twice a day and you miss one dose, it is usually safe to take the missed dose when you remember, but talk with your prescribing physician and ask if you should wait until it is time for your next dose and double up on the next dose. If a morning or evening dose of a once a day medication is missed, that dose should be taken as soon as you remember.

A system for refilling prescriptions can be established with your prescribing physician that is easy for both of you to follow. This ensures that you won't run out of a medication late at night or on a weekend when your physician and pharmacist are unavailable.

What About Driving an Automobile While Taking Anticonvulsant Medications?

Individual states regulate licenses to operate automobiles. Many states require physicians to report patients with seizures to their motor vehicle departments. Motor vehicle departments usually allow individuals with seizures to drive if they are seizure free for 6 to 12 months. Some departments require physicians to file yearly reports substantiating that seizures are controlled and that anticonvulsant medication levels are in a therapeutic range. As long as seizures are completely controlled, individuals with seizures are allowed to drive an automobile.

Goal

The goal for this session is to make a joint decision with your prescribing physician about the central question of Session 3: Is your anticonvulsant drug therapy optimum for you, or does it need to be changed (increased, decreased, or discontinued) before or while proceeding with Sessions 4 through the end of this *Workbook*?

Several guiding concepts may be helpful to you in answering this question:

1. Trust yourself. If you have questions or anxiety about your medication, discuss these concerns with your doctor. Choose a doctor who is open to joint discussion.
2. If you experience *severe* side effects with a medication, it is probably not good for you to take it.
3. Positive effects of an anticonvulsant drug should be evident within a month. After adjusting dosages, if you take a particular medicine for a month and it has not reduced seizure frequency or severity, it should most likely be stopped. If it is not helping you, it may be hurting you.

Obstacles

Select the statements below that may be obstacles for you.

- Lack of understanding about the benefits of anticonvulsant drug therapy.
- Lack of understanding of the possible side effects of drug therapy—and how to work with your physician to deal with them.
- Lack of communication with your physician about medications, for example: "When I did not like feeling so sleepy on my medicines, I just stopped taking them."
- Seeing your physician as a person who is telling you what to do—that you *have* to take your pills—rather than as someone who can help you find the best medication program that will help you to live more happily with seizures.

- Some physicians do tend to treat people with seizures like children who must be told to take their medicine. (If you feel that your physician has this attitude, discussing the subject may help you develop a more cooperative relationship.)
- Many people have strong feelings about taking medicines, for example: "I just do not want to take pills for the rest of my life—I do not care if they are helping me."
- Reluctance to take responsibility for your own care, for example: "You cannot expect me to remember to take medicine every day!"
- Lack of information about what to expect from anticonvulsant drug therapy, for example: "If my medicines don't stop all my seizures, why should I bother taking them?"

Tools

Tool #1: The Written Explanation About Central Nervous System Active Medicines Already Given in This Chapter

The purpose of this tool is to provide you with the basic information you need in order to be an informed participant in your drug therapy program. The text and Tables 4.1 and 4.2 have been designed to answer many of the common questions people have about the whys and wherefores of anticonvulsant drugs. Because there is a lot of material packed into this one chapter, you may wish to read this section over several different times before the appointment in order to learn as much as you need to know about anticonvulsant medications.

Tool #2: Communication With Your Prescribing Physician and Your Seizure Counselor About Your Medicines

Improving communication with your physician and seizure counselor about your medicines is essential for establishing the best drug therapy program for you—one that maximizes benefits and minimizes side effects and possible toxicity. Most important of all, communication enables you to become an active partner in decisions about your drug therapy program. An active partner is well-informed and participates in the decision-making process, especially when trade-offs are involved, such as tolerating more small seizures to minimize side effects or, alternatively, having fewer seizures but feeling slightly off-balance or drowsy. You can use the healthy communication tools you learned in Session 2 to aid you in your discussion.

A passive partner, on the other hand, when he or she feels dissatisfied with a medication program, often stops taking drugs or takes them irregularly. Usually this means that this person loses out on having the best possible advantages of anticonvulsant therapy. In contrast, an active partner gets questions answered, expresses negative feelings about drug-taking when they come up, and carefully watches out for side effects or signs of toxicity. As a result, the active partner becomes the most important person in the partnership because after all, *it is you—not your doctor—who takes the medication and gets the benefits from it.*

In-Office Discussion

Read these sections and make notes in your *Workbook* prior to your appointment, as preparation for the in-office discussion with your seizure counselor.

Use the following section of your *Workbook* to write down your questions and concerns about anticonvulsant drug therapy. You may wish to reread the material given in the first part of this session in order to clarify the following questions and issues. Your written input below will form the basis of the in-office discussion with your prescribing physician and/or seizure counselor at your next visit.

Note: The purpose of writing your answers to the following questions is to give you a basis for improving communication with your prescribing physician about anticonvulsant drugs. Although it takes a lot of work, this is what is required for you to become an active, informed participant in your drug treatment plan. Let your prescribing physician know the date and time when you will be discussing your medications during your appointment with your seizure counselor, if he or she is able to call in and join the discussion.

Worksheet: Questions About CNS Medications

What questions did you write down after reading the initial information about anticonvulsants and antidepressants (i.e., CNS medications)?

what make medications so strong?

What side effects, if any, have you noticed with your CNS active medications?

depression, anixtey

Do you think these side effects will interfere with your participation in Sessions 4 through completion of this workbook?

yes because that causes alot of the Serzers.

What benefits do you feel you are now getting from taking your medicines, or from not taking your medicines, if you have stopped them?

The benefits I'm getting I'm alot clamer and alot more laid back.

Do you have any special concerns about the effects of your medicines, such as how they affect pregnancy, nutrition, alcohol, or other drugs?

NO

Are you wondering about any other drug options, such as taking a different medicine or combination, changing dosages, or going off medication?

NO

Do you take your medicines regularly? Yes ✓ **No____ Sometimes ____**

Reasons I take my pills regularly:

To feel better

Reasons I do not:

Because I Hate being on them

How do you feel about taking medicines? (Many people have conflicting feelings, so do not hesitate to express both positive and negative feelings.)

I don't like taking medicine because a negative about it gives you side effects. Postive makes you feel better

With regard to prescription drugs in particular, how do you think communication could be improved between you and your prescribing physician and seizure counselor? (Be specific about what problem areas you think need to be discussed.)

I think we need to talk about what meds I need to be on together.

Any ideas about how you might take a more active role in your drug therapy program?

doing my workbook everyday note taking.

WHAT ARE YOUR PRIORITIES? PUT AN (*) BESIDE THE THREE QUESTIONS ABOVE WHICH ARE MOST IMPORTANT TO YOU. IN ADDITION TO THE CHECKLIST AT THE BEGINNING OF THIS CHAPTER, THESE WILL BE THE QUESTIONS YOU AND YOUR PHYSICIAN DISCUSS FIRST AT YOUR NEXT APPOINTMENT.

Review of Assignments

Seizure Log

Go over your Seizure Log from the preceding week. Your counselor will ask to look at your Seizure Logs at the beginning of each appointment in order to get information about any patterns in the occurrence of your seizure activity. In the long run, this information will be of great benefit to you as you progress through this "taking control" program.

Journal-Keeping

If you wish to do so, now is the time to read excerpts or to discuss your journal assignment from last session to talk with your support person about something that is bothering you. Were you able to get the support you wanted? Is there any aspect of your journal or getting support you would like to discuss now with your seizure counselor?

Goal Review from Prior Session

Were you able to meet the goal you set for yourself from your last session? If so, give yourself a lot of credit for following through. If not, use this as a learning experience. What can you do to plan more carefully in future so you will be able to be successful in meeting your goal?

Review of Obstacles

What obstacles do you notice in yourself, with regard to understanding your anticonvulsant medications? What are the obstacles to your active participation in decision-making about your anticonvulsant drug therapy?

Topic #1: Discussion About Anticonvulsant Drugs

1. **Your priorities**: Look back on the notes you made in answer to the many issues raised in the section entitled "Preparation for In-Office Discussion." Talk with your seizure counselor about the three topics that you indicated with an asterisk (*) as being the highest priority for you. Also refer to the answer you made on the checklist at the beginning of this session.
2. **Your Doctor's Priorities**: Your prescribing physician or seizure counselor may have topics about drugs that she or he feels are important

to discuss with you. Or your counselor may be concerned about areas where communication between you could be improved. Take some time to discuss these priorities now.

3. **Other topics related to drugs**: If time allows, it is useful to go over and discuss your responses and questions that you have noted in your *Workbook*. If any areas that you think are important do not get discussed, mark them in your *Workbook* and bring them up at your next appointment. Also make a note of new questions that arise about drugs; maintaining good communication with your prescribing physician and seizure counselor is an ongoing process.

Deciding About Your Drug Therapy

The goal of Session 3 is to decide with your prescribing doctor about whether to change your current medication regimen. Be sure to allow enough time in your appointment with your doctor to make this important decision.

Worksheet: Decision About Your Medication

The following are some possible changes that you and your prescribing physician might consider:

1. Increase the dosage of your current antidepressant medication.
2. Decrease the dosage of your current anticonvulsant medication.
3. Change the number of times per day that you take your medication(s).
4. Change the type of medication that you take (AED to anxiolytic).
5. Stop taking a CNS active medication.
6. Start taking a CNS active medication.
7. Take the same CNS active medication, now knowing it is not for nonepileptic seizures, but may be indicated for another disorder (bipolar disorder/migraines).

After you and your seizure counselor have considered these and other alternatives, write down the decision you and your prescribing physician have jointly made about your drug therapy:

☑ **We have jointly decided that my drug therapy is as optimum as possible and that no changes are currently necessary.**

Or

☐ **We have jointly decided to make the following changes to my anticonvulsant drug therapy:**

_____

_____

yes because I dont want more Serizure

In making these changes, we are hoping to accomplish the following positive effects:

By keep doing the therp

We are scheduling a follow-up appointment with my prescribing physician and me (with the input of my seizure counselor) to assess the effects of these medication changes on the following date and time:

Assignments _(to Complete Prior to Your Next Session)_

Seizure Log

Keep your Seizure Log throughout the upcoming week, recording the details daily, as explained in the Assignment section of Session 1. Two Seizure Log forms are provided at the end of this and all subsequent sessions.

Medications List

Bring a list of your up-to-date, current medications. Record the medicines you are taking, your drug dosages, times taken, any side effects noted, reasons for taking and not taking your medicines, and any other relevant information.

Journal-Keeping

Continue writing a daily entry in your journal. Also write a specific entry where you describe the different feelings that you notice you have about taking medications. Try to include good feelings and bad feelings, as well as feeling that are mixed. For example, "Today I like taking these pills because they make me have less seizures—but I hate the idea of having to remember to take a pill, no matter what else I'm doing." Record your feelings in your journal on different days to capture as many different moods and emotions as possible. Bring your journal to your appointment.

Preparing for Your Next Appointment

After completing this session and discussing it with your seizure counselor, you will read and complete "Session 4: Learning to Observe Your Triggers" in preparation for your next appointment.

Resources for Further Reading

Chadwick, D., Shukralla, A., & Marson, T. Comparing drug treatments in epilepsy. *Therapeutic Advances in Neurological Disorders*, 2009;May 2(3):181–187.

Devinsky, O., & Friedman, D. We need proof on marijuana. *New York Times*, Op-Ed, February 12, 2014.

Engel, J., Jr. *Seizures and Epilepsy*, 2nd ed., Chapters 14–15. New York: Oxford University Press, 2012.

Laidlaw, J., & Richens, A. *A Textbook of Epilepsy*. London: Churchill Livingstone, 1982.

Miller, J. W. Slim evidence for cannabinoids for epilepsy. *Epilepsy Currents*, 2013;13:81–82.

Oto, M., Espie, C., Pelosi, A., Selkirk, M., & Duncan, R. The safety of antiepileptic drug withdrawal in patients with non-epileptic seizures. *Journal of Neurology Neurosurgery, and Psychiatry*, 2005;76(12):1682–1685.

Schachter S. C., LaFrance W. C. Jr., editors. *Gates and Rowan's Nonepileptic Seizures*, 3rd ed. Cambridge; New York: Cambridge University Press, 2010.

Webmd.com/epilepsy/tc/epilepsy-medications

SEIZURE LOG   For the Week of ____/____/____to ____/____/____

Init:_____
ID:_____
Week: _____
Type:_____

Instructions: Please fill in the diary at the end of each day to record the number and descriptions listed. This information will be reviewed with your physician at each appointment.

SUNDAY __/__/__ (day 1)
Number of Seizures:_____
Time(s) of day:_____
Duration (sec or min):_____
Description:_____
Location(s):_____
Severity (1: mild, 2: mod, 3: severe):_____
Trigger(s):_____
Precursor(s):_____
Improved with:_____
Impact on your day:_____
Impact on others:_____

MONDAY __/__/__ (day 2)
Number of Seizures:_____
Time(s) of day:_____
Duration:_____
Description:_____
Location(s):_____
Severity (1: mild, 2: mod, 3: severe):_____
Trigger(s):_____
Precursor(s):_____
Improved with:_____
Impact on your day:_____
Impact on others:_____

TUESDAY __/__/__ (day 3)
Number of Seizures:_____
Time(s) of day:_____
Duration:_____
Description:_____
Location(s):_____
Severity (1: mild, 2: mod, 3: severe):_____
Trigger(s):_____
Precursor(s):_____
Improved with:_____
Impact on your day:_____
Impact on others:_____

WEDNESDAY __/__/__ (day 4)
Number of Seizures:_____
Time(s) of day:_____
Duration:_____
Description:_____
Location(s):_____
Severity (1: mild, 2: mod, 3: severe):_____
Trigger(s):_____
Precursor(s):_____
Improved with:_____
Impact on your day:_____
Impact on others:_____

THURSDAY __/__/__ (day 5)
Number of Seizures:_____
Time(s) of day:_____
Duration:_____
Description:_____
Location(s):_____
Severity (1: mild, 2: mod, 3: severe): _____
Trigger(s):_____
Precursor(s):_____
Improved with:_____
Impact on your day:_____
Impact on others:_____

FRIDAY __/__/__ (day 6)
Number of Seizures:_____
Time(s) of day:_____
Duration:_____
Description:_____
Location(s):_____
Severity (1: mild, 2: mod, 3: severe): _____
Trigger(s):_____
Precursor(s):_____
Improved with:_____
Impact on your day:_____
Impact on others:_____

SATURDAY __/__/__ (day 7)
Number of Seizures:_____
Time(s) of day:_____
Duration:_____
Description:_____
Location(s):_____
Severity (1: mild, 2: mod, 3: severe): _____
Trigger(s):_____
Precursor(s):_____
Improved with:_____
Impact on your day:_____
Impact on others:_____

Use **the space below or on back** to describe any significant information not covered in this record:

_____
_____
_____
_____
_____
_____

Were you successful in stopping any seizures this week:
yes ☐   no ☐

Please mark which seizures you stopped with an asterisk (*).

Total: _____   Rater: _____

SEIZURE LOG   **For the Week of** ____/____/____ **to** ____/____/____   **Init:**_____

Instructions: Please fill in the diary at the end of each day to record the number and descriptions   **ID:**_____
listed. This information will be reviewed with your physician at each appointment.   **Week:** _____

   Type:_____

SUNDAY ___/___/___ (day 1)
Number of Seizures:_____
Time(s) of day:_____
Duration (sec or min):_____
Description:_____
Location(s):_____
Severity (1: mild, 2: mod, 3: severe):_____
Trigger(s):_____
Precursor(s):_____
Improved with:_____
Impact on your day:_____
Impact on others:_____

MONDAY ___/___/___ (day 2)
Number of Seizures:_____
Time(s) of day:_____
Duration:_____
Description:_____
Location(s):_____
Severity (1: mild, 2: mod, 3: severe):_____
Trigger(s):_____
Precursor(s):_____
Improved with:_____
Impact on your day:_____
Impact on others:_____

TUESDAY ___/___/___ (day 3)
Number of Seizures:_____
Time(s) of day:_____
Duration:_____
Description:_____
Location(s):_____
Severity (1: mild, 2: mod, 3: severe):_____
Trigger(s):_____
Precursor(s):_____
Improved with:_____
Impact on your day:_____
Impact on others:_____

WEDNESDAY ___/___/___ (day 4)
Number of Seizures:_____
Time(s) of day:_____
Duration:_____
Description:_____
Location(s):_____
Severity (1: mild, 2: mod, 3: severe):_____
Trigger(s):_____
Precursor(s):_____
Improved with:_____
Impact on your day:_____
Impact on others:_____

Total: _____   **Rater:** _____

THURSDAY ___/___/___ (day 5)
Number of Seizures:_____
Time(s) of day:_____
Duration:_____
Description:_____
Location(s):_____
Severity (1: mild, 2: mod, 3: severe): _____
Trigger(s):_____
Precursor(s):_____
Improved with:_____
Impact on your day:_____
Impact on others:_____

FRIDAY ___/___/___ (day 6)
Number of Seizures:_____
Time(s) of day:_____
Duration:_____
Description:_____
Location(s):_____
Severity (1: mild, 2: mod, 3: severe): _____
Trigger(s):_____
Precursor(s):_____
Improved with:_____
Impact on your day:_____
Impact on others:_____

SATURDAY ___/___/___ (day 7)
Number of Seizures:_____
Time(s) of day:_____
Duration:_____
Description:_____
Location(s):_____
Severity (1: mild, 2: mod, 3: severe): _____
Trigger(s):_____
Precursor(s):_____
Improved with:_____
Impact on your day:_____
Impact on others:_____

Use **the space below or on back** to describe any significant
information not covered in this record:
_____
_____
_____
_____
_____

Were you successful in stopping any seizures this week:
yes ☐   no ☐

Please mark which seizures you stopped with an
asterisk (*).

CHAPTER 5 ▶ Session 4: Learning to Observe Your Triggers

Triggers are factors that often bring about, or "trigger," seizures. Common examples are situations leading to an emotional state of excitement or frustration, missed medications, or lack of sleep. As noted in Chapter 1, *thoughts, mood, environment, physical reactions*, and *behaviors* are interrelated and can also be triggers. Many people with seizures are unaware of their triggers, which are personal to each individual. In Session 4, you will begin to identify and observe your own specific triggers.

In the medical literature about seizures, triggers are called "precipitants of seizures." A great deal of research has been done to determine various seizure precipitants, which you will find summarized in the list of Common Triggers to Seizures, provided later in this chapter. The most important emphasis in this session, however, is the idea that *you* can do a lot to control your own seizure frequency by becoming aware of your own personal triggers. This idea is corroborated by two well-known British epileptologists, Dr. C. D. Marsden and Dr. E. H. Reynolds, as quoted in Laidlaw and Richens's *A Textbook of Epilepsy*:

It is always useful to inquire closely for any precipitatory cause of (seizures), for such a discovery may enable the patient to avoid specific dangerous circumstances and learn to control his own seizure pattern to some extent.[1]

---

[1]Laidlaw, J., & Richens, A., eds., *A Textbook of Epilepsy* (London: Churchill Livingstone, 1982), p. 109.

Identifying triggers is an important step in taking control of your seizures and your life. It is especially useful because eventually you may be able to avoid some of your triggers, thereby decreasing the frequency of your seizures. With other triggers, you may develop alternative outlets or coping patterns that may prevent the onset of a seizure. Investigating your triggers involves becoming a keen observer of your own lifestyle, feelings, and behavior. It is a challenging process of self-awareness that can be richly rewarding.

How Do Triggers Lead to Seizures?

In order to understand how triggers lead to seizures, bear in mind that your brain/mind is constantly processing input that may influence your seizure disorder, not just when you are having a seizure. For epileptic seizures, the weakness or damage in the brain that is responsible for your seizure disorder is there all the time. But the seizures certainly do not occur all the time. This means that there are other factors—including triggers—that may impact your brain/mind to produce a seizure. The same is true for nonepileptic seizures (NES), although the propensity is not related to a specific area of brain damage, but rather to a way of processing stressors. As you read and observe more about triggers, it will become clear that a wide variety of factors can increase the irritability of the brain/mind and thereby aggravate your tendency to have seizures.

In fact, these same kinds of triggers seem to exist for every person, not just those with seizures. Researchers who study how life stress affects health use the term "target organ" to describe the part of the body that is most often affected by stress. Everyone seems to have at least one "target organ" that produces symptoms under certain stressful circumstances. Common examples of these symptoms include back or stomach pains, headaches, frequent colds, or insomnia.

In this *Workbook*, the term "trigger" is used to describe those stressful circumstances, which might be an *external event*, such as an argument or a poor night's sleep, or an *internal event*, such as a feeling of anxiety. The term "target symptom" is used to describe the symptom that a particular individual experiences in response to various triggers. For one person, the target organ might be the lower back (because of a chronic

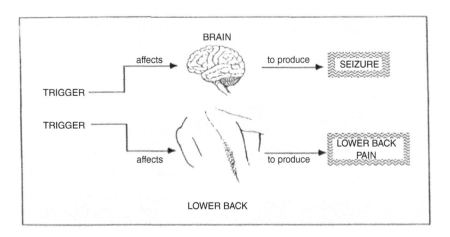

Figure 5.1

Target Organs and Symptoms

weakness in the back muscles, for example), and therefore, the target symptom would be back pain. For a person with seizures, the brain/mind is the target organ (because of a pre-existing disturbance in some part of the brain and/or the way the mind processes stressors, thoughts and emotions), and the target symptom is a seizure. The impairment or damage of the target organ may be there all the time, but the target symptom comes and goes—often in response to triggers. Figure 5.1 illustrates this process.

At this point, it is useful to look at one middle step in the process of how triggers lead to symptoms. Triggers do not *always* lead to symptoms, but they do lead to a feeling of "dis-ease"—a sense of disharmony of body, emotion, or thought. In this *Workbook*, this sense of dis-ease is described by the term "negative state." A trigger brings about a negative state, which may in turn lead to a target symptom. Figure 5.2 summarizes this process.

TRIGGER ------------------------> NEGATIVE STATE -----------------> TARGET SYMPTOM		
Examples:		
Triggers	**Negative States**	**Target Symptoms**
Not enough sleep	Fatigue, irritability	Headache
Criticism from parent or spouse	Feelings of inadequacy and anger	Seizure
Worry about a job interview	Fear of failure	Insomnia

Figure 5.2

Examples of Trigger, Negative State, Target Symptom Pattern

As you can see from examples listed in Figure 5.2, triggers are far from exotic. On the contrary, they are a familiar part of human experience. Triggers are simply the factors in a person's life that lead to negative emotions, thoughts, and physical sensations, which in turn produce symptoms. Although these negative states and symptoms are unpleasant, they are a strong message from your body and mind that you have some work to do in order to gain a feeling of health and well-being. This work usually involves getting to know and understand your triggers and the negative states they produce.

If Triggers Are That Common, and if It Is So Important to Take Control of Your Seizures, Then Why Has Your Doctor Not Discussed the Concept With You More Extensively, or Has Even Called Some of Your Seizures "Unprovoked"?

Standard medical practice may only screen for limited types of seizure triggers, mainly personal habit risk factors, such as missed meals or medications, menses or a lack of sleep, and/or specific external triggers for which clear-cut EEG evidence for epilepsy has been established in a scientific setting, such as flickering light. If these factors are not present, the seizures may be considered to occur as "random" or "spontaneous" or "unprovoked" events.

To find your triggers, be your own scientist by conducting your own experiment. Identifying triggers for your seizures is a search for the relationship between triggers and symptoms.

Psychological and emotional seizure precipitants do not always follow the same time relationships, as do physical triggers. With some seizures, a mind-based reaction to an external event can take place long after the external event is over; it can re-visit and change its qualities. If this mental event—whether an emotion or a thought—gives rise eventually to a seizure, the delay between the mental trigger and the seizure may make it difficult to figure out a conventional "cause and effect" relationship that can be verified scientifically and is based on external measurement.

Therefore, *you need to become your own systematic scientist to study yourself.* Learning to observe your thoughts, feelings, and behaviors will allow you to analyze the relationship between mental events and a seizure that may occur later. With the help of your seizure counselor, you can develop theories about the cause and effect relationships in your life that ultimately lead to seizures. This process will allow you to arrive at your own unique conclusions that are specific for you.

Triggers to seizures and other target symptoms can be categorized as physical, external, and internal:

- **Physical triggers** are physical factors that affect your body and brain in such a way as to increase the tendency to have seizures. Some common examples include missed medications, drug or alcohol abuse, and illness itself. Physical triggers also include stimuli such as light, sound, touch, or movement, which produce seizures in some people with specific reflex epileptic seizures or in some with NES. (If your seizures are predictably produced by flickering of light, music, or abrupt movements, it would be useful to bring this to the attention of your physician and seizure counselor.)

- **External triggers** are factors that come from outside yourself and that lead to negative feelings and thoughts, which in turn may lead to seizures. Examples include difficult interactions such as arguments and rejections, and anxiety-producing situations such as job demands or school pressure.

- **Internal triggers** are negative thoughts or emotions that are self-generated: bad feelings that seem to come for no obvious reason and have a life of their own. Examples include feelings of sadness, anger, or inadequacy. Sometimes the feeling starts as a direct response to a person or event (an external trigger) but continues or recurs long after the situation that triggered it is over. At other times, a bad feeling (negative state) will occur spontaneously without any apparent cause. Internal triggers are usually the most difficult triggers to identify because people tend to ignore or fight these uncomfortable feelings to try to make themselves feel better. As you begin to look for your triggers, remind yourself that knowing your true feelings, rather than denying them, will help you to become more accepting of yourself and more in control of your seizures.

The Common Triggers to Seizures list includes examples of common triggers, under categories of physical, external, and internal. As you read over the chart, ***mark any triggers that you think might apply to you***. (*This will help you later in this session, when you are asked to list your own personal triggers and in the "Going Further" questions.*)

Common Triggers to Seizures

(Place a check by the triggers that apply to you, and write an example. Use for Triggers on page 111.)

Physical Triggers

Missed medications

Lack of sleep

Menses

Overexertion

Underexertion (too sedentary)

Illness

Injury

Fever

Hyperventilation

Holding your breath

Pain

Overuse of alcohol, speed, cocaine, caffeine, nicotine, other stimulant drugs

Withdrawal from alcohol, barbiturates, or benzodiazepines

Skipping meals

Poor nutrition

Specific light, sound, or touch stimuli

External Triggers

Criticism

Failure

Arguments

Loss or threatened loss of relationship

Loss or threatened loss of job

Death of a loved one

Pressure from school, job, marriage, financial problems, and so on

Overwork (job, home, school, etc.)

Internal Triggers

Anger

Fear

Anxiety

Boredom

Worry

Grief

Tension

Depression

Excitement

Feeling of inadequacy

Agitation

Emotions can affect seizures. Dr. Donna Andrews's research indicates that emotional triggers with complex partial epileptic seizures may be different when the seizure focus is in the left or right hemisphere.[2] A group of 23 patients with left hemisphere seizure onset reported anger, frustration, and excitement as triggers for their seizures. In contrast, a group of 16 patients with right hemisphere seizures onset reported fear, anxiety, and sadness as triggers for their seizure.

The Work

Goal

The goals for this session are:

1. To recognize your "triggers"—the physical, external, or internal factors and events that lead to negative states and often result in seizure episodes.
2. To learn to modify triggers when possible as a means of reducing seizure frequency.

Obstacles

Select the statements below that may apply to you, or write in your own.

- Most people are unaware of this process. They may view their seizures as purely random or as happening for "no good reason."
- Unwillingness to take any responsibility for triggers, negative states, and/or seizures. For example, "I cannot help the way I feel," or "I did not feel like going to bed on time last night—what does that have to do with having seizures?"
- Not being accustomed to self-observation. (It takes time and practice to develop self-observation skills, in order to become aware of triggers and negative states.)
- Disconnection from how you really feel. (not knowing how you feel; denial of how you feel—both to yourself and others)
- Thinking your reactions should be a certain way when actually you feel the opposite way. For example, "I should be pleased that I was

---

[2]Andrews D., Reiter J., Schonfeld W., Kastl A., & Denning P. A neurobehavioral treatment for unilateral complex partial seizure disorders: A comparison of right- and left- hemisphere patients. *Seizure*, 2000;9(3):189–197.

picked to be interviewed for this job," when in fact, you feel scared and wish you did not have to go.

- Feeling frustrated, angry, or depressed about trying to identify your triggers. Blaming yourself and feeling like a failure if you cannot observe your triggers immediately.

Blame and Guilt: A Cautionary Note

The last obstacle above refers to a particularly important obstacle that warrants further discussion. When people are told that they have some capacity for taking control of a problem such as seizures, there is a tendency to take that piece of information and blame oneself. A person may then tell him- or herself: "It's all my fault I have seizures—I should have been able to get control of this before." Another person might feel an ongoing sense of guilt for not following all of the guidelines in a program such as this one. That person might ignore the suggestion to take on only a few, small, attainable goals at a time. Or that person might use this program as an excuse to reproach him- or herself with inner comments like "You didn't do *all* the homework—no wonder you're such a failure!"

No one can follow all the suggestions in a program such as this one all the time. **You are not a failure**. This program offers you an opportunity to gain more control over the troublesome symptom of seizures. No one is expected to do this quickly or easily. Nor can everyone expect to get the same results, because each person is working with a unique personality, a different brain, and his or her own individual set of life circumstances.

Slacking Off: What to Do Instead of Feeling Guilty

On the other hand, people certainly do slack off in programs such as this one. They stop reading and do not work on their assignments at home. Self-observation goes out the window. Or they just do not show up for their appointments. Sometimes they know why, and sometimes they do not. Sometimes life crises occur that interfere, and sometimes people create crises so they do not have to continue with this process. Some people feel guilty and blame themselves when this happens, and other people feel justified or unworried.

Whatever the case, slacking off calls for some definitive measures. Rather than feeling guilty or getting caught up in all your justifiable reasons, go back to Session 1 and review your initial decision. Do you really want to begin the process of taking control—now, at this particular time in your life? (It is okay to make the decision to wait a while.) Are you meeting with unexpected resistance from yourself? Are there some obstacles to taking control of your seizures that you need to face?

Because this is important, you will have a chance to discuss your obstacles each week with your seizure counselor. And if you notice yourself feeling guilty or blaming yourself, whether or not you are slacking off, be sure to bring it up with your seizure counselor.

Examples of Two People's Experiences With Their Triggers and Seizures

---

L. B.

L. B. had complex partial seizures starting at age 12. In his early twenties, his seizures became less frequent. At the age of 25, his seizures consisted of twitching of the left arm and face, with stiffening of his left leg—sometimes causing him to fall.

L. B. lived with his parents while he attended a community college. He wanted very much to please his family. Most of all, he tried to please his father, who expected a lot from him and would often tell L. B. that he could get better grades even when he got B's.

During office visits, L. B. would focus on the positive aspects of his life: he enjoyed school, went out with friends, and played guitar in a band. But sooner or later, he would mention his father. Often at that moment, his left arm and face would begin to twitch slightly. If his seizure counselor noticed the slight seizure and reminded him to do some relaxed deep breathing, the twitching would stop.

During a self-observation practice session, L. B.'s counselor asked him to think about his father and observe the feelings that resulted. L. B. thought about a recent conversation they had had in which his father had urged him to think about his career plans, to consider going to law school or business college. He was able to observe that he felt inadequate to meet his father's expectations—and very much afraid of failure.

L. B. noticed later that these conversations with his father, in which he listened passively to his father's high expectations of him, frequently triggered his seizures. He observed that even thinking about his father was sometimes a trigger for seizures. The negative state that resulted was one of feeling inadequate and afraid he would fail. And his target symptom was seizures, from a mild twitching of his face or arm to a more severe seizure in which he actually fell down.

During subsequent sessions with his seizure counselor, L. B. worked on developing ways to avoid or reduce this particular trigger. He also learned to channel his

---

negative state (fear of failure) into positive outlets, instead of having seizures. (You will read about some of his solutions in future chapters.) L. B. later told his counselor that identifying this particular trigger was one of the most useful insights he gained during his sessions of this "taking control" program.

A. W.

A. W., who was in her mid-thirties and worked as a waitress, called her doctor and left a message that she was "having seizures all the time." From age 8 she had absence seizures, which were in good control as long as she took her medication. During her teenage years she stopped taking her medicine several times and had a flurry of seizures.

When A. W. came in to see her doctor, she told him quickly that she knew why she was having seizures again. She had a new boyfriend, and she started taking some stimulant street drugs when they were out together. She also had been missing out on a lot of sleep. At her doctor's suggestion, she wrote down three physical triggers that in her experience brought about seizures:

"My triggers: Skipping medicine (teenage years), taking drugs, missing sleep."

A. W. decided she would try avoiding these three triggers and see if she still had seizures. As she and her doctor had hoped, her seizures promptly stopped.

In-Office Discussion

Read these sections and make notes in your *Workbook* prior to your appointment, as preparation for the in-office discussion with your seizure counselor.

Review of Assignments

Seizure Log

Your counselor will ask to look at your Seizure Logs for the past weeks in order to get information about any patterns in the occurrence of your seizure activity. In the long run, this information will be of great benefit to you as you progress through this "taking control" program.

Medication Questions

If you have questions or concerns about your medications, discuss them now with your seizure counselor.

Journal-Keeping

If you wish to do so, read excerpts or discuss some of your feelings about taking medications that you wrote about in your journal with your support person or seizure counselor.

Goal Review from Prior Session

Review of Obstacles. What obstacles do you have to observing your triggers? How are you coping with these obstacles?

Tools

Topic #1: Self-Observation

Do this exercise at home to discuss in your upcoming appointment.

Self-observation can occur on at least three levels: physical sensations, emotions, and thoughts. Self-observation means directing your attention to your experience of being alive and aware at this very moment—here and now. *To prepare for your appointment discussion, find a quiet place at home or someplace, read and do the following:*

1. Begin by sitting comfortably and quietly. Allow your breathing and body posture to relax. Simply sit without attempting to direct your attention for about 3 minutes.
2. At the end of this period of relaxation, begin to observe your physical sensations. Direct your attention to your body, noticing sensations of tension, comfort, warmth, cold, how the chair or clothing feels against your skin, and so on. Spend 5 to 10 minutes rotating your attention from one part of your body to the next, in the following sequence: left foot, left ankle, left knee, left thigh, left hip, right foot, right ankle, right knee, right thigh, right hip, left hand, left forearm, left upper arm, right hand, right forearm, right upper arm, lower back, middle back, abdomen, upper back, chest, shoulders, neck, jaw, mouth, nose, cheeks, eyes, forehead, scalp, and back of head.
3. Begin to observe your emotions. For about 3 minutes, ask yourself, "How do I feel?" (If no specific emotions are apparent, ask yourself, "How do I feel about the prospect of learning to observe my triggers?")
4. Begin now to observe your thoughts. Ask yourself, "What am I thinking?" Allow 3 more minutes to complete the exercise.

Worksheet: Discussion of Self-Observation Session

Write down an example of one sensation, emotion, and thought that you observed.

Physical Sensation: <u>Falling down staris</u>

Emotion: <u>Feeling upset</u>

Thought: <u>Tried</u>

Comment on any difficulties or benefits you experienced with the exercise.

<u>None</u>

Examples of what others have stated

- "I noticed a bodily sensation of heaviness, fatigue, and tension around my eyelids, especially the right eye."
- "I found myself feeling angry that I hadn't done the assignment from last week."
- "I was thinking about what I need to tell a person I'm going to see later today. Then I thought—'I shouldn't be thinking this right now.'"

You will discuss what you have written with your seizure counselor in the upcoming appointment.

Discussion of Triggers and the Negative States They Produce

Use the blank Trigger Chart on page 111 to write down your own triggers, negative states, and target symptoms. *Begin filling in this* Trigger Chart *at home before coming to the appointment*, where this will be the topic of your in-office discussion. Under Target Symptoms, include the type and frequency of your seizures, as well as any other target symptoms you may experience, which may include headaches, pains, tremors, and so forth.

Use your own "Inner Dialogue" to identify seizure triggers. Review how you will identify your triggers most efficiently. Keep in mind that the best way to identify triggers is to work backward from your last seizure; that is, as soon as you can, after your next seizure, ask yourself: "How did I feel right before that seizure? What happened that day, before the seizure occurred?" Some people tend to be disappointed when they cannot answer these questions immediately, and they might end up saying, "I don't know what caused the seizure." Once again, the way your inner voice puts your assessment into words has a huge influence on the likelihood of a successful outcome. Saying the words "I don't know" is like a directive to the brain to stop searching for the answer. If you have not yet successfully identified the trigger to your last seizure, it is much better to simply say to yourself and/or your seizure counselor: "I need to think about what caused my last seizure." Open-mindedness is more likely to produce a sudden insight into what might have been the trigger. And whenever another seizure occurs, do this same kind of detective work to gradually fill in the trigger chart with all the information you can possibly gather about your negative states and seizures.

Topic #2: Change Your Attitude Toward Your Seizures: Respect Your Brain

Change your attitude toward seizures. Build a respectful working relationship with your brain. It is common to react with anger, frustration, and/or sadness once a seizure has happened. Having started the process of taking control of your seizures, you can now make a choice: You can decide to fundamentally shift your attitude and accept your seizures as a means of communication by your brain to let you know that you have crossed your physical or mental limits (or "seizure threshold")—either by exposing yourself to a single very potent seizure trigger or by accumulating multiple physical, internal, and/or external triggers. This attitude turns any seizure that occurred into an opportunity to learn.

Some people are angry with their brains and express this anger in an internal dialogue, by saying: "You stupid brain, it is all your fault that I keep having seizures. Why do you have to keep doing that?" It might be helpful for you to change this angry/blaming relationship with your brain. While no one can blame you for the fact that you have an increased seizure disposition, you can take responsibility for crossing your seizure threshold or "overloading your brain."

Some people imagine their brain is like a small child. If you have ever observed a caring parent attend to his child's needs, you will have seen that—ideally—the child's needs have priority over the parent's needs. Applying this concept to your working relationship with your brain would mean that—even if you would like to continue working on a project or celebrating with your friends, but you are tired (which is your brain's way of telling you that it needs you to go to sleep)—you put your brain's needs first.

Another helpful analogy is working with a computer. Have you ever overloaded your computer by being impatient and entering too many commands at the same time? What happened? Usually your computer will freeze and you might even have to shut it down completely before you can continue working. The parallel to a seizure event becomes obvious. Even though you could say, "I wish I had a faster computer," it was you who were working on too many tasks at the same time. So, you can also imagine that your mind is like the computer's software and your brain is the hardware. While you cannot exchange the hardware (your brain), you can reprogram your mind's software to create a more efficient and sustainable workflow.

Topic #3: The Concept of "Thought Cancellation"

"Cancel that thought." Even though the following sessions will provide you with the tools for an in-depth exploration of your triggers and your search for compensatory measures, there is a specific thought-form that can potentially lead to seizures that you should start to become increasingly aware of. Have you ever noticed that a thought like "this would be a really embarrassing situation in which to have a seizure—I hope I will not have a seizure," or "I have not had a seizure today—I wonder if I am going to have one later today … ?" was followed by a seizure? Such anticipatory or somewhat fearful thoughts that circle around the occurrence of seizures can at times be a setup for a self-fulfilling prophecy. In other words, such thoughts may increase the potential for a seizure.

While we cannot control the thoughts that enter our minds, we have some level of control over the decision of which thoughts we want to support and cultivate and which thoughts we do not want to support and cultivate. Reprogramming the relationship between your mind and your brain can be a powerful tool when you learn to catch yourself in the act of thinking non-supportive thoughts. Instead of feeling bad and guilty for having had a specific thought in the first place, tell yourself to "cancel that thought."

However, when we order ourselves *not* to think something, it just makes the thought that we "do not want to think" reappear even more forcefully. The process of "thought cancellation," therefore, needs to be followed by the replacement of the non-supportive thought by a supportive thought. This has been described as "taking the thought captive" to change strongholds in our lives. Here, the same rules that were discussed in Session 1 regarding the phrasing of goals in order to increase the likelihood of success need to be applied: Be positive and confident in the way you formulate the supportive thought with which you want to replace the initial non-supportive thought.

Trigger Chart

Complete this chart to discuss in your upcoming appointment.

TRIGGERS *(from page 102)*	NEGATIVE STATES	TARGET SYMPTOMS

Physical

Injury	Broken Foot	
Menses		
Lack of Sleep		
Fever		
Pain		

External

Failure		
Arguments		
Death loved one		
Over work		
Criticism		

Internal

Anger		
Worry		
Tension		
Anxiety		
Fear		
Boredom		

Seizure Log

Continue recording seizure activity and severity as before. For each seizure that you have, see if you can identify any triggers that preceded it. Write one or two words to remind you what the trigger was, for example, "Forgot meds" or "Upset re: brother." Whenever possible, write about the situation or circumstances that you observed, as well as any negative states you observed, in more detail in your journal.

Use your journal to record more detailed information regarding different triggers for seizure that occur each day.

Journal-Keeping

The name of this session's journal-keeping assignment is *"A Day in the Life."* Pick one day and try to observe yourself as much as possible during the day. Practice "self-observation" (as described in this chapter) at least once for 15 to 20 minutes. Write down some of your observations from that session and from the entire day. Concentrate on your feelings, but also include some of the thoughts and physical sensations that you were able to observe. In addition, describe any negative states that you notice during the day.

Goal-Setting for Session 4

Read through the following Goal List, which provides a good summary of the ideas presented in this session. In addition to the journal-keeping assignment described above, choose **one** goal from the following Goal List related to learning how to observe your triggers. If desired, you may also choose one goal from the Goal List for "Session 2: Getting Support." Check off the goal or goals you have selected and write in the specifics of how you plan to meet that goal in the space provided below. *Show this written goal to your seizure counselor before you leave today's appointment.*

Goal List *(select one goal from the list below)*

Understanding the Idea of Triggers

___ In your own words, write a definition of the following concepts in your journal: trigger, negative state, target organ, target symptom.

___In your own words, write a definition of the three types of triggers in your journal: physical trigger, external trigger, internal trigger.

___Discuss the terms mentioned above with a friend or family member.

___Other: _____

Developing the Tool of Self-Observation

___Practice the self-observation exercise described in Session 4 at home. (Fill in _____# of times/ week).

___Make a digital recording (mp3, mp4, iPhone, iPod, or similar device) of the self-observation exercise to use when practicing.

___Record self-observations in your journal.

___Keep a daily diary (_____# times/week) that includes events, thoughts, feelings. Note possible triggers.

___Ask your counselor to review your self-observations in your journal and to comment on how they relate to triggers.

___Other: _____

Identifying Your Own Triggers

___As soon as you can remember after your next seizure, ask yourself "What was the trigger?" and write it down.

___The next time you notice yourself in a negative state, ask yourself "What was the trigger?" and write it down.

___Review your journal entries for possible triggers.

___Review your Trigger Chart and add new information from recent observations.

___Show your Trigger Chart to your support person and ask if he or she noticed any additional triggers.

___Ask your seizure counselor to review your Trigger Chart and make comments or additions.

___Other: _____

Addressing Triggers

___ Review your Trigger Chart. Place a star beside the triggers that you think might be modifiable.

___ Select one physical trigger and make a plan for how you will address it.

___ Select one external trigger and make a plan for how you will address it.

___ Select one internal trigger and make a plan for how you will address it.

___ Get help with a problem trigger (such as alcohol, drugs, serious marital conflict or family problem, strong negative feelings such as depression) if needed. Bring up the problem with your seizure counselor and ask about where to go for help.

___ Other: _____

After you have selected *one* of the above goals, write down in your own words specifically what you plan to do to meet this goal during the coming week. The more specific you are, the easier it will be to meet your goal.

My goal for the week ending (give date) ___/___/___ is to:

is to work on understanding
how to use my medication probaly

Sometime during the week that you are planning to meet this goal, write in the following information to show your counselor at your next appointment:

On (give date) ___/___/___, I tried to meet his goal with the following results:

I want to meet my goal by
keep writing in my notebook
everyday.

I consider that I did ___, did not ___ meet the goal that I set out for myself this week.

Trigger Chart

Continue to add any new triggers that you identify to the Trigger Chart in Session 4 of your workbook.

Addressing Triggers

Now that you have identified some of your triggers, Session 4 contains a special section entitled "Going Further: Learning to Address Triggers." This section is designed for you to complete after you have used your self-observation skills and identified triggers.

Complete this section now; you may wish to make a plan with your seizure counselor to set up an appointment for another session in a few weeks to talk about triggers again, with an emphasis on learning to address the triggers you have identified.

Going Further

Now that you have identified some of your triggers, you can make a plan for addressing one or more of those triggers as a way to reduce the frequency of your seizures. But before you make a plan for addressing triggers, you will first need to know which of your triggers are avoidable and which are not. The goal here is to address triggers in a healthy manner, sometimes modifying them, sometimes avoiding them. The following examples illustrate the differences between avoidable and unavoidable triggers:

Avoidable Triggers:	**Unavoidable Triggers:**
Not enough sleep	Having the flu
Drinking too much alcohol	Test anxiety
Getting into an argument (which you start or encourage)	Feeling inadequate, depressed, angry, and so on

There is an additional category of triggers that are "sometimes avoidable," depending on the circumstances and the person. These include pressures, overwork, criticism, tension, and excitement—triggers that seem unavoidable if you let them happen, but which you might be able to address by changing some aspects of your life and improving your coping mechanisms.

To prepare for discussion of this session with your seizure counselor, *fill in the following chart now*, indicating which of your triggers are *avoidable*, *unavoidable*, and *sometimes avoidable*. Choose one of your avoidable triggers and make a plan for how you will avoid it. Write your plan in the space provided, and *show it to your seizure counselor at your next appointment* after putting your plan into action.

Note: The following section of Session 4 is designed for you to complete by referring to the observations you made about your triggers and documenting these triggers on the Trigger Chart provided in the "Assignments" section of this session. Discuss any questions you may have about it with your seizure counselor.

Worksheet: Addressing Triggers

Triggers that I can probably address:

anxeity, Depression.

Triggers that I probably cannot avoid:

Depression

Triggers that I may be able to modify sometimes:

My hands will start shakeing

I want to make a plan to address the following trigger:

Track my triggers

This is my plan for addressing this trigger:

Writeing in my notebook

After trying to follow this plan, these are my observations about how it went:

It went really good

Preparing for Your Next Appointment

After completing this session and discussing it with your seizure counselor, you will read and complete "Session 5: Channeling Negative Emotions Into Productive Outlets."

LAST BUT NOT LEAST

Read over the Thought Record page near the end of this chapter to prepare for discussion. You will be doing a Thought Record with your seizure counselor at the end of your appointment after you discuss your triggers.

Resources for Further Reading

Andrews, D., Reiter, J., Schonfeld, W., Kastl, A., & Denning P. A neurobehavioral treatment for unilateral complex partial seizure disorders: a comparison of right- and left- hemisphere patients. *Seizure*, 2000;9(3):189–197.

Devinsky, O., Schachter, S., & Pacia, S. *Complementary and Alternative Therapies for Epilepsy.* New York: Demos, 2005.

Fenwick, P. Behavioral treatment of epilepsy. *Postgraduate Medical Journal*, 1990; 66: 336.

Laidlaw, J., & Richens, A., eds. *A Textbook of Epilepsy.* London: Churchill Livingstone, 1982.

Nakken, K., Solaas, M., Kjeldsan, M., Friis, M., Pellock, J., & Corey, L. Which seizure-precipitating factors do patients with epilepsy most frequently report? *Epilepsy and Behavior*, 2005;6(1):85–89.

Pelletier, Kenneth R. *The Best Alternative Medicine.* New York: Simon and Schuster, 2007.

Richard, A., & Reiter, J. *Epilepsy: A New Approach.* New York: Walker, 1995.

Selye, Hans. *The Stress of Life.* New York: McGraw-Hill, 1976.

Selye, Hans. *Stress Without Distress.* New York: The New American Library, (Signet) 1974.

THOUGHT RECORD

Patient Example

1. Situation	2. Moods	3. Automatic Thoughts (Images)	4. Evidence That Supports the Hot Thought	5. Evidence That Does Not Support the Hot Thought	6. Alternative/Balanced Thoughts	7. Rate Moods Now
Riding in the car to the store with wife	Angry 90%	The movers are changing the pick up time. I have too many things to do before the move.	I got kicked out of school for fighting.	Later, I got my GED and got an Associate degree.	I am not a failure. 75%	Angry 15%
Saturday at noon.	Anxious 90%	I am being taken advantage of by them.	I made poor grades.	I am working on my health by coming to the appointments.		Anxious 20%
Got into an argument over the phone with the movers.		My father would just show up at any hour. This is how my father did me and my mother when I was a boy.	I got a DUI 8 years ago. I lost a good paying job. I haven't talked with my father in 2 years.	I help my wife out around the house. I take care of my daughter.		Happy 30%
Had a seizure.		I got expelled from school. (I am a failure.)				
		Answer some or all of the following questions:				
Who were you with? What were you doing? When was it? Where were you?	Describe each mood in one word. Rate intensity of mood (0-100%).	What was going through my mind just before I started to feel this way? What does this say about me? What does this mean about me? my life? my future? What am I afraid might happen? What is the worst thing that could happen if this is true? What does this mean about how the other person(s) feel(s)/think(s) about me? What does this mean about the other person(s) or people in general? What images or memories do I have in this situation?	Circle the one hot thought in previous column for which you are looking for evidence. Write factual evidence to support this conclusion. (Try to avoid mind-reading and interpretation of facts).	Ask yourself questions to help discover evidence which does not support your hot thought. (e.g. If my best friend or someone I loved thought this, what would I tell them?) If my best friend or someone I loved knew I had this thought, what would they tell me?)	Ask yourself questions to generate alternative or balanced thoughts. (e.g. Based on both evidence columns, what is another way of thinking about this?) Write an alternative or balanced thought. Rate how much you believe in each alternative or balanced thought (0-100%).	Copy the feelings from Column 2. Rerate the intensity of each feeling from 0 to 100% as well as any new moods.

Completed from *Mind Over Mood* by Dennis Greenberger and Christine A. Padesky. © 1995 The Guilford Press. 7-Column Thought Record © 1983 Christine A. Padesky, www.MindOverMood.com

Thought Record

SEIZURE LOG   For the Week of ____/____/____ to ____/____/____

Instructions: Please fill in the diary at the end of each day to record the number and descriptions listed. This information will be reviewed with your physician at each appointment.

Init:_____
ID:_____
Week: _____
Type:_____

SUNDAY __/__/__ (day 1)
Number of Seizures:_____
Time(s) of day:_____
Duration (sec or min):_____
Description:_____
Location(s):_____
Severity (1: mild, 2: mod, 3: severe):_____
Trigger(s):_____
Precursor(s):_____
Improved with:_____
Impact on your day:_____
Impact on others:_____

MONDAY __/__/__ (day 2)
Number of Seizures:_____
Time(s) of day:_____
Duration:_____
Description:_____
Location(s):_____
Severity (1: mild, 2: mod, 3: severe):_____
Trigger(s):_____
Precursor(s):_____
Improved with:_____
Impact on your day:_____
Impact on others:_____

TUESDAY __/__/__ (day 3)
Number of Seizures:_____
Time(s) of day:_____
Duration:_____
Description:_____
Location(s):_____
Severity (1: mild, 2: mod, 3: severe):_____
Trigger(s):_____
Precursor(s):_____
Improved with:_____
Impact on your day:_____
Impact on others:_____

WEDNESDAY __/__/__ (day 4)
Number of Seizures:_____
Time(s) of day:_____
Duration:_____
Description:_____
Location(s):_____
Severity (1: mild, 2: mod, 3: severe):_____
Trigger(s):_____
Precursor(s):_____
Improved with:_____
Impact on your day:_____
Impact on others:_____

THURSDAY __/__/__ (day 5)
Number of Seizures:_____
Time(s) of day:_____
Duration:_____
Description:_____
Location(s):_____
Severity (1: mild, 2: mod, 3: severe): _____
Trigger(s):_____
Precursor(s):_____
Improved with:_____
Impact on your day:_____
Impact on others:_____

FRIDAY __/__/__ (day 6)
Number of Seizures:_____
Time(s) of day:_____
Duration:_____
Description:_____
Location(s):_____
Severity (1: mild, 2: mod, 3: severe): _____
Trigger(s):_____
Precursor(s):_____
Improved with:_____
Impact on your day:_____
Impact on others:_____

SATURDAY __/__/__ (day 7)
Number of Seizures:_____
Time(s) of day:_____
Duration:_____
Description:_____
Location(s):_____
Severity (1: mild, 2: mod, 3: severe): _____
Trigger(s):_____
Precursor(s):_____
Improved with:_____
Impact on your day:_____
Impact on others:_____

Use **the space below or on back** to describe any significant information not covered in this record:

_____
_____
_____
_____
_____
_____

Were you successful in stopping any seizures this week:
yes ☐   no ☐

Please mark which seizures you stopped with an asterisk (*).

Total: _____   Rater: _____

SEIZURE LOG   **For the Week of** _____/_____/_____ **to** _____/_____/_____

Instructions: Please fill in the diary at the end of each day to record the number and descriptions listed. This information will be reviewed with your physician at each appointment.

SUNDAY ___/___/___ (day 1)
Number of Seizures:_____
Time(s) of day:_____
Duration (sec or min):_____
Description:_____
Location(s):_____
Severity (1: mild, 2: mod, 3: severe):_____
Trigger(s):_____
Precursor(s):_____
Improved with:_____
Impact on your day:_____
Impact on others:_____

MONDAY ___/___/___ (day 2)
Number of Seizures:_____
Time(s) of day:_____
Duration:_____
Description:_____
Location(s):_____
Severity (1: mild, 2: mod, 3: severe):_____
Trigger(s):_____
Precursor(s):_____
Improved with:_____
Impact on your day:_____
Impact on others:_____

TUESDAY ___/___/___ (day 3)
Number of Seizures:_____
Time(s) of day:_____
Duration:_____
Description:_____
Location(s):_____
Severity (1: mild, 2: mod, 3: severe):_____
Trigger(s):_____
Precursor(s):_____
Improved with:_____
Impact on your day:_____
Impact on others:_____

WEDNESDAY ___/___/___ (day 4)
Number of Seizures:_____
Time(s) of day:_____
Duration:_____
Description:_____
Location(s):_____
Severity (1: mild, 2: mod, 3: severe):_____
Trigger(s):_____
Precursor(s):_____
Improved with:_____
Impact on your day:_____
Impact on others:_____

Total: _____   **Rater:** _____

THURSDAY ___/___/___ (day 5)
Number of Seizures:_____
Time(s) of day:_____
Duration:_____
Description:_____
Location(s):_____
Severity (1: mild, 2: mod, 3: severe): _____
Trigger(s):_____
Precursor(s):_____
Improved with:_____
Impact on your day:_____
Impact on others:_____

FRIDAY ___/___/___ (day 6)
Number of Seizures:_____
Time(s) of day:_____
Duration:_____
Description:_____
Location(s):_____
Severity (1: mild, 2: mod, 3: severe): _____
Trigger(s):_____
Precursor(s):_____
Improved with:_____
Impact on your day:_____
Impact on others:_____

SATURDAY ___/___/___ (day 7)
Number of Seizures:_____
Time(s) of day:_____
Duration:_____
Description:_____
Location(s):_____
Severity (1: mild, 2: mod, 3: severe): _____
Trigger(s):_____
Precursor(s):_____
Improved with:_____
Impact on your day:_____
Impact on others:_____

Use **the space below or on back** to describe any significant information not covered in this record:

_____
_____
_____
_____
_____

Were you successful in stopping any seizures this week:
yes ☐   no ☐

Please mark which seizures you stopped with an asterisk (*).

CHAPTER 6 | Session 5: Channeling Negative Emotions Into Productive Outlets

In Session 4, you learned how triggers often lead to strong negative states, which in turn produce target symptoms such as seizures. It was suggested that getting to know and understand your triggers would enable you to prevent some of the powerful negative states that your triggers produce. For example, physical triggers, such as excessive alcohol or insufficient sleep, and external triggers, such as verbal criticism or an overload of work, can often be avoided by personal choice.

Trigger → **Negative State** → **Target Symptom**

Insufficient sleep → **Fatigue or Anger** → **Seizure**

In the above example, adequate sleep would prevent the negative state, which could in turn help to prevent the seizure.

Identifying and avoiding triggers can do a lot to prevent frequent negative states. But some triggers cannot be avoided, and strong negative states are a common human experience. If it were necessary to prevent all negativity—all fear, anger, and hurt—to prevent seizures, the situation would be close to hopeless. But preventing all negative feelings and states is neither possible nor necessary, and the situation is far from hopeless. In this session, we focus on learning to channel negative states into productive outlets that do not produce seizures or other target symptoms.

```
┌─────────────────────────────────────────────────────────────────────────────┐
│ Trigger  ----//---->  Negative State  ----//---->  Target Symptom (e.g., seizure) │
│                                                                               │
│        Session 4                          Session 5                           │
│                                                                               │
│   Block negative                    Block target symptom, e.g. seizure,       │
│   state by addressing               by channeling negative state              │
│   and/or accepting                  into productive outlets.                  │
│   Trigger.                                                                     │
└─────────────────────────────────────────────────────────────────────────────┘
```

Figure 6.1

Trigger, Negative State, Target Symptom Pattern

Figure 6.1 illustrates the key tasks of Sessions 4 and 5 of this *Workbook*.

What Is Meant by Productive Outlets for Negative States?

When a person is experiencing a deeply depressed mood or extreme anger, it is hard to imagine that there could exist a "productive" or "positive" outlet for such powerful negative feelings. It is a difficult process—a "pull-yourself-up-by-your-own-bootstraps" operation—but it is certainly possible. The following four guidelines will help you work on channeling negative states into productive outlets. In this process, you can learn to take destructive responses and turn them into constructive ones.

1. *Expression—to yourself and others*
2. *Self-acceptance*
3. *See your negative state as a demand for action*
4. *Take action*
   —toward positive change
   —toward productive and/or non-destructive outlets

Look at this process closely, one point at a time:

Expression

First and foremost, "expression" means expressing your thoughts and feelings honestly to yourself. Remember that you can be your own best friend. This is by no means easy, because most of us judge or criticize ourselves for feeling a certain way that we consider negative or "bad." Nonetheless, it is very important to work on observing oneself, asking oneself, "How do

I *really* feel right now?" "What are my true thoughts?" Express these feeling and thoughts honestly, without censorship, to yourself. As a reminder, our primary moods/emotions are

- *mad (angry)*
- *sad (depressed)*
- *glad (happy)*
- *bad (ashamed/guilt)*
- *anxious (worried)*
- *afraid (fearful)*
- *surprised.*

Part of the process is to observe the inner commentary that you make about yourself, for example, "it's stupid to feel or think that way."

When you have expressed your negative state as clearly as you can and have acknowledged your accompanying negative fears or judgments to yourself, then consider whether you want to express yourself to other people. Sometimes "talking about your feelings" to a supportive person can be a great release, a truly "productive outlet." At other times, expressing yourself honestly to others may compound your problems. Only **you** can decide in each instance whether talking to another person will be helpful or not.

Expression is connected with the issue of "Getting Support," which was discussed in Session 2. Certainly no one can expect to have supportive people available to listen at every moment. All of us, however, do need to have a "support system" of people who care for us and are willing to listen to our troubles—our "negative states"—at least, at times. When these other people are not available to listen, self-expression becomes particularly important. Self-expression might take the form of an inner statement or dialogue with oneself ("I sure got bummed out when that policeman gave me a ticket!"), writing in your journal, or some other form of expression such as playing music.

EXPRESSION: AN EXAMPLE

E. S. noticed she was feeling particularly tense in her shoulders and generally uncomfortable.

"What am I really feeling?" she asked herself. "Upset because Jim barely said 'hello, good morning,' much less talked to me. It hurt."

"What else do I feel?"

> *"Inner criticisms, like, 'It's stupid to feel upset, when I know Jim is just in a bad mood about his job today.'"*
>
> *"So that's the whole picture. I feel hurt, and I feel stupid for being hurt. Do I want to talk to him about it now?"*
>
> *"No. He has to leave in 10 minutes to get to work. I'll talk to him later if I still feel this way tonight."*

In this example, E. S. was able to take a sensation of tension in her shoulders and a general feeling of being uncomfortable—and explore her true feelings that underlay these signals. She expressed her thoughts and feelings fully to herself but decided not to express them to the other person involved at that particular time. This inner process of self-expression became in itself a "productive outlet" for her negative state.

Self-Acceptance

Self-acceptance is the attitude and "feeling tone" that all of us need to cultivate while working on self-observation and self-expression. Becoming more aware of your feelings, thoughts, and impulses makes it increasingly important to develop a compassionate, self-accepting attitude toward oneself. Self-acceptance means seeing oneself as a worthy person, deserving of understanding, forgiveness, and respect. It means taking good care of oneself, without blaming or holding others responsible and without guilt or recrimination toward oneself.

In his book, *Compassion and Self-Hate*, psychiatrist Theodore Rubin (1998) presents these two contrasting states of mind that people adopt toward themselves. *Self-hate* consists of inner attacks on oneself—criticisms, judgments, the sense of not measuring up to perfectionistic standards, not being good enough to deserve love and pleasure and all the positive things life has to offer. *Compassion*, on the other hand, means accepting one's limitations and humanity while reaffirming one's own worthiness as a person. With regard to the work you are doing to become more aware of your true feelings and thoughts, Rubin makes a plea for compassionate self-acceptance:

"In other than a compassionate atmosphere and process, careless and uncaring revelation of hitherto buried aspects of ourselves often brings on massive self-hating onslaughts and further repression. The solemn, deep promise to be gentle with ourselves must be invoked again and again, before and during any process of self-revelation."

Some developmental environments plant the seeds for and foster a sense of inadequacy. An example is a child who grows up in a home with an alcoholic parent. The thought that "if I can just be 'good-enough', then maybe he won't have another argument with mom again" is a thought that crosses the mind of a number of children with substance-abusing parents. The internal need for perfection feeds a people-pleasing attitude, hopefully to avoid punishment or to someday garner praise. The cycle is fed by a sense of apprehension or fear. This "need to please" later translates into the inability to say "no" either in relationships or at work. Soon, trying to do everything results in not being able to do anything, creating a self-fulfilling prophecy of failure. This coping model is illustrated in Figure 6.2.

Figure 6.2

Fear - Failure Cycle

In light of possible past rejections and hurts, how do you cultivate an attitude of compassionate self-acceptance? It can be a difficult, slow process. Begin by noticing your inner attitude to yourself. Perhaps you have a tendency to reproach yourself, as soon as you observe something about yourself you do not like. Or maybe you have a tendency to blame other people when things are not going well. Or possibly, you take on responsibility for other people's sadness or anger, seeing yourself as at fault.

Whether you blame yourself or blame others, the harsh inner voice that blames is the voice of self-hate. Whenever you recognize that voice, remind yourself of the "solemn, deep promise to be gentle" with yourself and hence with others. Coin a phrase to describe this gentle, self-accepting attitude, such as, "I wish to accept myself as I really am," or "I am really OK." Use this phrase whenever you need to, as a helpful reminder of your commitment to learn to accept yourself. This attitude of compassionate self-acceptance will gradually free you of the need to judge yourself, blame others, or assume responsibility for the difficulties of other people.

For many in our society, what we do defines us. A man is not known so much for his devotion to his family or giving help to those in need; he is defined by his job. A woman who serves her children is not validated for her work as a "homemaker" as much as she is for what she does in her professional life. When seizures or chronic illness disable, and what you do at work is now limited, many people feel that they are now "worthless." Many people say, "Now that I have my seizures, I can't do what I used to do. It's like I'm of no value to anyone." It cannot be emphasized enough: *your worth is not tied to what you do.*

Consider the life of Christopher Reeve, the actor who played Superman. After sustaining a spinal cord injury, was his life as a paraplegic *worthless*? Some would argue that his contributions to society and to research were greater when he was in the wheelchair than when he was able to walk.

Sometimes people find themselves thinking that there is something about themselves that just is not normal or acceptable, no matter how much they try to tell themselves that they are OK. If you are not sure if your particular feelings or wishes are human and normal, seek out validation from other people. Consider discussing these issues with a trusted friend or family member. It also may be helpful to bring up your worst fears about yourself with your doctor or seizure counselor. While it takes courage to do this, sometimes sharing your concerns about yourself—your reason for self-hate and non-acceptance—is the only way to get over such a major obstacle to compassionate self-acceptance.

Close supportive relationships with others, as well as professional counseling, may be needed to help you develop a sense that your particular set of "baggage" or negative qualities are OK, and you are worthy of self-acceptance. Keep plugging away at this effort, which is a long process. Self-acceptance—giving yourself permission to have the thoughts and feelings you really have—becomes in itself a "productive outlet" for your negative states.

See Your Negative States as a Demand for Action

Many people view their negative states as completely "negative" and undesirable—something to be avoided, if only that were possible. To counter this viewpoint, you may find it helpful to see your negative states as important survival mechanisms, each of which is a valid demand for action.

What is meant by the concept that negative states are survival mechanisms? Remember that negative states can occur at any or all of the four levels of human experience: (1) physical, (2) emotional, (3) intellectual, and (4) spiritual. Pain is an example of a "negative" physical state, which is clearly a survival mechanism. The experience of physical pain leads you to withdraw your hand from a scorching hot casserole dish. Pain is a dramatic "demand for action," which screams at your nervous system to "get your hand away from that burning hot dish, right this second!" And that is exactly what you or any other person would do. You take action in a way that stops or relieves the "negative state." In this case, the survival mechanism of pain prevented a deep, serious hand burn.

Now take an example of a negative emotional state: fear. If you are being chased by a raging rhinoceros toward a 100-foot precipice overlooking an ocean with huge swells, you would no doubt feel afraid. This fear would probably include feeling afraid of injury from the rhino's horn, fear of falling off a cliff, and fear of drowning in the ocean waves, if you survived the fall in one piece. This emotional state of fear helps to mobilize all your resources toward survival, so that when you see a tree near your path, you climb it faster and higher than you have ever climbed a tree before in your life. You reach safety and survive.

But what if the fear does not concern physical survival, but deals instead with emotional safety?

> *Take the situation of F., a woman who finds herself feeling "negative" about a dinner invitation from her parents. When she asks herself what this negative state is about, she notes that she is afraid that her parents will criticize her at this dinner, particularly about the fact that she has not yet found a good full-time job. Closer scrutiny of her feelings may tell her that she has a good reason to feel fear, because her emotional survival is indeed threatened by the prospect of her parents' criticism.*
>
> *As her parents' daughter, she also tends to attach her self-esteem, her feeling of being a worthwhile person, to her success in the working world. In other words, she is afraid that her parents' disapproval will only add to her own inner sense of failure—so she is right in seeing that there is a threat to her self-esteem. Her emotional survival is at risk.*
>
> *F. notices that along with fear, she is feeling angry with her parents. "Why can't they be supportive? Why can't they just encourage me in my job search—instead of judging me as a failure because I haven't found a job? Why don't they respect me as a grown woman instead of treating me as a helpless little kid?"*

Anger often accompanies fear as one combined negative emotional state, for some very good reasons. When a person's self-esteem and boundaries are threatened, fear and anger work together to help that person protect his or her sense of safety and self-worth. Although it is more difficult to see it that way, F.'s negative state is just as much a survival mechanism as the negative state experienced by the person who touched the hot dish or the person running to escape from the rhino. Her negative state is also an important ***demand for action***. She needs to ***do something*** to remove the emotional threat of her parents' potential criticism. She has many options in terms of what kind of action she could decide to take. But the most important point at this stage of the process is ***to see the negative state as a demand for action***.

To see your negative state as a survival mechanism, and in particular as an important, valid demand for action, is a positive step for a number of reasons. One reason is that it enhances self-expression of one's true feelings and states. If F. had begun by saying to herself, "I shouldn't feel this way toward my parents," she probably would not have discovered her true feelings. Another reason is that this viewpoint helps to encourage the attitude of self-acceptance described above. It provides a healthy alternative to the inner voice that most of us have, which says something like "you shouldn't be feeling this way," or "it's your fault that you feel so negative," in response to any uncomfortable feeling or thought. Seeing negative states as a demand for action is therefore a productive outlet in itself. In addition, this viewpoint will help you take appropriate, effective action, as described below.

Take Action

In the discussion of how to channel negative states into productive outlets, the three points explored thus far are primarily internal—taking place within your own mind and feelings. The task of expression is mostly internal; you need to be able to express your negative state and understand as much as you can about the reasons you feel that way ***to yourself*** first and foremost. Both self-acceptance and seeing your negative state as a demand for action are also inner processes that deal with how you view yourself and how you feel about yourself. All three of these points involve learning to see ourselves and our negative state in an accepting, compassionate light. With this inner work under our belt, now is the time to consider taking action as a productive outlet for negative states.

There are two categories of "action" that people have found to be productive outlets for negative states:

1. Action aimed at relieving the *source* of the negative state

    and

2. Action aimed at relieving oneself of the *effects* of the negative state.

Action Aimed at Relieving the *Source* of the Negative State

Removing one's hand from a scalding hot dish and climbing a tree to escape a charging rhino are two simple examples of taking action to relieve the source of a negative state. In these cases, the person takes action to avoid an obvious threat to health and survival. But what kinds of action might F. take, who finds herself fearful and angry about having dinner with her parents?

She might begin by asking herself, "What exactly is the source my anger and fear—my negative state?" She answers herself by summarizing the situation as follows: "The source of my negative state seems to be the thought that my parents will probably make critical comments to me about my inability to find a job. This really gets to me because of my own sense of failure at not yet 'making it' in the working world. I really want a good job so I can be independent, feel better about myself (less inadequate), and also to show my parents I can do it."

Her detailed understanding of the source of her current state of fear and anger enables her to think of a wide variety of possible actions. As you read F.'s list, see if you can think of other alternative actions she might consider that could relieve the source of her negative state:

1. Tell my parents I'm too busy to accept their dinner invitation.
2. Tell my parents I would like to accept their dinner invitation, but only with the understanding that my job situation will not be a topic of conversation during the evening.
3. Stop feeling that not finding a job means that I am an inadequate person. (F. later crossed this possibility off her list because she realized that at this time, she could not change how she felt about this.)
4. Arrange a time to talk with both of my parents privately about how I feel when they make critical, judgmental comments about me. Let

them know that I value seeing them, but I will not put up with any more of their negative comments.

5. Attend an upcoming seminar at a local community college on "How to market yourself in today's job market."

6. See a career counselor about taking some computer or other business courses that might improve my chances of finding employment.

7. Telephone the businesses that I sent applications to before, to check if they have any new openings.

8. Let myself get openly angry with my parents. Tell them to lay off the put-downs. Let them know I do not think they are any better than I am, so why should I let them judge me? They are never happy with what I am doing and that is their problem, not mine. But it is really aggravating!

9. Consider seeing a psychological counselor about my feeling that I am inadequate, no matter what I do.

As you can see from this list, and perhaps from some other actions that you have thought of, there are a wide variety of actions that a person might choose to take in order to relieve the source of a negative state. Successful actions might include avoiding a stressful situation, as in 1 on her list, or communicating her needs clearly in an attempt to change a stressful situation, as in 2 and 4. Often communication of this kind involves expressing clearly how the person's actions or words make you feel. Sometimes it may be necessary to set limits with other people by letting them know what you are willing and unwilling to accept from them in order to continue the relationship on a positive basis.

Third, you might choose to try to change your own thoughts and feelings about yourself, as in 3 and 8, remembering that this is particularly difficult. Often long-term efforts are necessary in order to feel less sensitive or threatened about certain situations.

A fourth kind of action, as seen in 5, 6, and 7, involves those actions you take to reach an important personal goal and to improve your own self-esteem. Clearly, finding a job immediately would probably relieve F.'s negative state—but so far she has not been able to achieve this. Instead, she could take a number of steps to improve her chances of excellent employment in the next few months or years, a few of which are listed above. Any one of those actions might help to relieve her negative state because she would know that she was taking a new, potentially productive step in her job search.

Action Aimed at Relieving Oneself of the *Effects* of a Negative State

As mentioned above, there is a whole other category of action that a person can chose to take as a method of channeling negative states into productive outlets. This type of action is aimed at relieving oneself of the effects of the negative state. In order to illustrate this type of action, let us change slightly the situation of the woman whom we have been discussing.

Suppose that F. is 21 years old and is currently living with her parents. She has told her parents repeatedly over the past year that she strongly dislikes their negative, judgmental comments about her, but they are either unable or unwilling to change this pattern. They have told her that if she does not like what they say about her, she should either prove to them that their view of her as a loser is not true, or she should live on her own. She would very much like to live independently, but her low income from part-time employment will not allow her to move out. She avoids frequent contact with her parents, particularly mealtimes, which she often shares with friends. Today, she is particularly angry and afraid about this evening's dinner with her parents, in which she anticipates a lot of comments about her recent rejection for a job she hoped to get. She has decided not to avoid this dinner because she simply needs a nutritious meal and cannot afford to repeatedly eat out.

Although the actions she listed in 5, 6, and 7 above are still viable options for her, they probably will not make a big difference for her today. She plans to take action to relieve the source of her negative state as soon as possible, by finding a job and moving out on her own. But since that may take weeks or months, *what can she do to relieve herself of this negative state right at this very moment?*

It is useful here to note that she is facing exactly the kind of trigger—her parents' harsh criticism—that often leads to a negative state, which in turn might lead to a seizure or some other target symptom such as a migraine headache. What can she do to help herself feel better, given this difficult situation? What actions can she take to relieve her own negative state, channeling it into a productive outlet instead of a target symptom such as a seizure?

Some possible actions are listed below (*check ones that you may do*).

1. Telephone a close friend to talk.
2. Take a brisk 3-mile walk.
3. Spend an hour before dinner working in her room on a favorite hobby.
4. Work in the yard pulling weeds.

5. Write in her journal about her feelings, fears, anger, plans to improve the situation, and so forth.
6. Listen to music that she finds particularly soothing or enjoyable.
7. Make a plan with a friend to go out to a movie after dinner.
8. Clean out her room and/or garage storage area.
9. Go to the gym for some exercise. Look into the cost of a regular exercise program while she is there.
10. Settle down in a comfortable chair with a book or enjoyable magazine.

Your own list of "top 10" actions for dealing with a negative state will certainly differ somewhat from the one above. But it is useful to look at the above list to learn more about which kinds of actions are particularly effective channels for negative states. The following summary indicates six different kinds of actions that many people find helpful for relieving negative states:

1. Physical exercise, as in examples 2 and 9, above.
2. Obtaining social support, as in examples 1 and 7.
3. Self-expression and/or talking about your worries, as in 1 and 5.
4. Vigorous activity, especially when it gives a sense of accomplishment, such as in 4 and 8.
5. Active relaxation (i.e., activities such as hobbies that are relaxing for a particular person), as in 3 and 10.
6. Escape into recreation, as in 6, 7, and the book or magazine in 10.

The first kind of action, which merits some explanation, is physical exercise. You might choose other forms of exercise than those listed in 2 and 9, but the important fact is that *physical exercise is the single most effective stress-reducing activity* that a person can choose to engage in. Exercise reduces both physical and emotional tension and works powerfully to decrease negative states.

Another type of action that is effective in relieving negative states is to seek some social support, especially when you choose to get in touch with a person you can talk honestly to about some of your negative feelings. Expression is a third method of helping yourself to feel less negative, whether you express yourself to another person or engage in some form of self-expression such as writing, art, or music. Alternatively, any form of vigorous activity involving hard work and a sense of accomplishment will often help you to get out of a negative state.

Finally, negative states can be relieved by purposely doing something relaxing and enjoyable instead of allowing yourself to wallow in bad feelings. You might choose to do something particularly relaxing for you, such as a hobby, or you might escape into recreation by watching a favorite TV show or reading an absorbing novel. Later in this session, when you are making your own list of actions to relieve negative states, refer back to this section and try to include at least one from each of the six categories suggested above. Taking action to ease negative states will allow you to move into a different place in your relationships with others as well as with yourself.

Fear and Anger

Session 4 pointed out that fear and anger tend to be common seizure triggers. Research conducted by the Andrews/Reiter Epilepsy Program has shown that fear and anger require different outlets for expression.

Fear: Address With Courage to Overcome What You Are Afraid of—A Demand for an Activity-Oriented Outlet

Fear can play a major role in triggering seizures. Based on the experience of the authors, unrealistic fear usually demands an activity-oriented outlet; that is, the individual will have to gently summon the courage to meet the challenge of carrying out the very activity of which he or she is afraid in order to overcome the fear. The reward is not only the sustainable resolution of fear but also newly built confidence in the skill that was required in order to address the fear.

What is meant by unrealistic fear? This question can be answered easily by giving examples of realistic fears: Being afraid of getting too close to the edge of a high building constitutes a realistic fear; that is, it will keep you from doing something that is potentially dangerous. Not to hand in the application for a promotion even though all of your coworkers encourage you to do so because it is clear to them that you are capable of doing the job and deserve to be recognized for your capabilities, is an unrealistic fear; that is, the fear itself turns into an obstacle that keeps you from doing something beneficial for yourself. In some cases it might be difficult to determine if your fear is a realistic warning of a potential danger or if it indicates a challenge that should encourage you to summon the courage that will be necessary to meet the opportunity. If you have a hard time determining the right strategy to address a specific fear, discuss your concerns with your seizure counselor.

Anger: Need to Address With Communication to Yourself or Others—A Demand for a Communicative Outlet

Anger can also play a role in triggering seizures. Anger tends to get sparked by dissatisfaction with an event that may or may not be within your control to be changed. Anger is on a continuum of emotions that includes frustration and can eventually lead to depression if it remains unresolved. Since the resolution of the cause of angry feelings may not be within one's control, the authors have found that anger requires communication in order to relieve the tension that it creates.

Session 4 described various examples of communicative opportunities, including honest expression to yourself in the form of an inner dialogue or journal writing, as well as talking to a friend, a family member, or your seizure counselor. Direct communication with the person who has caused you to be angry can be quite a challenge, but it is especially important to learn how to use assertive communication in the form of direct communication. *If you communicate with the subject of your anger without obvious anger in the tone of your voice, it will make your communication more readily acceptable to that person.* Otherwise, raising your voice and using disrespectful verbal expressions will give the recipient of the communication an easy excuse to dismiss anything you say. Soon the conversation will not be about the cause of your anger, but will be consumed by the communicative spiral of the angry emotion itself. If you are not sure that you can temper yourself or you feel uncomfortable addressing the subject matter in person, it may be a good idea to organize your thoughts by composing a letter. Letter writing is a somewhat forgotten, "old-fashioned," but very efficient method to relieve anger while directly addressing the person who made you angry. Letter writing refers to a handwritten or typed, well thought-out letter, not a reactive email or brash text response, which are misused (and many times, later regretted) forms of modern communication. The letter also gives *the recipient* the opportunity to consider your thoughts, at his or her leisure. At times, it can even be beneficial to simply start writing the letter and make the decision later about whether you want to send it or not. Some letters end up being a complete and therefore satisfying communication. This may be especially true if a long time has passed between the incident that incited the anger and the time when you finally decide to communicate it by letter. You may want your support person or seizure counselor to review the letter to help process some of your thoughts and feelings before considering sending it.

A CAUTIONARY NOTE

At times it may be beneficial to conduct a quick "reality-check" in order to determine if your anger is actually justified or if it is an expression of "other-blame," in order to avoid responsibility. In particular, if you choose to directly communicate with the person who has caused you to be angry, you need to aim at complete communication, while neither overstepping the socially acceptable boundaries nor allowing yourself to give in to oversensitive traits of character. A helpful maxim is to "speak the truth in love." Complete communication allows you to let go of the anger and avoid future ruminations, resentment, and/or frustration. As soon as you have fulfilled your responsibility to communicate your anger, it becomes your responsibility to let go of this emotion as quickly as possible. You have to be aware that you cannot make the decision to let go of the anger dependent on the recipient's reaction, since that response is clearly outside your control. You can review some examples of activities that may help you let go of the anger after you have achieved a complete communication, which are listed in the prior session.

Putting It All Together: A Summary

Figure 6.3 summarizes the process described in Sessions 4 and 5.

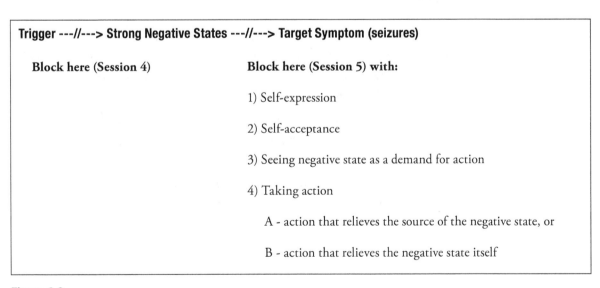

Trigger ---//---> Strong Negative States ---//---> Target Symptom (seizures)

Block here (Session 4) **Block here (Session 5) with:**

1) Self-expression

2) Self-acceptance

3) Seeing negative state as a demand for action

4) Taking action

    A - action that relieves the source of the negative state, or

    B - action that relieves the negative state itself

Figure 6.3
Tools to Block Progression of Negative State to Target Symptom

Goal

The goal for this session is to learn to take positive action in response to negative states, that is, to channel negative states into productive outlets instead of target symptoms.

Obstacles

Select the statements below that may apply to you, or write in your own.

- Feeling powerless and helpless ("There's no way I can help myself out of my negative states.")
- Blaming other people for negative states
- Blaming yourself for negative states
- Blaming circumstances for negative states
- Difficulty getting in touch with how you really feel
- Difficulty accepting how you really feel, when you do become aware of it
- Wanting to forget about negative states when you are not experiencing one
- Feeling resistant to planning how you are going to deal more effectively with the next negative state you experience.

Tools

Some effective tools for learning to channel negative states into productive outlets have been discussed thus far in Session 5. Now is the time for you to apply these tools to your own particular needs. Before your next office visit, in each category below, write in your own ideas of how you might utilize the different methods we have discussed. Refer to the earlier sections of this session for relevant examples and a detailed explanation of each category. Try to be as practical and specific as possible, keeping in mind that the lists you make will be your personal guidelines for learning to channel negative states into productive outlets.

Worksheet: Your Productive Outlets

1) Expression

(for example, write in journal, talk to friend, engage in expressive art)

_____

_____

_____

_____

2) Self-Acceptance

Identify aspects of yourself that you find difficult to accept or like. Make a list of these:

_____

_____

_____

_____

_____

_____

_____

Read over your list, reminding yourself that you can be compassionate toward yourself with regard to these aspects of yourself. Utilize a phrase such as "I'm only human" or "nobody's perfect" or "it's okay to be like this," while you think about each item on your list. At other times when you find yourself not liking or accepting yourself, use this same phrase to help you cultivate a compassionate attitude toward yourself and others. Give yourself and others permission to be human—to be less than perfect.

3) See Your Negative State as a Demand for Action

List at least five of your recent negative states: What was the demand for action?

_____

_____

_____

_____

_____

_____

_____

4) Take Positive Action

A) Action aimed at relieving *the sources* of the negative state:

List the actions you might choose to relieve the source of one or more negative states that you listed above:

_____

_____

_____

_____

_____

_____

_____

B) Actions aimed at relieving oneself of *the effects* of the negative state:

List actions you might take to channel your negative states into positive outlets. Refer to the example list given earlier in the text of Session 5. Then spend some time thinking and writing down your own list of "top 10" actions for relieving a negative state.

1) _____

2) _____

3) _____

4) _____

5) _____

6) _____

7) _____

8) _____

9) _____

10) _____

The Most Important Tool Is Practice

Refer frequently to the work you have just done in your *Workbook*.

- Practice all four different methods that have been discussed as useful for channeling negative states into productive outlets.
- Use your journal to record your progress, noting which methods and actions seem to be most effective for you.
- Remind yourself that this is a long, complex process; give yourself plenty of time to practice and to learn.

The goal of this process is not *to eliminate all negative states*—positive and negative emotions are part of who we are as human beings! You can rightly congratulate yourself for "small successes," such as taking a powerful negative state and making it slightly weaker and more manageable by some positive action that you take. Such achievements may seem small, but they have a major effect on reducing target symptoms—and on helping you reach your goal of taking control of your life.

In-Office Discussion

Please read these sections and make notes in your *Workbook* prior to your appointment, as preparation for the in-office discussion with your seizure counselor.

Review of Assignments

Seizure Log

If you experienced seizure activity since your last appointment, how often were you able to identify a trigger? Do you remember the negative state that the trigger produced?

Journal-Keeping

If you wish, read one or more passages from "A Day in the Life" to your support person or seizure counselor. If possible, select material that contains observations of your negative emotions and how you cope with them.

Goal Review From Prior Session

Were you able to meet the goal you set for yourself at your last session? If so, good for you! If not, discuss with your seizure counselor how you might choose more realistic, achievable goals for yourself.

Trigger Chart

Discuss any new triggers you have identified since last session. Be sure to add them to your Trigger Chart in the Discussion section of Session 4. Continue to add to this chart whenever you identify a new trigger for your seizures.

Thought Record

You will discuss again how to go through a Thought Record with your seizure counselor. Complete Thought Records with your symptoms. Here are some instructions and ways you may find Thought Records helpful:

- Thought Records help you to develop a set of skills that can improve your mood and relationships and lead to positive behavior change and fewer target symptoms.
- The first three columns of a Thought Record distinguish a situation from the emotions and thoughts you had in the situation. In Column 1, describe the situation in detail: date, time, place, who was there, what were you doing. In Column 2, rate the intensity of your moods at the time of the situation. In Column 3, list any thoughts you had accompanying the event.
- Identifying and listing Automatic Thoughts may reveal a Hot Thought (or Core Belief)—a charged thought that fuels your negative feelings. Use the questions in the column example to drill down to the Hot Thought.
- In the next two columns, you then list evidence that does and does not support the Hot Thought that you identified.
- In the Alternative Thought column, you provide a Balanced Thought, which is an opportunity to develop new ways of thinking that can lead to feeling better. Rate how much you believe it.
- After the Balanced Thought, in the last column, list your current moods and re-rate their intensity.
- As in developing any new skill, you may need to practice completing many Thought Records before you achieve consistent results.
- The Thought Record can be used at the onset of symptoms to prevent the progression, or can be used afterward to process what may have triggered the symptoms, including seizures.

Review of Obstacles

What obstacles have you noticed with regard to observing triggers? If you tried to avoid any of your triggers, did you experience any obstacles or resistance? Which of the obstacles listed above, regarding channeling negative states into productive outlets, seem to apply to you? Have you noticed any others?

Discussion of Methods for Channeling Negative States Into Productive Outlets

Session 5 focuses on the work you have done at home. Think through and list your own methods for channeling negative states into productive outlets. Write down your own personal strategies that you have used, in preparation for your next appointment. Use what you wrote to discuss and clarify or to generate new ideas with the help of your seizure counselor.

Worksheet: Personal Strategies for Productive Outlets

Select three methods of channeling negative states from the many ideas you have listed above. Make a specific plan for how and when you will utilize these three methods and write them down now in the space provided below to review at the end of your discussion with the seizure counselor:

1) _____

_____

_____

_____

_____

2) _____

_____

_____

_____

_____

3) _____

_____

Seizure Log

Continue to record seizure activity, severity, and triggers, daily, as explained in Session 4. In the upcoming week, begin recording your emotional state as well. On the Seizure Log forms, write descriptive terms to convey your emotional state or moods, such as, "angry, afraid, worried, excited." Write one or more of these words if you experience those states during the day (whether you had a seizure or not.) Whenever possible, and especially when your negative state is not well described by any of these four words, write more about how you feel in your journal. Indicate that you made a journal entry by circling the word "journal" on the Seizure Log form.

Journal-Keeping

Observe yourself while you are experiencing a negative state. Describe your observations in your journal, including the many different aspects of the experience, which are listed below:

a. Triggers that brought about the negative state
b. Any efforts to block or address triggers? If so, how effective were these efforts?
c. The negative state (how you felt, thoughts, sensations, etc.)
d. Expression and acceptance of the negative state
e. In what way was this negative state a demand for action? What action could you/did you consider to relieve the *source* of this negative state?
f. What actions could you consider to relieve yourself of the *effects* of the negative state?
g. Did you actually take any action? If so, describe what you did and any effects that you observed.
h. Any target symptoms?

Bring your journal to discuss any responses you want with your seizure counselor.

Goal-Setting for Session 5

Read through the following Goal List for Session 5. In addition to the journal-keeping assignment described above, choose one goal that relates to channeling negative emotions into productive outlets. If desired, you may also choose one goal from the Goal Lists for Sessions 2 or 4. Check off the goal you have selected and write in the specifics of how you plan to meet that goal on the bottom of the Goal List in the space provided. If you have chosen to work on a goal from an earlier session, include a written plan for that goal as well. Show your written goals to your seizure counselor before you leave today's appointment.

Goal List

Expression—to Yourself and Others

___Ask yourself, "How do I really feel right now?" one or more times this week.

___Write about your thoughts and emotions in your journal three times this week.

___Call a close friend when you have some feelings to talk about, at least one time this week. (In order to be sure to be able to carry out this goal, you may want to ask your friend ahead of time if it is OK to call next time you are feeling negative or down.)

___Plan ahead to engage in a particular expressive art (playing music, painting or drawing, dance, creative writing, and so on) the next time you experience a negative state at home, or at least one time this week.

___Arrange to get together this week with a friend to talk about a recent experience or situation that upset or bothered you.

___Other: _____

Self-Acceptance

___Remind yourself of "the solemn, deep promise to be gentle with yourself before and during any process of self-revelation" at least three times this week.

___Write in your own phrase to describe a compassionate, self-accepting attitude toward yourself, such as "It is OK to be human," or "I wish to accept myself as I really am."

___ Think about an example of someone who suffered a trial or who has a disability and ended up making an impact in his or her life and the life of others.

_____

_____

_____

___ Say the compassionate phrase to yourself at least three times this week.

___ Plan a time in the next week to discuss some part of yourself that you think of as "unacceptable" with a close trusted friend or with your seizure counselor.

___ If not addressed in these therapy sessions, ask your seizure counselor or physician to refer you to a psychologist, psychiatrist, or other professional counselor with whom you can work on self-understanding or self-acceptance.

___ Other: _____

See Your Negative State as a Demand for Action

___ The next time you observe yourself feeling fearful, angry, or upset, ask yourself: "How is this negative state a demand for action? What exactly is the source of this negative state and what could I do to relieve it?" (Do this at least one time this week.)

___ List three to five negative states that you recently experienced. Write down at least one demand for action for each negative state you listed.

___ Other: _____

Taking Action to Relieve the Source of the Negative State

___ Address/modify the following stressful situation at least one time this week:

_____

___ Attempt to change a stressful situation with another person by communicating your needs clearly, using the assertive communication techniques described in Session 2. Pick a specific, ongoing situation that you will have the opportunity to deal with in the next week. Briefly describe the situation and what you plan to say:

_____

___ Make a list of five or more possible actions you might take to relieve the source of a negative state that you experienced recently.

___ Plan an action that will help you reach an important personal goal, improve your self-esteem, and relieve a potential source of negative states. (See earlier in this chapter for examples.) Briefly describe your plan:

_____

_____

Taking Action to Relieve the Effects of a Negative State

___ Engage in physical exercise three times this week (at least once, while in a negative state).

___ Call or seek out a friend the next time you experience a negative state. (Arrange ahead with a particular friend or family member who is willing to provide social support this way.)

___ Plan a particular vigorous activity that will give you a sense of accomplishment, that you will do the next time you experience a negative state while at home (e.g., clean out the garage, wash the windows, yard work):

_____

_____

___ Choose some activity that is actively relaxing (e.g., a hobby, craft) that you will do the next time you experience a negative state at home:

_____

_____

___ Plan an escape into recreation (e.g., book, taped TV show or video, magazine) that you will save specifically for the next time you experience a negative state while at home:

_____

_____

___ Other: _____

After you have selected one of the above goals, write down in your own words specifically what you plan to do to meet this goal during the coming week. The more specific you are, the easier it will be to meet your goal.

My goal for the week ending (give date) ___/___/____ is to:

_____

_____

_____

_____

_____

On (give date) ___/___/_____ , I tried to meet this goal with the following results:

_____

_____

_____

_____

I consider that I did ___, did not ___ meet the goal I set for myself this week.

Trigger Chart and Avoiding Triggers

Continue to add any newly discovered triggers to your Trigger Chart. If you have not done so yet, when you and your counselor feel you are ready, begin work on a plan for triggers that you can avoid. (See the "Going Further" section of Session 4.) Make sure you and your seizure counselor have planned a time to talk about this work, preferably at a session that you will both decide will be devoted to discussion of avoiding triggers.

Relaxation Exercise

To prepare for Session 6, please begin to spend 10 to 15 minutes each day training yourself to reach an awake relaxed state. You may wish to practice the self-observation exercise described in Session 4, or to utilize any relaxation exercises you have used in the past. Instructions are included in the next session to help you practice this relaxation exercise.

Preparing for Your Next Appointment

After completing this session and discussing it with your seizure counselor, please read and complete "Session 6: Relaxation Training: Experiencing the Sensation of the Brain Changing Itself."

Additional Assignments

- Complete a Thought Record on your own, which you can review with your counselor to help with the exercise of channeling negative emotions. Use the prompts at the bottom of the columns of the Patient Example Thought Record (page 119) to guide you in filling out each column.
- On another piece of paper, write out the following: *"What makes me angry"* and *"What makes me sad"* and provide responses. **Bring this to the session**.

Resources for Further Reading

Biebel, D.B., & Koenig, H.G. *New Light on Depression: Help, Hope and Answers for the Depressed and Those Who Love Them*. Grand Rapids, MI: Zondervan, 2004.

Cousins, Norman. *Anatomy of an Illness as Perceived by the Patient*. New York: W. W. Norton, 1979.

LaHaye, Tim. *How to Win over Depression*. Grand Rapids, MI: Zondervan, 1996.

McGee, R. S. *The Search for Significance: Book and Workbook*. Revised and expanded. Nashville, TN: W Publishing Group, 2003.

Rubin, Theodore Isaac. *Compassion and Self-Hate*. New York: Touchstone, 1998.

Other Resources

If not addressed in the following sessions, you may wish to consider a referral to a psychologist, psychiatrist, or other trained counselor after you finish the Workbook to help you continue with your work on observing triggers, coping with negative emotions, and other issues that affect the process of taking control of your seizures. If you are considering this, please discuss this possibility with your physician or seizure counselor. This question will be explored further in "Session 9: Dealing with Internal Issues and Conflicts."

Thought Record

SEIZURE LOG   For the Week of ____/____/____ to ____/____/____

Instructions: Please fill in the diary at the end of each day to record the number and descriptions listed. This information will be reviewed with your physician at each appointment.

Init:_____
ID:_____
Week:_____
Type:_____

SUNDAY __/__/__ (day 1)
Number of Seizures:_____
Time(s) of day:_____
Duration (sec or min):_____
Description:_____
Location(s):_____
Severity (1: mild, 2: mod, 3: severe):_____
Trigger(s):_____
Precursor(s):_____
Improved with:_____
Impact on your day:_____
Impact on others:_____

MONDAY __/__/__ (day 2)
Number of Seizures:_____
Time(s) of day:_____
Duration:_____
Description:_____
Location(s):_____
Severity (1: mild, 2: mod, 3: severe):_____
Trigger(s):_____
Precursor(s):_____
Improved with:_____
Impact on your day:_____
Impact on others:_____

TUESDAY __/__/__ (day 3)
Number of Seizures:_____
Time(s) of day:_____
Duration:_____
Description:_____
Location(s):_____
Severity (1: mild, 2: mod, 3: severe):_____
Trigger(s):_____
Precursor(s):_____
Improved with:_____
Impact on your day:_____
Impact on others:_____

WEDNESDAY __/__/__ (day 4)
Number of Seizures:_____
Time(s) of day:_____
Duration:_____
Description:_____
Location(s):_____
Severity (1: mild, 2: mod, 3: severe):_____
Trigger(s):_____
Precursor(s):_____
Improved with:_____
Impact on your day:_____
Impact on others:_____

THURSDAY __/__/__ (day 5)
Number of Seizures:_____
Time(s) of day:_____
Duration:_____
Description:_____
Location(s):_____
Severity (1: mild, 2: mod, 3: severe):_____
Trigger(s):_____
Precursor(s):_____
Improved with:_____
Impact on your day:_____
Impact on others:_____

FRIDAY __/__/__ (day 6)
Number of Seizures:_____
Time(s) of day:_____
Duration:_____
Description:_____
Location(s):_____
Severity (1: mild, 2: mod, 3: severe):_____
Trigger(s):_____
Precursor(s):_____
Improved with:_____
Impact on your day:_____
Impact on others:_____

SATURDAY __/__/__ (day 7)
Number of Seizures:_____
Time(s) of day:_____
Duration:_____
Description:_____
Location(s):_____
Severity (1: mild, 2: mod, 3: severe):_____
Trigger(s):_____
Precursor(s):_____
Improved with:_____
Impact on your day:_____
Impact on others:_____

Use **the space below or on back** to describe any significant information not covered in this record:

_____
_____
_____
_____
_____
_____

Were you successful in stopping any seizures this week:
yes ☐   no ☐

Please mark which seizures you stopped with an asterisk (*).

Total: _____   Rater: _____

SEIZURE LOG   For the Week of ____/____/____ to ____/____/____

Init:_____
ID:_____
Week: _____
Type:_____

Instructions: Please fill in the diary at the end of each day to record the number and descriptions listed. This information will be reviewed with your physician at each appointment.

SUNDAY ___/___/___ (day 1)
Number of Seizures:_____
Time(s) of day:_____
Duration (sec or min):_____
Description:_____
Location(s):_____
Severity (1: mild, 2: mod, 3: severe):_____
Trigger(s):_____
Precursor(s):_____
Improved with:_____
Impact on your day:_____
Impact on others:_____

MONDAY ___/___/___ (day 2)
Number of Seizures:_____
Time(s) of day:_____
Duration:_____
Description:_____
Location(s):_____
Severity (1: mild, 2: mod, 3: severe):_____
Trigger(s):_____
Precursor(s):_____
Improved with:_____
Impact on your day:_____
Impact on others:_____

TUESDAY ___/___/___ (day 3)
Number of Seizures:_____
Time(s) of day:_____
Duration:_____
Description:_____
Location(s):_____
Severity (1: mild, 2: mod, 3: severe):_____
Trigger(s):_____
Precursor(s):_____
Improved with:_____
Impact on your day:_____
Impact on others:_____

WEDNESDAY ___/___/___ (day 4)
Number of Seizures:_____
Time(s) of day:_____
Duration:_____
Description:_____
Location(s):_____
Severity (1: mild, 2: mod, 3: severe):_____
Trigger(s):_____
Precursor(s):_____
Improved with:_____
Impact on your day:_____
Impact on others:_____

THURSDAY ___/___/___ (day 5)
Number of Seizures:_____
Time(s) of day:_____
Duration:_____
Description:_____
Location(s):_____
Severity (1: mild, 2: mod, 3: severe): _____
Trigger(s):_____
Precursor(s):_____
Improved with:_____
Impact on your day:_____
Impact on others:_____

FRIDAY ___/___/___ (day 6)
Number of Seizures:_____
Time(s) of day:_____
Duration:_____
Description:_____
Location(s):_____
Severity (1: mild, 2: mod, 3: severe): _____
Trigger(s):_____
Precursor(s):_____
Improved with:_____
Impact on your day:_____
Impact on others:_____

SATURDAY ___/___/___ (day 7)
Number of Seizures:_____
Time(s) of day:_____
Duration:_____
Description:_____
Location(s):_____
Severity (1: mild, 2: mod, 3: severe): _____
Trigger(s):_____
Precursor(s):_____
Improved with:_____
Impact on your day:_____
Impact on others:_____

Use **the space below or on back** to describe any significant information not covered in this record:

_____
_____
_____
_____
_____

Were you successful in stopping any seizures this week: yes ☐   no ☐

Please mark which seizures you stopped with an asterisk (*).

Total: _____   Rater: _____

CHAPTER 7

Session 6: Relaxation Training: Experiencing the Sensation of the Brain Changing Itself

If your experience is similar to that of other people with seizures, your seizures started suddenly and unexpectedly. You were told that you have a brain disturbance, either with a cause such as head injury or without any known cause. Most likely, it was emphasized that your condition may be referred to as "organic," which is an older term referring to a process caused by a problem in the structure or function of your brain and therefore out of your control. Medication was prescribed and subsequently adjusted to reduce the frequency and severity of your seizures. From the onset of your seizures, your understanding has probably been that your brain does whatever it feels like, and you have no control in this process.

Do you have control over your brain? The answer to this question seems obvious. Most of the time, of course you do! You determine when you want to speak, walk, write, or talk. You are constantly sorting information and impulses in your brain and making choices, which are under your conscious control. Like most other people, you have moments when you do not have control over your brain—such as when you are in a negative state or experiencing a target symptom. But these moments make up only a small part of your life—and are universally experienced by all human beings, with or without seizures. During most of your waking hours, you are in charge of what you are doing.

But do you feel in control? The answer to this question is less obvious, and most often people with seizures will respond by saying, "No, I don't feel in control of my own brain."

The experience of having seizures leads many people with seizures to see themselves as out of control, of both their brains *and* their bodies. A brief lapse of consciousness, especially if it is accompanied by involuntary movements and/or loss of bladder control, can be a painful and humbling experience. While other people might have "invisible" target symptoms such as headaches or stomach pains, your seizures are much more visible to other people. It is easy to forget that most people are no more in control of their target symptoms than you are of yours—and that most of the time, you *are* in control of your own brain, just like anyone else. Each time you have a seizure, your own embarrassment is often enough to make you feel helpless and out of control.

So What Can You Do to Gain a Sense of Being in Control?

Suppose you could develop the sense that you are in control of your brain, and that you have the ability to change the state of your brain at will. This might allow you to use your awareness of seizure triggers, negative states, and auras more effectively—to actually change your brain's state at the moment that you sense yourself going into a seizure. But to most people with seizures, at first this idea sounds impossible.

We know, however, that it is possible for people to change their brain state, predictably and at will. Yogis have done this for centuries, and modern-day physicians and physiologists have documented the reality of these phenomena. Westerners traditionally are not taught these techniques as schoolchildren, or as part of their faith tradition. Most of us simply have never had the opportunity to feel comfortable and to gain skill with techniques such as relaxation and meditation. Some faiths also discourage meditation because of its use in Eastern religions. While reservations about using transcendental meditation are warranted for the possibility of "opening" oneself for unorthodox experiences, realize that certain forms of meditation are even *scriptural*. Even the Psalmist wrote about meditating on the law of the Lord day and night (Psalm 1:2).

Whenever you decide to practice relaxation techniques, in the process you are allowing yourself to perceive your internal messages. Over time you will increase your awareness of what is going on inside you and how this internal landscape can be transformed by minor changes. This awareness will allow you to understand your body's language. You might catch yourself holding your breath while you concentrate, or you might notice how you raise your shoulders while you check your bank account on your computer. Unconscious muscular tightening and poor breathing can be a result, as well as a cause, of physical and mental stress. Your mind, your muscles, your body, and your brain are constantly communicating. Thus by relaxing your body, you also relax your brain, and by relaxing your mind, you relax your muscles. This session acknowledges their connection and encourages you to find strategies that help you to relax your mind and your muscles, your brain and your body.

Will Relaxation Actually Help You to Reduce Your Seizure Frequency?

For many individuals with epileptic and nonepileptic seizures, working with relaxation will in fact help to reduce seizure frequency. While this has been demonstrated by the authors' experience with numerous patients, as well as by other researchers, the reasons for this improvement are not fully understood. Most likely, it is the process of learning to change and control physiological and emotional states that helps to reduce seizure frequency and to give people a sense of being in control of seizure onset.

Another explanation for the benefits of relaxation training is that it helps you learn to truly relax—your mind as well as your body. Relaxation, whether achieved through vigorous exercise, progressive relaxation exercises, meditation, or biofeedback, helps to reduce the overall arousal level of the body and brain. This means that the person who practices relaxation regularly is less susceptible to stress, less tense, and less likely to have target symptoms such as seizures. While you will be learning about many different ways to relax and reduce tensions in Session 10, relaxation training is a good way to begin now to lower your level of tension and arousal and therefore decrease symptoms.

Relaxation training may help you learn to change your brain wave state at times when you are likely to have a seizure. For example, when you are having a negative state such as anxiety following a trigger, you may be able to change your state to "awake, relaxed" (alpha) in order to prevent yourself from having a seizure. Another example is when you are experiencing a pre-seizure aura (an unusual sensation that may precede your seizures, described fully in Session 7), you may also be able to change your state to "awake, relaxed" in order to stop yourself from having a seizure. While no one can expect to always control their inner state in situations such as these, relaxation may help to familiarize you with this "awake, relaxed" brain wave state enough that you can sometimes achieve this feeling during tense moments when you might otherwise have experienced a seizure.

Relaxation is a relatively new tool in the treatment of seizures. It is not a "proven" method of improving seizure control, but experimentally it has been found to be extremely beneficial. There are no harmful side effects of relaxation and there are no contraindications. There have been no reported instances of people experiencing a worsening of symptoms after relaxation, and many people have had permanent symptom improvement after a complete series of relaxation training sessions. Because of these promising research results, and the fact that no side effects are known to occur, this *Workbook* highly recommends relaxation for anyone whose seizures are not fully controlled with medication and other self-care treatment methods.

Our experience with relaxation with many patients with nonepileptic seizures (NES) is similar to that in epilepsy. That is, many patients with NES who learn relaxation and use it have reduced the number of seizures they experience over time and have stopped the progression of seizures when they experience their aura.

Will Relaxation Training Actually Give You the Sensation of Your Brain Changing Itself?

Yes, relaxation training is a powerful way for you to gain the experience of your brain changing itself—of being in control. For many with seizures, the "out of control" feeling does more to undermine self-esteem than all the other aspects of having seizures. It makes it doubly hard to work seriously on the task of taking control of your life, as outlined in the sessions of this *Workbook*. Learning to change your brain wave states through systematic practice sessions with relaxation will do a lot to change a self-image of being "helpless" and "out of control." If you work on relaxation patiently and regularly, you will truly gain a control over your brain wave states that most people do not have—and which will give you a well-deserved sense of mastery and control over your own brain and inner experience.

How Will You Go About Your Relaxation Training?

The first step is to train yourself to go into your "awake, relaxed state." This helps to teach you to relax your mind as well as your body at will.

Once you have learned to go into your awake, relaxed state, you will then be one step closer to taking control of your seizures.

With practice, you will come to recognize how your subjective experience of the relaxed state feels different from how you feel in the non-relaxed state. As you learn to go into this awake, relaxed state, you will experience "the sensation of the brain taking control of itself." Once you learn to do this, repetition becomes easier and easier. Some of you who have doubted the ability to control your brain state, through this experience, will actually become convinced of your brain's ability to do so.

What If You Are Agitated Much of the Time?

This is another example of a situation where an individual can benefit from developing an ability to relax. Some people, with or without seizures, experience themselves as tense, agitated, and often unable to "shut off their minds." These people do not know what it feels like to be awake and relaxed.

Even if you experience this kind of agitation most of the time, you will be able to learn to use relaxation techniques that will enable you to drift into an awake, relaxed state at times. As you become more familiar with the experience of being in an awake, relaxed state, you will be able to return to this state more and more easily. In your practice, you will learn to quiet your mind and to experience a relaxed, awake state in different situations.

Will You Benefit From Relaxation Training?

Yes. In our experience, anyone with seizures that are not completely controlled with medications and other self-help measures can benefit a great deal from relaxation, deep breathing, and body awareness exercises. The relaxation techniques detailed later in this chapter will allow your body to recognize when you are applying these techniques successfully—in other words, when you have actually reached an awake, relaxed state. This training then offers you the possibility of learning to change your brain state when you want to, from one of agitation or drowsiness into one of awake relaxation. You will gain the experience of your brain taking control of itself.

We have mentioned how relaxation can help you to recognize when you are taking charge of your own brain wave state. Remember, however, that relaxation does not do the work for you. As with all of the sessions in this *Workbook*, you are the one who does the hard work—and you are the one who gets the benefits. Detailed instructions for a series of relaxation sessions are outlined in the section of this chapter entitled "Tool: In-Office Practice Session: Relaxation." Following these instructions, with the help of your seizure counselor, will enable you to verify and maximize your progress with relaxation training techniques.

Can Relaxation "Cure" Seizures?

No, relaxation cannot "cure" seizures, epileptic or nonepileptic. There is not a specific EEG brain wave state that actually "cures" seizures. Our research has simply shown that training individuals to go into a relaxed, awake brain state can help them to reduce seizure frequency and to develop a sense of being in control. In the majority of our research participants, this improvement was a lasting one.

Relaxation training is an established field of research, and there is increasing literature showing its medical benefits. Studies on relaxation have revealed a decrease in the following—heart arrhythmias in cardiac patients; chronic headache pain; the depression and anxiety associated with rheumatoid arthritis; and glucose levels and insomnia in hemodialysis patients. Relaxation is a non-pharmacological, free intervention that relieves both mind and body symptoms.

How Does Relaxation Actually Work to Reduce the Frequency of Seizures?

We simply do not know the answer to this question because the science of relaxation is still young. In looking at the various approaches to research for individuals with seizures, it is interesting to note that a variety of different approaches have been found to be helpful. All of them teach people to change their brain state, resulting in decreased seizure frequency, and they seem to give people a greater sense of being in control. It appears that learning to change the brain state, on a moment-by-moment basis, has a major effect both on seizure frequency and on how much a person feels "in control."

As previously mentioned in this chapter, it may simply turn out that short sessions of the awake, relaxed state are effective because they relieve stress and produce mind/body relaxation. Relaxation sessions may act like meditation or vigorous exercise to lower a person's level of tension and arousal. This reduction of tension could then act to prevent target symptoms of all kinds, including seizures. Some individuals with seizures use relaxation techniques to prevent seizures, incorporating relaxation in a daily routine. Others use relaxation techniques at the onset of a seizure or in a stressful situation to stop the progression of the symptoms. Either or both can lower the number of seizures that one experiences.

It may be that the greatest benefit of relaxation training for people with seizures is that it gives them the sensation of being in control. It is undoubtedly of great value for people to regain a sense of being in control of their own brains, after suffering a loss of self-esteem from a malady that makes them feel helpless and out of control. Additionally, some people have reported that when they sense an aura, or a negative state prior to a seizure, relaxation training has enabled them to go into an awake, relaxed state that can help prevent the seizure. The experience of "the brain changing itself" may be the factor that makes relaxation training such an effective tool for people working to take control of their seizures.

The Work

Goal

The goal for this session is to experience the sensation of the brain changing itself, through the use of relaxation training.

Obstacles

Select the statements below that may apply to you, or write in your own.

- Expecting to be able to change your brain state right away, without repeated practice sessions.
- Difficulty "tuning in" to your state. (This is a skill you will develop through the practice of relaxation, deep breathing, and self-observation exercises, as well as through relaxation training.)

- Resistance to "taking control." Wanting to remain helpless about changing your brain wave state or controlling seizures.
- Fear of increased responsibility for your own inner state.
- Having to be "in control" at all times and not being able to become relaxed.
- It is difficult to apply what you learn with relaxation training to situations out in the world when you sense a seizure coming on (but you *can* learn to do it!).

In-Office Discussion

Please read these sections and make notes in your *Workbook* prior to your appointment, as preparation for the in-office discussion with your seizure counselor.

Review of Assignments

Seizure Log/Thought Records

Show your Seizure Logs to your seizure counselor. How are you doing with identifying and listing triggers and emotional states? Discuss your Thought Records. Do they help you understand how your negative emotions sometimes trigger seizures?

Journal-Keeping

If you wish to do so, read some pertinent observations about the negative state that you described this week in your journal.

Goal Review From Prior Session

Did you meet the goal(s) you set for yourself at your last session? If so, good work! If not, discuss with your seizure counselor how you might choose more attainable goals for yourself.

Trigger Chart and Avoiding Triggers

Discuss if any new insights occurred since your last session.

Relaxation Exercise

Review your practice relaxation at home this week with the counselor.

Review of Obstacles

With regard to undertaking relaxation training, which of the obstacles listed above do you feel apply to you? Are there any other obstacles that you can identify? If you have trouble with relaxation, it may be associated with the sense that you always have to be "in control." Realize that a paradoxical situation exists, where sometimes *to gain control over the seizures, you may have to relinquish control over some things in your life*.

Undertaking Relaxation Training

Who Will Do the Relaxation Training?

The most desirable option is to see your own seizure counselor for relaxation training because you are already on your way toward building a therapeutic relationship together. If counselors are not already trained in the use of relaxation, they can obtain training by attending a seminar or from one of the resources mentioned at the end of this chapter. If this is impossible, you can consider a referral to a relaxation specialist to assist with this aspect of your "taking control" program while continuing to see your seizure counselor weekly to discuss your progress and to proceed with Sessions 7 to the end.

Adding Relaxation to Your Schedule

Relaxation training is usually initially practiced daily for 5–6 weeks. The total number of sessions required depends on individual progress and interest. You may choose to practice relaxation sessions up to 30 minutes, but this may vary from 10–30 minutes, depending on how long each person can concentrate optimally on the training.

Making the Decision: Do You Want to Begin Relaxation Training?

___yes ___no

If your answer is "no," talk to your seizure counselor about what reservations you have about relaxation. Some seizure counselors may feel comfortable with eliminating the relaxation phase of this program, providing that you practice other relaxation training techniques. Other counselors may not.

If your answer is "yes," to prepare for the session with your counselor, practice the parts below over the days preceding your appointment.

Practice Part 1: Getting Familiar With the Basics of Relaxation

1. Lie back and relax in a comfortable lounge chair. The purpose of this exercise is to help the brain associate a slow deep breath with going into the awake, relaxed state. (After practice, you may be able to go into this state simply by taking a relaxed deep breath.) To the count of 4, take a slow deep breath through your nose. Hold breath for one second. Slowly release this breath, through your mouth, to the count of 4. Repeat this slow deep breathing a few times.

2. Free interaction with the relaxation exercise: Think about different things that make you happy, sad, or worried. See what kind of relaxation state you are in while you are feeling or thinking different things. Ask questions, experiment, and indulge your curiosity. This is your chance to learn to feel comfortable with the relaxation process, as well as to become more knowledgeable about different brain wave states.

Practice Part 2: Finding What Works to Produce an Awake, Relaxed State

1. Practice a relaxation technique such as this one, where you read aloud or your support person will lead you through the exercise by slowly reading something like this:

> *Sit in a comfortable position. ... Let your breathing become slow and relaxed. ... Become aware of the palms of your hands ... sense the palms of your hands ... now become aware of the soles of your feet ... sense both soles of your feet at the same time. ... Good ... now in your mind, begin to warm up your palms, forearms, and upper arms at the same time. ... Keep all your attention on your arms as you make them feel warm and heavy ... warming your hands from the palms all the way up to the shoulders ... good. ... Now move attention to your legs ... your legs are becoming warm and heavy ... beginning with the soles of your feet and moving up to the ankles, calves, knees, thighs ... all your attention is on your legs ... your legs feel heavy and warm ... good. ... Now move your attention to your shoulders ... your shoulders are becoming warm, heavy, and relaxed ... you feel your shoulders melting into the chair ... good. ...*

2. You may choose to continue this exercise with other parts of the body or to switch to another relaxation exercise, depending on how you are responding. The goal is to try to achieve relaxation 40% of the time during this or similar exercises.

3. Proceed with Practice Part 3.

Practice Part 3: Finding What Works to Produce an Awake Relaxed State

1. The purpose of this session is to try various visualization methods that may produce an awake, relaxed brain state.

2. Practice a positive visualization, which might include an ocean beach, or walking through the forest along a dirt path. Once you find a scene that has peaceful and relaxing associations for you, you can verbalize this, or your support person can describe this visualization for a few minutes. Then you will have a period of silence to practice your visualization on your own, being aware of any body muscle tension, to reach an awake, relaxed state.

3. A second method of reaching an awake, relaxed brain state involves positive thoughts or a prayer. You might pick a positive thought such as peace, love, or well-being. Or you could concentrate on an affirmation such as "God loves me." Thoughts have great power and can be useful in teaching oneself to relax and feel at peace. Pick one of these, or another thought or affirmation of your choice. Concentrate on this positive thought for a period of time, trying to produce an awake and relaxed state.

4. Note that much of this session may be conducted with your support person out of the relaxation training room, while you practice these various methods of learning to become awake and relaxed. Many people find it easier to concentrate when they are alone, but if you are not comfortable with this arrangement or feel the need for frequent comments and assistance, let your support person know about these needs. Be sure to allow 10 minutes or so at the end of your practice session for comments and discussion.

Tool: In-Office Practice Session—Relaxation

The instructions (above and below) provided in this session are intended for you to use with the assistance of your seizure counselor in the appointment, after you have attempted them initially on your own. Because relaxation is a skill that takes practice to learn, the instructions are provided here for you to refer back to when you practice progressive relaxation. Many people find that making their own recording, either in their own voice or the voice of a person who has a calming effect, is a good way to practice. With your counselor, you can decide what will work best for you.

Practice Part 4: Progressive Relaxation (Practice at Home to Prepare for the Office Appointment)

1. Explanation of what will be done in the session.
2. Discussion of any questions and concerns you may have.
3. In this session, you will utilize a progressive relaxation exercise in order to reach an awake, relaxed state. This exercise is the same one that was mentioned in the Assignments section of Session 5. You will listen to a prerecorded version of this exercise, or your seizure counselor will read it aloud to you. Being able to go through the exercise *without* the use of a recording is ideal so that you are not dependent on any equipment. This way, you can use relaxation anywhere, anytime. As in previous relaxation sessions, you may hear background noises going on around you, whenever you are in an awake, relaxed state. Even if you hear this background noise, try to sustain your state with relaxation for as long as possible.

4. Listen to your counselor read or to the recorded version of the following script during the appointment:

Begin by getting into a comfortable position, preferably sitting with your legs uncrossed and your hands resting on your thighs or armrests. ... Notice if your body feels comfortable, and adjust your position and clothing if you need to. ... Let your eyes close gently, and let your shoulders drop into a relaxed position. ... Allow your breathing to become quiet, rhythmic, and relaxed. ... Remind yourself that your mind will remain awake and active throughout this exercise. ...

Now use your mind to concentrate on the palms of your hands. Let yourself sense your palms so that they tingle and become strongly present with you and your body. [Pause 5–10 seconds.] Now move your attention to the soles of your feet. Try to sense the soles of your feet so that they begin to tingle and feel strongly present. [Pause 5–10 seconds.] When you can clearly sense the soles of your feet, imagine that a wave of warm, calming relaxation is beginning to form at the soles of your feet. ... Slowly over the next few minutes, this wave of relaxation will spread throughout your entire body. ...

Feel the wave of warmth and relaxation passing up through your feet, relaxing all the muscles of your feet and ankles. ... Now the wave of relaxation is moving up to your calves. ... Feel the warm, relaxing wave flow up, reaching your knees ... your thighs ... letting all the tension leave your muscles, until your legs are warm, heavy, and relaxed. ...

Now the wave of relaxation moves into your hips and buttocks. ... You can sense the muscles of your buttocks becoming relaxed ... your hips. ... your pelvic area. ... relaxing all the organs of your pelvis. ... The wave of relaxation now begins to travel through your abdomen ... relaxing your stomach muscles ... letting go of the tension in your abdominal wall. ... Now the wave of relaxation passes through all the internal organs ... your intestines ... your stomach ... your kidneys. ...

The wave of relaxation now spreads to your lower back ... encompassing the muscles of your spine as it flows from your seat up to your middle back ... upper back ... shoulder blades. ... Now the wave of relaxation forms a ring around your body at the level of your heart ... relaxing and warming the muscles of your chest, diaphragm, and upper back. ... The wave of relaxation now enters your heart itself. ... Take a slow, deep breath inward, and as you slowly let it out, gently release the tension around your heart. ... Feel the wave of relaxation encompassing the entire upper chest region of your body, moving up to reach your shoulders. ...

Now the wave of relaxation travels down your arms ... beginning with your shoulders ... upper arms ... elbows ... forearms ... wrists ... hands and fingers. ... The warmth of relaxation spreads through your palms ... and slowly moves back up your arms ... to your elbows ... and up to your shoulders. ... The wave of relaxation reaches the base of your neck ... and slowly moves up your neck, vertebra by vertebra. ... As your neck muscles relax, the bones of your neck separate and you may feel as though your neck is growing longer as it becomes more and more relaxed. ...

> *Now the wave of relaxation moves up past your neck into your head. … The wave of relaxation travels into the center of your brain and begins to spread from there to relax your thoughts … your scalp muscles … your forehead. … eyes … cheeks and nose … mouth and tongue … and the muscles of your jaw. … You may feel your jaw drop and your mouth open slightly as your face becomes completely warm and relaxed.*
>
> *Become aware again of the relaxation state present in the very center of your brain. … Take a slow, deep breath in, and let any tension flow out through the top of your head … . As you exhale, allow any tension that remains in your body, heart, and brain to slowly release through the top of your head. … Take another slow, deep breath in, and as you exhale, remind yourself of the words "Let go." … Let go of any tension that remains in your muscles … quieting your mind … feeling your body becoming warm and deeply relaxed—Try to stay in this state for a few minutes longer, gently telling yourself "Let go" whenever you notice your mind wandering or any part of your body feeling tense…*
>
> *(Wait 3–5 minutes in this state) … As you finish … slowly open your eyes with the feeling of relaxation, and come back into the room. … Try to carry this feeling of relaxation with you for the rest of the day.*

5. Along with proceeding with work on Sessions 7–11, integrate the relaxation exercises. If you feel this has helped you relax after walking through the exercise with your counselor, continue using the script of the exercise, which you can review and internalize on your own at home.

Practice Part 5: Further Practice for Progressive Relaxation

1. Continue practicing your progressive relaxation exercise as a method for reaching an awake, relaxed state. This time, you will first attempt the exercise yourself *without* your written script, verbal instructions, or use of a recorded version. Later, as you practice, you can utilize the script again if you need, or have your counselor read aloud the relaxation script when you meet again. It is important here that you not become dependent on your counselor's voice or presence (or on a recorded version) in order to reach an awake, relaxed state.

2. Try a progressive relaxation exercise on your own, utilizing slow deep breathing and attention on relaxing different parts of your body. Do as much as you remember of the exercise that was introduced at your last session, but don't worry if you forget parts of it or make up your own variations. The important thing is to learn to relax on your own.

3. If you wish, practice with the script or with the pattern memorized. Reinforce the time you are in a relaxed state by taking a deep breath.

4. As part of your homework assignment, continue practicing about 10 minutes a day of progressive relaxation. Learn to do this exercise on your own internally.

Practice Part 6 and Subsequent Practice Sessions

1. The purpose of your relaxation practice sessions are to work on spending more time in an awake, relaxed state. Once you can reach this goal, try to sustain it as long as possible in your relaxation sessions.

2. Practice progressive relaxation exercise or deep breathing. Try to maintain longer and longer periods of an awake, relaxed state. Plan to spend most of your relaxation session on your own.

3. Once you have reached the goal of being able to go into an awake, relaxed state, you will then spend time in your relaxation sessions learning how to use this new skill. You can use your ability to change your brain state when you are tense or over-aroused, when you experience a powerful emotion such as anger or fear, and when you sense your pre-seizure aura. Between relaxation sessions, begin to work on taking a deep breath and trying to change your brain wave state to awake and relaxed, whenever you remember or feel the need to do so. Discuss progress with your seizure counselor in applying these skills to various life situations at every subsequent relaxation or counseling session.

4. Proceed with work on Sessions 7–11. Integrate relaxation according to a schedule that works for you.

Assignments *(to Complete Prior to Your Next Session)*

Relaxation Exercise

Set for yourself the goal of practicing the relaxation exercise you utilized in this week's relaxation session (or the exercise above) for 10 minutes or more each day. Remember to allow yourself uninterrupted time for this, with your door closed and your phone turned off. These home practice sessions will help considerably with your relaxation training. For your personal record, you may wish to make a note of the relaxation exercise you do on your Seizure Log forms.

Goal-Setting for Session 6

Your most important goal for this week is to work on your daily relaxation exercise, as described above. If you wish to select an addition goal for this week, use the space below to record your plan:

_____

_____

_____

_____

Trigger Chart and Modifying Triggers

Continue to work on observing triggers, updating your Trigger Chart, and modifying your triggers. Use your journal to record your experiences with modifying triggers.

Preparing for Your Next Appointment

After completing this session and discussing it with your seizure counselor, you will read and complete "Session 7: Identifying Your Pre-Seizure Aura."

Additional Information on Relaxation Techniques

The following additional techniques are included in Appendices at the end of the *Workbook* to help you and your counselor decide whether they would help you with relaxation and to better understand the relationship between your brain, mind, and body.

Biofeedback: Experiencing the Sensation of the Brain Changing Itself

Some individuals and counselors may choose to use biofeedback training to augment relaxation training. The biofeedback procedures in Appendix I are guidelines that the Andrews/Reiter Epilepsy Research Program has utilized with biofeedback training.

Yoga

Yoga entered Western culture many years ago. Millions of people practice yoga on a regular basis, and public demand has led to widespread availability of yoga studios. Surveys investigating the use of complementary and alternative medicine (CAM) in individuals with neurological conditions have found that yoga is one of the most used and helpful CAM modalities. Consequently, many individuals with epilepsy wonder if practicing yoga might produce health benefits for the mind and body. Appendix II is intended to help you decide whether you are interested in trying yoga.

Meditation

Meditation is a method of relaxation that also helps to calm feelings and thoughts. Historically, almost all human cultures and religions have practiced some form of meditation as a means of finding inner peace. While there are many ways to meditate, most of them simply involve concentration on one thought, picture, or idea. The benefits of meditation include increased tranquility and well-being, a sense of oneness with oneself and God, and fewer target symptoms as a result of the deep relaxation experienced with the regular practice of meditation. Drs. Robert Emmons and Michael McCollough performed a study[1] of the effects of gratitude, comparing people who meditated on things to be thankful for to those who focused on life's hassles. Interestingly, the people who focused on the gratitude list reported heightened well-being, emotionally and physically, proving the benefits of "counting your blessings." Appendix III briefly describes the meditation process, which can be used for relaxation.

Resources for Further Reading

Andrews-Reiter Epilepsy Research Program, Inc. www.andrewsreiter.com.

Devinsky, O., Schachter, S., & Pacia, S. *Complementary and Alternative Therapies for Epilepsy.* New York: Demos, 2005.

Emmons R. A., & McCullough, M. E. *The Psychology of Gratitude.* Oxford; New York: Oxford University Press, 2004.

Foster, Richard J. *Celebration of Discipline: The Path to Spiritual Growth,* 3rd ed. San Francisco: Harper, 2002.

Swenson, Richard A. *Margin: Restoring Emotional, Physical, Financial, and Time Reserves to Overloaded Lives.* Colorado Springs, CO: NavPress, 1992.

Swingle, P. G. Neurofeedback treatment of pseudoseizure disorder. *Biol Psychiatry,* 1998;44(11):1196–1199.

---

[1] Emmons, R. A., & McCullough, M. E., *The Psychology of Gratitude* (Oxford; New York: Oxford University Press, 2004).

SEIZURE LOG   **For the Week of** ____/____/____ **to** ____/____/____

Init:_____
ID:_____
Week: _____
Type:_____

Instructions: Please fill in the diary at the end of each day to record the number and descriptions listed. This information will be reviewed with your physician at each appointment.

SUNDAY ___/___/___ (day 1)
Number of Seizures:_____
Time(s) of day:_____
Duration (sec or min):_____
Description:_____
Location(s):_____
Severity (1: mild, 2: mod, 3: severe):_____
Trigger(s):_____
Precursor(s):_____
Improved with:_____
Impact on your day:_____
Impact on others:_____

MONDAY ___/___/___ (day 2)
Number of Seizures:_____
Time(s) of day:_____
Duration:_____
Description:_____
Location(s):_____
Severity (1: mild, 2: mod, 3: severe):_____
Trigger(s):_____
Precursor(s):_____
Improved with:_____
Impact on your day:_____
Impact on others:_____

TUESDAY ___/___/___ (day 3)
Number of Seizures:_____
Time(s) of day:_____
Duration:_____
Description:_____
Location(s):_____
Severity (1: mild, 2: mod, 3: severe):_____
Trigger(s):_____
Precursor(s):_____
Improved with:_____
Impact on your day:_____
Impact on others:_____

WEDNESDAY ___/___/___ (day 4)
Number of Seizures:_____
Time(s) of day:_____
Duration:_____
Description:_____
Location(s):_____
Severity (1: mild, 2: mod, 3: severe):_____
Trigger(s):_____
Precursor(s):_____
Improved with:_____
Impact on your day:_____
Impact on others:_____

THURSDAY ___/___/___ (day 5)
Number of Seizures:_____
Time(s) of day:_____
Duration:_____
Description:_____
Location(s):_____
Severity (1: mild, 2: mod, 3: severe):_____
Trigger(s):_____
Precursor(s):_____
Improved with:_____
Impact on your day:_____
Impact on others:_____

FRIDAY ___/___/___ (day 6)
Number of Seizures:_____
Time(s) of day:_____
Duration:_____
Description:_____
Location(s):_____
Severity (1: mild, 2: mod, 3: severe):_____
Trigger(s):_____
Precursor(s):_____
Improved with:_____
Impact on your day:_____
Impact on others:_____

SATURDAY ___/___/___ (day 7)
Number of Seizures:_____
Time(s) of day:_____
Duration:_____
Description:_____
Location(s):_____
Severity (1: mild, 2: mod, 3: severe):_____
Trigger(s):_____
Precursor(s):_____
Improved with:_____
Impact on your day:_____
Impact on others:_____

Use **the space below or on back** to describe any significant information not covered in this record:

_____
_____
_____
_____
_____

Were you successful in stopping any seizures this week: yes ☐   no ☐

Please mark which seizures you stopped with an asterisk (*).

Total: _____   **Rater:** _____

SEIZURE LOG   For the Week of ____/____/____ to ____/____/____

Instructions: Please fill in the diary at the end of each day to record the number and descriptions listed. This information will be reviewed with your physician at each appointment.

Init:_____
ID:_____
Week: _____
Type:_____

SUNDAY ___/___/___ (day 1)
Number of Seizures:_____
Time(s) of day:_____
Duration (sec or min):_____
Description:_____
Location(s):_____
Severity (1: mild, 2: mod, 3: severe):_____
Trigger(s):_____
Precursor(s):_____
Improved with:_____
Impact on your day:_____
Impact on others:_____

MONDAY ___/___/___ (day 2)
Number of Seizures:_____
Time(s) of day:_____
Duration:_____
Description:_____
Location(s):_____
Severity (1: mild, 2: mod, 3: severe):_____
Trigger(s):_____
Precursor(s):_____
Improved with:_____
Impact on your day:_____
Impact on others:_____

TUESDAY ___/___/___ (day 3)
Number of Seizures:_____
Time(s) of day:_____
Duration:_____
Description:_____
Location(s):_____
Severity (1: mild, 2: mod, 3: severe):_____
Trigger(s):_____
Precursor(s):_____
Improved with:_____
Impact on your day:_____
Impact on others:_____

WEDNESDAY ___/___/___ (day 4)
Number of Seizures:_____
Time(s) of day:_____
Duration:_____
Description:_____
Location(s):_____
Severity (1: mild, 2: mod, 3: severe):_____
Trigger(s):_____
Precursor(s):_____
Improved with:_____
Impact on your day:_____
Impact on others:_____

THURSDAY ___/___/___ (day 5)
Number of Seizures:_____
Time(s) of day:_____
Duration:_____
Description:_____
Location(s):_____
Severity (1: mild, 2: mod, 3: severe):_____
Trigger(s):_____
Precursor(s):_____
Improved with:_____
Impact on your day:_____
Impact on others:_____

FRIDAY ___/___/___ (day 6)
Number of Seizures:_____
Time(s) of day:_____
Duration:_____
Description:_____
Location(s):_____
Severity (1: mild, 2: mod, 3: severe):_____
Trigger(s):_____
Precursor(s):_____
Improved with:_____
Impact on your day:_____
Impact on others:_____

SATURDAY ___/___/___ (day 7)
Number of Seizures:_____
Time(s) of day:_____
Duration:_____
Description:_____
Location(s):_____
Severity (1: mild, 2: mod, 3: severe):_____
Trigger(s):_____
Precursor(s):_____
Improved with:_____
Impact on your day:_____
Impact on others:_____

Use **the space below or on back** to describe any significant information not covered in this record:

_____
_____
_____
_____
_____
_____

Were you successful in stopping any seizures this week:
yes ☐   no ☐

Please mark which seizures you stopped with an asterisk (*).

Total: _____   **Rater:** _____

CHAPTER 8	Session 7: Identifying Your Pre-Seizure Aura

The term "pre-seizure aura" refers to a symptom or group of symptoms that precede a seizure. The aura may consist of an unusual sensation, a body movement, and/or a feeling state. Examples of common auras are visualizing lights flashing, tingling in an area of the body, an abrupt change in mood, sudden fear, an unpleasant smell, dizziness, and twitching of an extremity. Auras are experienced by people with epileptic seizures and with nonepileptic seizures (NES).

Learning to identify your own aura is an important step because you will be able to utilize this pre-seizure warning to take control. In some situations, you may be able to prevent the seizure itself. In other circumstances, you will be able to avoid injury because you are aware that a seizure is about to take place.

What Determines the Kind of Aura That You Experience?

With epileptic seizures, the type of physical or sensory aura that precedes a seizure is determined by the area of the brain from which the seizure originates. In epilepsy, the aura experience itself is the result of an electrical discharge in that particular area of the brain. The functions of some different parts of the brain, and common auras that result from electrical discharges in epilepsy in those same brain areas, are shown in Figure 8.1.

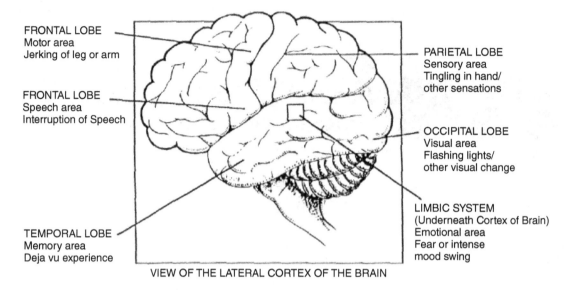

FRONTAL LOBE
Motor area
Jerking of leg or arm

FRONTAL LOBE
Speech area
Interruption of Speech

TEMPORAL LOBE
Memory area
Deja vu experience

PARIETAL LOBE
Sensory area
Tingling in hand/
other sensations

OCCIPITAL LOBE
Visual area
Flashing lights/
other visual change

LIMBIC SYSTEM
(Underneath Cortex of Brain)
Emotional area
Fear or intense
mood swing

VIEW OF THE LATERAL CORTEX OF THE BRAIN

Figure 8.1

View of the Lateral Cortex of the Brain

What Areas of the Brain Are Affected in Nonepileptic Seizures and Auras?

As was described in the introductory sessions, NES appear similar to epileptic seizures to an observer; however, no epileptiform activity is present on an EEG during NES. Neurophysiologic research reveals that no abnormal brain cell firing is present during NES. The same is true for the aura experienced before NES. The sensations experienced during an aura with NES are just as real as those of an epileptic aura, although *no electrical discharges are observed with an NES aura, just as no epileptiform activity is present during NES.*

What Determines Whether the Electrical Discharge That Produces an Aura in Epilepsy Will Also Produce an Epileptic Seizure?

Most people with seizures who have been able to identify their pre-seizure aura also note that their aura experience does not invariably lead to a seizure. Sometimes they experience their aura, followed by a seizure; sometimes they experience only the aura—with no subsequent seizure. This brings up the question, what determining factors sometimes lead to a seizure and other times result only in an aura? In order to answer this question, it is necessary to understand two processes of brain cell function: inhibition and excitation.

Inhibition and Excitation

Nerve cells work by forming a network where neighboring nerve cells tell each other what to do. Sometimes nerve cells give a message to their neighboring nerve cells to be quiet (a process called inhibition), and sometimes they give a message to neighboring nerve cells to be active (a process called excitation). These two processes of inhibition and excitation are equally important for coordinating brain cell function. In people with epileptic seizures, there is a disturbance of the nerve network in one area of the brain. Within this area, the process of inhibition at times does not work effectively, resulting in too much excitation. When this group of brain cells reaches a state of extreme excitation, a sudden electrical discharge is released—the beginnings of an epileptic seizure. If the electrical discharge remains isolated to one area of the brain, only an aura occurs. If the electrical discharge spreads slowly to other areas of the brain, the aura is followed by a generalized tonic-clonic ("grand mal") epileptic seizure. If the discharge spreads very rapidly, a generalized tonic-clonic ("grand mal") epileptic seizure occurs without any recognized aura.

Epileptic generalized and partial seizures are preceded by an electrical discharge in the brain that interrupts brain function and therefore produces an unusual experience, which is the aura. This pre-seizure aura may consist of a sensation, a body movement, or an emotional state. And because the aura in epilepsy results from an electrical discharge in one particular area of the brain, most people experience the same or similar aura every time it occurs—which means that once you identify your own particular aura, you can learn to recognize it whenever it recurs.

Patients with NES can also identify their aura(s). Some people with NES experience the same aura before every seizure, and others have different sensations as auras. Recognition of the symptoms that precede the NES can be very helpful.

What if You Have Never Noticed Any Pre-Seizure Aura Before?

People with complex partial epileptic seizures, with NES, and to a lesser extent those with other forms of seizures may have auras that are subtle and therefore easily overlooked. These individuals are more apt to experience auras as emotional states rather than physical symptoms. One common aura is a mood swing of sudden onset, such as intense fear. Other common auras are rushes of thought, feelings of unreality or strangeness, a sensation of floating, a sense of not belonging, and *déjà vu*—the feeling of having "already been here before." These auras are subtle experiences that you might not notice unless you were sensitized to look for them. In addition, anticonvulsant medications may make it more difficult for individuals to recognize the aura.

It is not expected that you should already be able to identify your aura. The purpose of Session 7 is to help you learn about the events that produce an aura, as well as the many different kinds of auras that are experienced by people with seizures. While not every individual with seizures has an aura, the great majority of people with seizures do experience one and will be able to identify their aura with repeated efforts. By becoming familiar with other people's aura experiences and observing yourself in the brief moments that precede your seizures, in time you will most likely begin to notice your own pre-seizure aura.

Why Is It So Important to Identify Your Aura?

Your aura is very important because it is your pre-seizure warning—your indicator that you are on the verge of having a seizure. It is specific and predictable for you. If you recognize your aura and continue to work with this step-by-step process of learning to take control of your seizures, you have a good opportunity of preventing many of your seizures. And when you cannot prevent the seizure itself, recognizing your aura will enable you to "take control" of your life by allowing you to avoid physical injury or emotional discomfort—because you know that a seizure is coming and can protect yourself if necessary. Learning to identify your aura is, therefore, a crucial step in the process of taking control.

Once You Learn to Recognize Your Aura, What Specifically Can You Do Differently That Will Help You "Take Control?"

There are two major ways that you can use the recognition of your aura to help you to "take control." One way is seizure prevention, and the second way is preventing unpleasant or unsafe effects of seizures.

Recognizing your aura will help you prevent seizures because you may be able to develop some conscious control over whether your aura will progress to a seizure. Some people report that changing their brain wave state (as you are learning to do with relaxation training) at the time that they sense an aura seems to prevent progression to a seizure. Others notice that deep breathing or relaxing in other ways—perhaps just lying down—will prevent seizures in many instances. Still others concentrate on being aware of a trigger or negative state that preceded their aura, and they are able to use one of many methods to channel negative emotions into productive outlets, as described in Session 5.

Noticing your aura can also help you prevent unsafe or unpleasant effects from seizures. Unsafe seizure effects include falling, which might result in cuts, bruises, concussion or other head injury; dropping objects, which may be sharp or breakable; and dangers from sports activities. Unpleasant effects from seizures might include social embarrassment from having a seizure, urinary incontinence, and disruption of social activities. Your aura may give you a few seconds of warning that a seizure is about to occur—at which point you can sit down to avoid injury, or put down any knives or sharp objects. Simply sitting down when you notice an aura may enable you to have a brief seizure unnoticed by those around you, after which you can resume your activities without any injury or undue concern from those around you.

The Work

Goal

The goal for this session is to identify your aura, and then to use your aura as a pre-seizure warning to prevent seizures and their effects.

Obstacles

Select the statements below that may apply to you, or write in your own.

- Some auras are subtle and difficult to observe.
- Lack of awareness, or unfamiliarity with the process of self-observation.
- Over-medication (e.g., drowsiness from anticonvulsant drugs or alcohol).
- 60% of the population with seizures claim no knowledge of a pre-seizure aura.

- When an aura itself is a powerful experience—like a sudden emotion—it is difficult to maintain a part of your mind that stays separate from this experience and is able to observe it enough to say, "Oh yes, this is my aura."
- Thinking that if the seizures are nonepileptic, then there should not be an aura.

Examples of Auras (Patients' Initials Are Listed With Aura Examples, Below) *Circle any auras that you experience.*

1. S. J.—agitation, a feeling of strangeness
2. C. O.—myoclonic jerks accompanied by fear
3. B. A.—dizziness
4. D. S.—anxiety and breathlessness
5. B. N.—a feeling of insecurity
6. D. G.—a sensation of electrical energy felt throughout the body
7. J. H.—weakness in the legs
8. R. M.—the sensation of being out of the body
9. C. K.—facial twitch
10. T. S.—a sinking sensation

In-Office Discussion

Read these sections and make notes in your *Workbook* prior to your appointment, as preparation for the in-office discussion with your seizure counselor.

Review of Assignments

Seizure Log/Thought Records

Show your Seizure Logs to your seizure counselor at the beginning of the appointment. Discuss your Thought Record(s) that you did for your symptoms.

Journal-Keeping

Are there any passages from your journal about how you are feeling about this process of "taking control" that you would like to read or talk about with your support person or seizure counselor?

Relaxation Exercise

How are you doing with your daily practice of relaxation at home? Which exercise(s) are you practicing? Are there any problems or experiences to report? Do you enjoy your relaxation process?

Goal Review From Prior Session

If you chose a goal in addition to practicing relaxation at home, let your seizure counselor know what it was and how it went for you. Discuss any questions or concerns you may have about goal-setting as a tool for personal change.

Trigger Chart and Avoiding Triggers

Discuss if any new insights occurred since your last session.

Identifying Your Aura: Discussion of Progress/Obstacles

Are you now aware of any aura? If so, how would you describe it? If not, have you ever noticed any unusual sensations or experiences prior to seizures? What obstacles come up for you with regard to identifying your aura? Or, if you have already identified your aura, what obstacles do you have to using this pre-seizure warning to your best advantage?

Tool #1: Self-Observation

Note: Follow the instructions below at home and complete prior to your session. If needed, you may also work on the exercise with your seizure counselor.

1. Begin by sitting comfortably and quietly. Allow your breathing and body posture to relax. Simply sit, without attempting to direct your attention, for about 3 minutes.
2. At the end of this period of relaxation, begin to observe your physical sensations. Direct your attention to your body, noticing sensations of tension, comfort, warmth, cold, how the chair or clothing feels against your skin, and so on. Spend 5–10 minutes rotating your attention from one part of your body to the next, in the following sequence: left foot, left ankle, left knee, left thigh, left hip, right foot, right ankle, right knee, right thigh, right hip, left hand, left forearm, left upper arm, right hand, right forearm, right upper arm, lower

back, middle back, abdomen, upper back, chest, shoulders, neck, jaw, mouth, nose, cheeks, eyes, forehead, scalp, back of the head.

3. Begin now to observe your emotions. For about 3 minutes, ask yourself, "How do I feel?" (If no specific emotions are apparent, ask yourself, "How do I feel about the prospect of learning to observe my aura?")

4. Begin now to observe your thoughts. Ask yourself, "What am I thinking?" Allow about 3 more minutes to complete the exercise.

For Discussion From Your Self-Observation Session

1. Write an example of one physical sensation, one emotion, and one thought that you observed during the self-observation session. (Discuss this with your seizure counselor during the upcoming appointment.)

Physical Sensation:_____

Emotion: _____

Thought:_____

2. Comment on any difficulties or benefits you experienced during this self-observation session.

_____

_____

Examples

- Physical Sensation—"I noticed a knot of tension between my shoulder blades."
- Emotion—"I felt frustrated about having to do this exercise again."
- Thought—"I started thinking about a TV program I watched last night. Then I said to myself, 'Stop thinking about that and start thinking about the exercise.'"

Once you have identified your pre-seizure warning, you have the opportunity to determine how you want to react to it. Many individuals tend to react with fear or even panic when they notice the sensations of a pre-seizure state. This reaction may increase muscular tension, breath-holding, and excitation, which in turn increase seizure potential. The following steps may help you to counteract these reactions and break the vicious cycle. Please feel free to modify the steps in collaboration with your seizure counselor.

When you sense a pre-seizure aura

1. **Get yourself in a safe position**. It is imperative that you get yourself into a safe position as soon as you notice the onset of seizure activity. Your preventive action will decrease the likelihood of physical harm.

2. **Take deep diaphragmatic breaths**. A fearful reaction to a seizure warning will lead to breath-holding in most people. Breath-holding introduces immediate changes in the oxygen and carbon dioxide levels in your blood, affecting the blood cells' ability to deliver oxygen to the cells throughout the body, and your brain is very sensitive to such changes. The practice of controlled deep diaphragmatic breathing can help to counteract those changes. Refer to Session 6 regarding proper instructions for deep diaphragmatic breathing, and practice the breathing technique with your seizure counselor. You will have to make sure that you avoid shallow high chest breathing (hyperventilation). In some instances, hyperventilation can precipitate seizures, so do not use this specific technique if breathing techniques precipitated your seizures.

3. **Visualize a relaxed place**. Individuals with seizures have described different visualization practices that they find helpful in addressing pre-seizure warnings. Use the techniques described in Session 6 to generate a visual image in your mind of a place where you are safe and relaxed.

Continue with those three steps until you are sure that the pre-seizure warning has passed.

4. **Ask yourself why you had the pre-seizure warning in the first place**. Some individuals describe that they had a subtle insight shortly before the pre-seizure warning occurred, for example, "I feel like taking a break. I am getting frustrated by this." Or "I should eat something. I am beginning to feel weak and dizzy." Or "I should have said something this morning when my boss made this unreasonable request. It was not fair and I am still angry." Realizing the validity and importance of those insights during the course of the day and learning to take them seriously enough to follow through with them are important steps toward taking control of your seizures. Remember to take notes of your observations and to write down any ideas that you might have to improve your technique of addressing pre-seizure warnings.

What if You Do Not Experience an Aura?

Remember that your aura may be subtle; for example, it may consist of a feeling state such as anxiety. If you do not identify a pre-seizure aura, continue self-observation and proceed through the process of taking control outlined in Sessions 8–11.

Relaxation Training

Continue with your relaxation training as directed in Session 6. Discuss and clarify any questions regarding the scheduling for these sessions, including whether you and your seizure counselor need to do more of this training before or after your session, during the in-office discussion.

Assignments *(to Complete Prior to Your Next Session)*

Seizure Log and Thought Records

Continue to record seizure activity, severity, triggers, and emotional state. In addition, *record whether you experience an aura each day* by indicating "yes" or "no." If "yes," describe your pre-seizure aura *in detail in your journal*. Continue doing Thought Records when you have uncomfortable experiences or intense emotions. Did you notice any of these feelings just before your aura?

Journal-Keeping

Describe in detail the sensations and feelings you notice just before one or more of your seizures. Is this your aura? Have you ever noticed it before? Do you know when you are going to have a seizure? If so, how do you know? Have you noticed whether you are able to use your aura as a warning, to give you time to sit down or seek privacy before a seizure?

Self-Observation Exercise

Practice the self-observation exercise that you did at home and discussed in the office, while you are at home, preferably once a day. This will help you develop the important skill of observing and noticing your physical sensations, emotions, and thoughts. Between now and your next appointment, this self-observation exercise should be done in place of the daily relaxation practice that you began in Session 6.

If you are unable to complete this assignment because no seizure happens this week or no aura is observable, then write in your journal about your experience of doing a self-observation exercise. Try to describe as many different sensations, emotions, and thoughts as you can remember observing during one of your practice sessions at home. You may choose to do a Thought Record.

Goal-Setting for Session 7

Read through the Goal List below, which provides a good summary of the information presented in Session 7. In addition to the assignments described above, choose *one goal* from the following Goal List related to identifying your aura. If desired, you may also select a goal from previous Goal Lists for Sessions 2–5.

The goal you select in order to proceed with Session 7 will depend on a number of factors related to your current obstacles and progress. If you are already familiar with your aura, you may wish to work on one of the goals related to your current obstacles and progress. If you are just beginning to look for your aura, you will probably choose to concentrate on self-observation as a tool for identifying your aura.

Check off the goal you have selected. Then write in the specifics of how you plan to meet that goal in the space provided below. Show your written goal(s) to your seizure counselor before you leave your appointment.

Goal List

What Is a "Pre-Seizure Aura?"

___Review the section of Session 7 that explains the different parts of the brain and the different kinds of auras that are produced.

___In your journal, list several examples of auras experienced by others, including some that are physical sensations, body movements, and emotional states. (See this *Workbook* chapter for examples.)

___Explain in your own words (to a friend, family member, or your seizure counselor) how an aura is produced in the brain and why it sometimes leads to a seizure.

___Other: _____

Identifying Your Own Aura

___For the upcoming week, remind yourself daily to try to observe yourself in the brief moments before your seizures. After any seizures that occur, write down your observations in your journal.

___For the upcoming week, remind yourself daily to observe yourself for any unusual sensations, feelings, or body movements that might constitute your aura. Write down any observations in your journal.

___After the next seizure you experience, try to remember any unusual sensation, emotion, or movement that preceded it. Write down your observations in your journal.

___Ask a friend or family member to observe you carefully when you look like you may be about to have a seizure. After the next seizure that this person witnesses, ask if he or she observed any unusual movement or apparent mood swing that might be your aura. Compare your own observations with those of this other person and record in your journal.

___Other:_____

NOTE

Begin work on the following goals when you have identified your aura.

Using Aura Recognition to Prevent Seizures

___When you notice your aura, sit or lie down and try to relax.

___When you notice your aura, sit or lie down and begin slow, deep breathing.

___When you notice your aura, sit or lie down and begin progressive relaxation.

___When you notice your aura, sit or lie down, take a deep breath, and attempt to go into an awake, relaxed brain wave state (as you are practicing in your relaxation training).

___When you notice your aura, sit down, take a deep breath, and try to identify your trigger and observe if you are in a negative state. Use one of the suggestions from the Goal List for Session 5 when you do find yourself in a negative state.

This is how I plan to work on dealing with my negative state:

_____

_____

_____

___Other:_____

Using Aura Identification to Prevent Unsafe and Unpleasant Effects of Seizures

___ Sit down when you experience your aura.

___ Lie down when you experience your aura.

___ When you notice your aura, put down any sharp or breakable objects you are holding, such as a knife, glass, or tool.

___ When you notice your aura, move away from any stairs or other hazards. Sit down if possible.

___ Other: _____

I have chosen the goal checked above in order to prevent one or more of the following unsafe or unpleasant effects of seizures:

___ Falling (with possible injury, such as bruises, cuts, or head injury)

___ Embarrassment

___ Injury from sharp objects

___ Dropping breakable objects

___ Too much attention from other people (when I have a seizure)

___ Other:_____

After you have selected *one* of the above goals, write down in your own words specifically what you plan to do to meet this goal during the coming week. The more specific you are, the easier it will be to meet your goal.

My goal for the week ending (give date) ___/___/____ is to:

_____

_____

_____

_____

_____

_____

On (give date) ___/___/____, I tried to meet this goal with the following results:

_____

_____

_____

_____

_____

_____

I consider that I did ___, did not ___ meet the goal I set for myself this week.

Preparing for Your Next Appointment

After completing this session and discussing it with your seizure counselor in your appointment, read and complete "Session 8: Dealing with External Life Stresses."

Resources for Further Reading

Andrews, D., & Schonfeld, W. Predictive factors for controlling seizures using a behavioral approach. *Seizure*, 1992;1:111–116.

Ettinger, Allen B., & Kanner, Andres M., editors. *Psychiatric Issues in Epilepsy*. 2nd ed. Philadelphia, PA: Lippincott Williams & Wilkins, 2007.

Richard, A., & Reiter, J. *Epilepsy: A New Approach*. New York: Walker, 1995.

Schachter, S. C., editor. *Brainstorms: Epilepsy in Our Words*. New York: Raven Press, 1993.

Tempkin, Oswei. *The Falling Sickness*. Baltimore, MD: The Johns Hopkins Press, 1945. (Reviews historical concept of seizure aura over the centuries.)

SEIZURE LOG   **For the Week of** ____/____/____ **to** ____/____/____

Instructions: Please fill in the diary at the end of each day to record the number and descriptions listed. This information will be reviewed with your physician at each appointment.

Init:_____
ID:_____
Week: _____
Type:_____

SUNDAY ___/___/___ (day 1)
Number of Seizures:_____
Time(s) of day:_____
Duration (sec or min):_____
Description:_____
Location(s):_____
Severity (1: mild, 2: mod, 3: severe):_____
Trigger(s):_____
Precursor(s):_____
Improved with:_____
Impact on your day:_____
Impact on others:_____

MONDAY ___/___/___ (day 2)
Number of Seizures:_____
Time(s) of day:_____
Duration:_____
Description:_____
Location(s):_____
Severity (1: mild, 2: mod, 3: severe):_____
Trigger(s):_____
Precursor(s):_____
Improved with:_____
Impact on your day:_____
Impact on others:_____

TUESDAY ___/___/___ (day 3)
Number of Seizures:_____
Time(s) of day:_____
Duration:_____
Description:_____
Location(s):_____
Severity (1: mild, 2: mod, 3: severe):_____
Trigger(s):_____
Precursor(s):_____
Improved with:_____
Impact on your day:_____
Impact on others:_____

WEDNESDAY ___/___/___ (day 4)
Number of Seizures:_____
Time(s) of day:_____
Duration:_____
Description:_____
Location(s):_____
Severity (1: mild, 2: mod, 3: severe):_____
Trigger(s):_____
Precursor(s):_____
Improved with:_____
Impact on your day:_____
Impact on others:_____

THURSDAY ___/___/___ (day 5)
Number of Seizures:_____
Time(s) of day:_____
Duration:_____
Description:_____
Location(s):_____
Severity (1: mild, 2: mod, 3: severe):_____
Trigger(s):_____
Precursor(s):_____
Improved with:_____
Impact on your day:_____
Impact on others:_____

FRIDAY ___/___/___ (day 6)
Number of Seizures:_____
Time(s) of day:_____
Duration:_____
Description:_____
Location(s):_____
Severity (1: mild, 2: mod, 3: severe):_____
Trigger(s):_____
Precursor(s):_____
Improved with:_____
Impact on your day:_____
Impact on others:_____

SATURDAY ___/___/___ (day 7)
Number of Seizures:_____
Time(s) of day:_____
Duration:_____
Description:_____
Location(s):_____
Severity (1: mild, 2: mod, 3: severe):_____
Trigger(s):_____
Precursor(s):_____
Improved with:_____
Impact on your day:_____
Impact on others:_____

Use **the space below or on back** to describe any signifi-cant information not covered in this record:

_____
_____
_____
_____
_____

Were you successful in stopping any seizures this week:
yes ☐   no ☐

Please mark which seizures you stopped with an asterisk (*).

Total: _____   **Rater:** _____

SEIZURE LOG   For the Week of ____/____/____ to ____/____/____

Instructions: Please fill in the diary at the end of each day to record the number and descriptions listed. This information will be reviewed with your physician at each appointment.

Init:_____
ID:_____
Week: _____
Type:_____

SUNDAY ___/___/___ (day 1)
Number of Seizures:_____
Time(s) of day:_____
Duration (sec or min):_____
Description:_____
Location(s):_____
Severity (1: mild, 2: mod, 3: severe):_____
Trigger(s):_____
Precursor(s):_____
Improved with:_____
Impact on your day:_____
Impact on others:_____

MONDAY ___/___/___ (day 2)
Number of Seizures:_____
Time(s) of day:_____
Duration:_____
Description:_____
Location(s):_____
Severity (1: mild, 2: mod, 3: severe):_____
Trigger(s):_____
Precursor(s):_____
Improved with:_____
Impact on your day:_____
Impact on others:_____

TUESDAY ___/___/___ (day 3)
Number of Seizures:_____
Time(s) of day:_____
Duration:_____
Description:_____
Location(s):_____
Severity (1: mild, 2: mod, 3: severe):_____
Trigger(s):_____
Precursor(s):_____
Improved with:_____
Impact on your day:_____
Impact on others:_____

WEDNESDAY ___/___/___ (day 4)
Number of Seizures:_____
Time(s) of day:_____
Duration:_____
Description:_____
Location(s):_____
Severity (1: mild, 2: mod, 3: severe):_____
Trigger(s):_____
Precursor(s):_____
Improved with:_____
Impact on your day:_____
Impact on others:_____

Total: _____   Rater: _____

THURSDAY ___/___/___ (day 5)
Number of Seizures:_____
Time(s) of day:_____
Duration:_____
Description:_____
Location(s):_____
Severity (1: mild, 2: mod, 3: severe):_____
Trigger(s):_____
Precursor(s):_____
Improved with:_____
Impact on your day:_____
Impact on others:_____

FRIDAY ___/___/___ (day 6)
Number of Seizures:_____
Time(s) of day:_____
Duration:_____
Description:_____
Location(s):_____
Severity (1: mild, 2: mod, 3: severe):_____
Trigger(s):_____
Precursor(s):_____
Improved with:_____
Impact on your day:_____
Impact on others:_____

SATURDAY ___/___/___ (day 7)
Number of Seizures:_____
Time(s) of day:_____
Duration:_____
Description:_____
Location(s):_____
Severity (1: mild, 2: mod, 3: severe):_____
Trigger(s):_____
Precursor(s):_____
Improved with:_____
Impact on your day:_____
Impact on others:_____

Use **the space below or on back** to describe any signifi-cant information not covered in this record:

_____
_____
_____
_____
_____

Were you successful in stopping any seizures this week:
yes ☐   no ☐

Please mark which seizures you stopped with an asterisk (*).

| CHAPTER 9 | Session 8: Dealing With External Life Stresses |

Now that you have completed Sessions 1–7 in this process, it is probably evident to you that your seizure disorder can be affected by almost every aspect of your life. In Session 8, you will be focusing on external life stresses—another key factor that affects both your seizure frequency and quality of life. A study completed in 2005 found that 53% of patients with seizures experience one precipitating factor, and 30% experience two or more precipitating factors. Emotional stress, sleep deprivation, and a feeling of tiredness were the three most frequently reported precipitants.[1] In the authors' experience, many individuals with seizures find that learning to deal with stress plays a major role in seizure control.

A stressor can be defined as any life circumstance that you find difficult to deal with—that is, any aspect of your life that causes strain and tension, therefore affecting your physical and emotional health. No human being is without external life stresses, so the work of this session is applicable to anyone seeking to cope more effectively with a chronic illness and/or to achieve high-level wellness. This material is included in this *Workbook* because our experience shows that while most people with

---

[1]Nakken, K., Solaas, M., Kjeldsan, M., Friis, M., Pellock, J., & Corey, L., Which seizure-precipitating factors do patients with epilepsy most frequently report? *Epilepsy and Behavior*, 2005;6:1, 85–89.

seizures are aware that they are experiencing stressful situations in their lives, they are not aware that these stresses have any effect on their seizures. When they become more aware of these stresses and the fact that they affect the frequency of seizures, they are able to learn to deal with external life stresses in ways that make them happier and healthier people.

Dealing with external life stresses means gaining awareness of factors in your life that are stressful for you—and taking responsibility for relieving those factors that are within your control. Long-term efforts can have the dramatic impact of reducing your seizure frequency and increasing well-being.

Are External Life Stresses Related to Seizure Triggers Described in Session 4?

The answer to this question is a definite "yes." In Session 4, we discussed factors known as "triggers," which produce negative states that in turn elicit seizures. We described three categories of triggers: physical (e.g., lack of sleep), external (e.g., criticism), and internal (e.g., anger, fear.). Your triggers will give you clues about the stresses in your life. They also will help you identify your internal issues and conflicts that you will be looking at in Session 9.

Take the time now to fill in the following Trigger Chart. It's okay to refer to the chart you filled out some weeks ago in Session 4, but be sure to add any new information that you have observed since that time. You will be referring to this chart frequently as you read the material in this chapter and formulate your list of major life stresses.

Trigger Chart

Complete this chart to discuss during your upcoming appointment.

TRIGGERS	NEGATIVE STATES	TARGET SYMPTOMS

Physical

_____

_____

_____

_____

_____

External

_____

_____

_____

_____

Internal

_____

_____

_____

_____

Any life situation that causes pressure or demands change is a source of stress. For example, life changes involving your family or job may cause stress. Relationship problems and financial worries often contribute to a high level of stress. In addition, personal loss through death or divorce, as well as serious health problems, may produce tension and strain—which are the telltale signs of feeling stressed.

Researchers have made some remarkable discoveries about the effects of stress on health—discoveries that are dramatically changing Western healthcare practices. In his classic book *The Stress of Life*, stress pioneer Hans Selye, MD, described the stress reaction, a universal response to a threatening situation.[2] The stress reaction results from the firing of the autonomic nervous system, which prepares the body for "fight or flight" when survival is threatened. Figure 9.1 illustrates how the body responds to a major source of stress.

By looking at this figure, it's easy to see why prolonged stress might make you sick. It is one thing to respond this way to an attacking saber-toothed tiger; in fact, the nervous system apparently developed this way so that human beings could mobilize all their resources toward "fight and flight" in prehistoric times, when this response was truly necessary for survival. Although the modern world has other threats—such as speeding cars or a mugger on a city street—which appropriately elicit this response, more often people today experience the stress reaction when the threat is *psychological* rather than *physical*.

For example, when the boss is reprimanding an employee, that employee may have a pounding heart and an increased level of muscle tension, even though the boss is not really going to attack that employee with his teeth and eat him for dinner. There is no immediate physical danger—but there is a definite emotional threat, such as loss of self-esteem and fear of losing one's job. The stress reaction experienced by this employee is illustrated in Figure 9.2.

In this figure, Point 1 represents a person's baseline level, neither particularly relaxed nor excited. Point 2 illustrates the body's stress reaction, which occurs when the autonomic nervous system reacts to a source of stress. There would actually be a peak like this if you were measuring

---

[2]Selye, Hans, *The Stress of Life* (New York: McGraw-Hill, 1976).

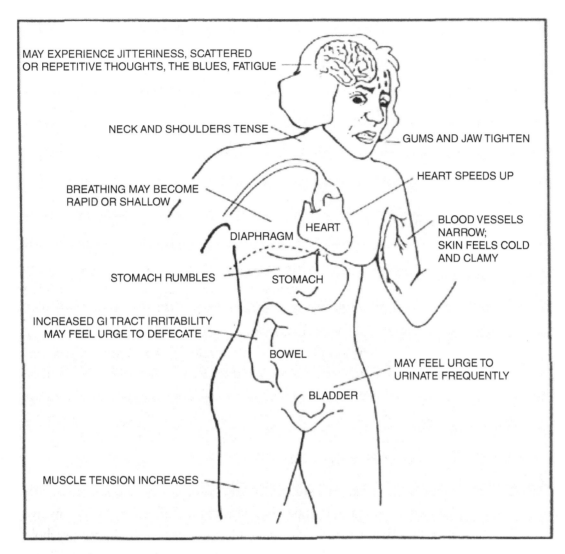

MAY EXPERIENCE JITTERINESS, SCATTERED
OR REPETITIVE THOUGHTS, THE BLUES, FATIGUE

NECK AND SHOULDERS TENSE

GUMS AND JAW TIGHTEN

HEART SPEEDS UP

BREATHING MAY BECOME
RAPID OR SHALLOW

DIAPHRAGM

HEART

BLOOD VESSELS
NARROW;
SKIN FEELS COLD
AND CLAMY

STOMACH RUMBLES

STOMACH

INCREASED GI TRACT IRRITABILITY
MAY FEEL URGE TO DEFECATE

BOWEL

MAY FEEL URGE TO
URINATE FREQUENTLY

BLADDER

MUSCLE TENSION INCREASES

Figure 9.1

The Body and Stress

blood pressure or muscle tension when an individual experiences a stress reaction. After the stress is passed, there is a period of compensatory relaxation, illustrated by Point 3. This happens because the autonomic nervous system allows the body to relax and return to baseline functioning. Point 4 shows that this return to baseline has occurred.

Everyone has experienced numerous episodes like the one shown in Figure 9.2, where the stress reaction is followed by compensatory relaxation and a return to baseline. But what happens to this employee, for example, if he continues to worry about this episode with the boss all day long? What if this employee goes home to a situation where arguments with his spouse are a daily occurrence, and financial worries are only one of many family problems? The answer is that there is no opportunity for

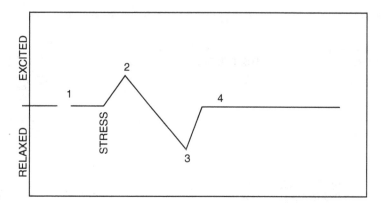

Figure 9.2

this person to experience the compensatory relaxation phase. Instead, he experiences one stress reaction on top of another one—a chronic stress pattern that Pelletier describes as follows: "What happens physiologically is that all the bodily functions accelerate as though your life were in danger, and they stay elevated, without release. We experience it as anxiety, frustration, tension, and worry. If we were to hook someone in this kind of worry pattern up to a monitor, we'd see something like the results shown in Figure 9.3. They continue at a level of high excitation without the compensatory relaxation phase. This is the kind of biological stress pattern that leads to disease."[3]

Sometimes external stresses are day-to-day, such as financial worries, job stress, and marital problems. Another kind of external stress involves life events that demand a change in life patterns or a significant psychological adjustment. In 1967, Holmes and Rahe[4] published a list of 43 stressful

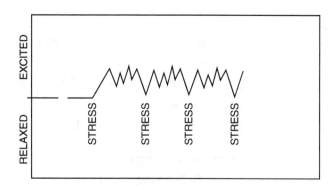

Figure 9.3

---

[3]Pelletier, Kenneth, Stress/Unstress, *Medical Self-Care*, Number Five (Inverness, CA: 1978), p. 4.
[4]Holmes, T. H., & Rahe, R. H., The social readjustment rating scale, *Journal of Psychosomatic Research*, 1967;11(2):213–218 (adapted by multiple authors since initial publication).

life events, which they rated according to how stressful each event was for most people studied.

Rate yourself according to the Holmes and Rahe Life Stress Scale. First, read the event list, and then, for each event, select the number for each event you have experienced in the past year (past 12 months). Once you are done with the list, add up your total score and write on the line.

Holmes and Rahe Life Stress Scale

Death of a spouse	100
Divorce	73
Marital separation	65
Imprisonment	63
Death of a close family member	63
Personal injury or illness	53
Marriage	50
Dismissal from work	47
Marital reconciliation	45
Retirement	45
Change in health of family member	44
Pregnancy	40
Sexual difficulties	39
Gain a new family member	39
Business readjustment	39
Change in financial state	38
Change in frequency of arguments	35
Major mortgage	32
Foreclosure of mortgage or loan	30
Change in responsibilities at work	29

Child leaving home	29
Trouble with in-laws	29
Outstanding personal achievement	28
Spouse starts or stops work	26
Begin or end school	26
Change in living conditions	25
Revision of personal habits	24
Trouble with boss	23
Change in working hours or conditions	20
Change in residence	20
Change in schools	20
Change in recreation	19
Change in church activities	19
Change in social activities	18
Minor mortgage or loan	17
Change in sleeping habits	16
Change in number of family reunions	15
Change in eating habits	15
Vacation	13
Christmas	12
Minor violation of law	11
TOTAL:	____

Reprinted from Thomas H. Holmes and Richard H. Rahe, "The Social Readjustment Rating Scale," *Journal of Psychosomatic Research*, 1967;11(2):213–218, Copyright © 1967, Published by Elsevier Science, Inc. All rights reserved. Permission to reproduce granted by the publisher.

Holmes and Rahe found that a score of 150 for events occurring within the last year gives you a 50-50 chance of developing an illness within 2 years. A score of 300+ gives you a 90% chance of getting sick within 2 years.

How Do These Recent Life Events Cause Stress?

If you look at the Holmes and Rahe Life Stress Scale, you can see that without exception, all of these events involve inner and outer change. The most stressful events affect one's closest relationships with people, often causing a profound loss of social support in one's life. Other life changes, such as moving or changing jobs, also affect connections with people, as well as increasing the demand to adjust to new circumstances. Another group of "life events" listed by Holmes and Rahe concern increased financial and/or relationship pressures.

All of these life events require change—and the fact of the matter is that change is stressful for human beings. The most stressful kinds of change are those that involve relationships with the most important people in our lives. Love, friendship, and social support are profound human needs, which is why "Getting Support" was chosen as one of the first chapters in this book. Whether you experience marriage or divorce, fewer arguments or more arguments with someone you love, you will be undergoing some major relationship changes that are stressful because they demand that you adjust in new ways. Anytime you have to adjust, you may repeatedly have thoughts, worries, and feelings of insecurity that elicit a stress response just like the boss's reprimand did in the example above. In addition, having to cope with any major change can cause enough of a baseline stress response that you rarely get to have a compensatory relaxation phase, as demonstrated in Figure 9.4.

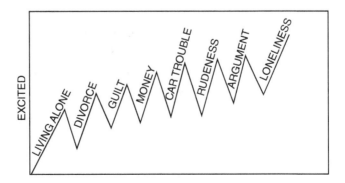

Figure 9.4

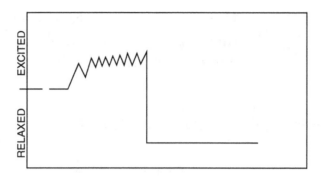

Figure 9.5

When Someone Experiences This Much Stress, What Happens to Allow Some Relaxation?

From the above discussion, you can see that day-to-day stresses can easily combine with stressful life events that may have occurred within the past year or so to produce a chronic stress pattern. This chronic stress pattern allows no opportunity for physical or psychological relaxation. Often a very stressed person will not break this pattern until a target symptom becomes so frequent or severe that the person is ill or an invalid for a period of time. Figure 9.5 illustrates this process of a sudden return to the relaxed state through illness, injury, or invalidism.

"This represents a state of complete nervous exhaustion, a nervous breakdown, a heart attack, a debilitating headache, an alcoholic binge—it can be any number of things. ... It's very often illness, because when you're sick there is a very different set of demands placed upon you. It's now OK to stay in bed and just take it easy."[5]

How Does This Model Relate to the Concept of "Triggers" Leading to Negative States Leading to Target Symptoms?

This model is simply another way of viewing the same process. Triggers and stresses are very similar concepts. Some triggers are also stresses, such as lack of sleep or an argument with your boss or spouse. Both of these external stresses can trigger a negative state, which may then elicit a target symptom. For example, an argument might make you feel angry and frustrated, and soon after, you develop a headache. From Pelletier's

---

[5]Pelletier, Kenneth, Stress/Unstress, *Medical Self-Care*, Number Five (Inverness, CA: 1978), p. 5.

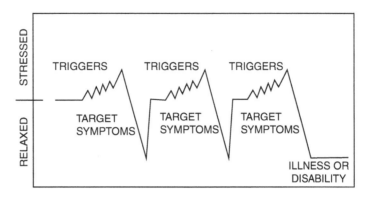

Figure 9.6

model, you can see that target symptoms usually happen when many triggers (or stresses) happen one after another and there is no time to relax or adapt in between.

The "negative state" is what you experience when your body is undergoing the stress reaction—Pelletier was quoted earlier describing this negative state as "anxiety, frustration, tension, and worry." The target symptom is the mechanism that allows relaxation to occur. Although it may seem ironic, a headache, a cold, or a seizure are all examples of target symptoms that can reduce stress.

Target symptoms act as stress reducers because they slow people down, take them out of a stressful situation, or give them a break from regular responsibilities. Of course, target symptoms are not the best way to reduce stress by any means, because having unpleasant symptoms adds to your stress level in the long run. A target symptom might develop into an illness or a disability when the symptom alone is not enough to adequately relieve stress. Figure 9.6 illustrates how this process works.

Why Is It That Some Triggers Seem Pretty Minor, Yet Affect You as if They Were Major Stresses?

Sometimes a trigger elicits a negative state because it symbolizes or reminds you of some wound—or sore point—that is a source of stress within you. For example, scoring poorly on a test would probably constitute a minor stress for just about anyone. Whether it was a driver's test, a law school exam, or a test for getting into college, most people would probably feel somewhat badly about not doing well on a test. But for some people, a low test score brings up memories from the past that make it a much more powerful trigger than it might be by itself in the present. It might cause that person to remember that one of his parents repeatedly gave him the message that "you're never going to have what it takes to succeed!"

He might actually remember his parent saying these things when he was a child, or he might remember unconsciously, without being aware of it. If this is the case, he might not think about any past events but simply notice that he keeps thinking, "I failed again—I'm no good!" whenever he remembers his low test score. In this case, the actual stress might be an internal feeling of inadequacy that began in childhood—and the trigger simply brought it up to the surface and made him feel badly about it, once again.

This is an example of how an external stress or trigger can bring up an internal issue, which then produces a much more powerful negative state than the trigger alone might elicit. The process of learning to recognize and deal with internal issues and conflicts, such as deep-seated feelings of inadequacy, will be discussed more fully in Session 9.

Examples of Individuals Who Experience External Stresses Leading to Target Symptoms

A Non-Seizure Example

Jennifer's most common target symptom is low back pain. When a series of external stresses builds up in her life, Jennifer becomes increasingly stressed, tense, and anxious (her negative state) until an episode of low back pain occurs. At that point, she stays home from work for a day or two, stays in bed, and allows her family to assume a lot of her responsibilities while she is laid up. This situation temporarily relieves the pressure she is under, allowing her to break the stress pattern she was in and to experience some compensatory relaxation.

Figure 9.7 shows how this pattern might occur over a period of weeks or months, where each time the target symptom occurs after a buildup of stress. Although the target symptom is certainly not pleasant or comfortable, it does have the effect of relieving an intolerable level of stress and allowing periods of physical and psychological relaxation.

If the level of stress in Jennifer's life continues to rise, and her coping mechanisms do not improve, she may reach a high enough level of stress where she experiences the "total nervous exhaustion" described previously

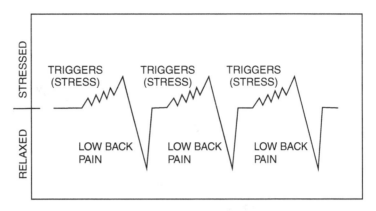

Figure 9.7

by Pelletier. There is a good chance that her usual target symptom will worsen to become a more long-term disability for a period of time. This means that her infrequent episodes of low back pain may worsen to make it impossible for her to get out of bed, to work, or to take on any family responsibilities. Jennifer may even have to go into the hospital for a period of time, if she is unable to get up to go to the bathroom or wash herself.

This serious illness is far from pleasant, but it does serve to break the stress pattern for a much longer period of time. During the period she is disabled, previous stresses may not just be postponed, but may actually diminish because of Jennifer's new status as an invalid. This allows her nervous system, as well as her psyche, to have a chance to achieve a state of relaxation; Figure 9.8 illustrates this sequence of events.

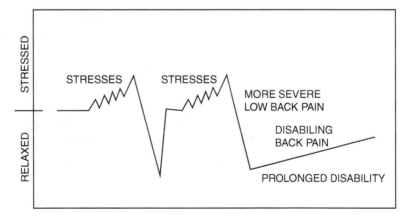

Figure 9.8

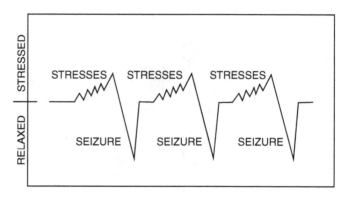

Figure 9.9

How Might This Process Occur With Seizures?

For people with seizures, the target symptom when stress builds up is often seizures. This process can happen exactly as it did with Jennifer, who had episodes of low back pain. Take the example of Dave, who takes his anticonvulsant drugs regularly and rarely has a seizure. But during a period of increased job and family stress, he begins to have more frequent seizures, both at home and at work. In Dave's case, seizures are the target symptom, which allow him some relief from stress. Although seizures at work might be embarrassing and disruptive, they do allow some tension release and a break from the pressure of his job. At home, seizures take attention away from marital and financial problems, allowing Dave a brief respite from family stresses.

We are not suggesting that people have seizures or develop low back pain on purpose to avoid stress and responsibility—but that *the body and psyche must find a way to relieve the stress*, and usually a target symptom is the result. Target symptoms force a stressed individual to slow down and often temporarily reduce pressures. Target symptoms can therefore be viewed as warnings that a person's stress level is too high.

Figure 9.9 illustrates this process of increasing stress leading to more frequent target symptoms (seizures).

Suppose the external stresses in Dave's life continue to increase, and he does not find any new coping mechanisms for dealing with his stresses. What might happen if he just can't find a way to resolve his marital or financial problems? There is a good chance that his target symptom will become more and more frequent, until his seizure disorder begins to interfere with his ability to function effectively at work. At home, his seizures

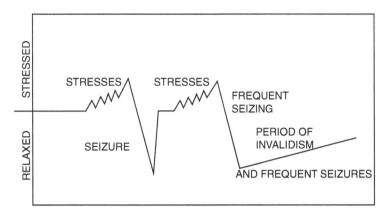

Figure 9.10

may occur so often that his relationships with family members begin to revolve around taking care of him after his seizures.

Eventually Dave loses his job and goes on disability, staying around the house, where his wife and children take care of him like an invalid. Figure 9.10 shows how this increasing frequency of seizures leads to a situation in which an individual becomes disabled, thereby reducing some of that person's life stress.

This model suggests that any target symptom can become an actual disability if stress continues to increase and the person involved is not able to cope or to reduce the stress through his or her own efforts. Table 9.1

Table 9.1 Target Symptoms and Prolonged Stress

Target Symptom	State of Disability After Prolonged Stress
Headaches	Severe, disabling headaches
Angina	Myocardial infarction (heart attack)
Minor injuries	Major injury, for example broken leg
Drinking bouts	Alcoholism, with inability to work
Low back pain	Disabling low back pain
Insomnia	Chronic insomnia and anxiety
Seizures	Frequent uncontrolled seizures
"The Blues"	Depression
Colds and minor illnesses	Serious illness, for example pneumonia

lists common target symptoms and the state of disability that may result if the target symptom increases in frequency and severity in response to unresolved stress.

The purpose of this discussion is to highlight that having seizures is not in a category by itself. On the contrary, having seizures is similar to other chronic illnesses or conditions that produce symptoms. This means that the same kind of health-enhancing measures and stress-reduction efforts that help people with back pain or heart problems can help reduce seizure frequency for people with seizures. Putting some effort into reducing external stresses in your life will help you minimize the disabling effects of having seizures.

Another point is that you may have to make a choice about whether you will allow your seizures to be a disability for you. Seizures can be a true disability, where a person is unable to work, to drive, to live independently and fully. Or, seizures can be a chronic disorder that does not control your life. You may need to take medications for the rest of your life; you may also need to pay more attention to maintaining your health and well-being than others who don't have a chronic illness. But if you are willing to put some effort into reducing the external stresses in your life, you have a good chance of avoiding the disability of frequent, uncontrolled seizures. The choice is yours.

If You Do Not Want Your Seizures to Be a Disabling Condition, How Do You Go About Learning to Deal With Stress?

Learning to deal with stress in such a way as to minimize target symptoms is not as mysterious a process as it may seem. First of all, in the remainder of Session 8, you will be involved in the task of identifying your external life stresses. The awareness that comes from looking at sources of stress is of great benefit in and of itself. Then you will do some problem-solving work to reduce or modify a few of these stresses. In Session 9, you will do some work to identify some of your internal sources of stress—the internal issues and conflicts that affect how you respond and feel about yourself. Then, in Session 10, you will use your relaxation methods, which will help you to reduce tension even when you are under stress.

But do not get the idea that anyone expects you to master stress reduction in three easy lessons, over the next 3 weeks! Learning to deal positively with stress is a big job. It takes time, patience, some trial and error, and a willingness to rethink life decisions and change some of your attitudes about where your priorities lie. Like many aspects of this program, it also requires some degree of self-awareness to observe your stresses and to see how they affect you.

If this is the first time you have looked at how your life and health are affected by stress, then use the rest of Session 8 as a guide for learning a stress-reduction approach that you can now begin to use over the next few years. On the other hand, if this approach is familiar to you, you can utilize the rest of this chapter as a "checkup" on how you are currently coping with stress. There is a lot of value in this approach for everyone, as long as there is the understanding that this is intended as a guide for ongoing stress reduction, rather than any kind of instant cure.

The Work

Goal

The goal for this session is to identify external stresses in your life and to make a plan to reduce and cope with these stresses.

Obstacles

Select the statements below that may apply to you, or write in your own.

- A sense of helplessness—"There's nothing that can be done to make things any easier."
- It may be difficult to identify the sources of stress in your life, either because of lack of practice with this kind of self-observation or because you take for granted these stresses and don't see them as modifiable.
- "All my stresses are out of my control. I'm stressed because of other people—there's nothing I can do about it myself."
- "I'm stressed because of seizures and there's nothing I can do about that!"
- Being overloaded with stresses may be a way to avoid the anxiety-provoking responsibility of health. In other words, for some people, maintaining high levels of stress in their lives is important as an excuse for health problems, or a reason that their life is not going as they would like it to.

- When approaching stress reduction, it is normal for people to experience anxiety—for example, "If I succeed in reducing some of my stresses, will I be able to handle the increased expectations I'll have of myself, and that other people may have of me?"
- If in trying to reduce external life stresses, you attempt to change too many aspects of your life at once, there is a good possibility that you will be unable to accomplish any positive changes whatsoever. Rushing and taking on too much are major obstacles to stress reduction, leading to a sense of hopelessness or failure.

Introduction to Stress Reduction

As you read through this section before your next session, write down a few things under each heading in preparation for talking with your seizure counselor. Then read the Case Study (on pages 210–212), which gives you an example of how one person used this stress reduction process to deal with external stresses in his life and improve seizure control. After reading the Case Study, go back and add any new ideas that occur to you.

In the actual appointment with your seizure counselor, try to allow enough time to briefly discuss each of the 4 steps below in the Stress Reduction Chart, writing down anything more you would like to add under each heading. Do not attempt to include everything in one session. We suggest that you try to address some important issues today, but realize that stress reduction cannot be accomplished all at once. We recommend that you return to this process once a month, adding to your lists and modifying your plans as necessary.

Stress Reduction Chart: Steps to Reduce External Life Stresses

1. Identify Major Stresses in Your Life

Consider your relationships, job or school, family and financial situation, environment and lifestyle. List elements of your life, including recent changes, that may cause pressure and stress:

_____

_____

_____

_____

_____

_____

2. List Stresses That You Can Realistically Modify or Reduce—Now, Later, or Probably Never

NOW	LATER	PROBABLY NEVER
_____	_____	_____
_____	_____	_____
_____	_____	_____

3. Set a few realistic short- and long-term goals to reduce those stresses that can be modified. Be as specific as possible.

SHORT-TERM GOALS:	LONG-TERM GOALS:
_____	_____
_____	_____
_____	_____

(**NOTE:** _While you may have identified many possible goals for reducing stress, we suggest that you pick only one for the following week._)

4. Try to Accept What You Cannot Change

Your list of stresses that you probably cannot change might include a chronic illness, a long-term debt, or divorce with subsequent family disruption. Frustration from trying to change something that is not within your control increases your stress level. Acceptance (until you can realistically change it) will help you to reduce it.

Worksheet: List of Stresses

To begin addressing the issue of acceptance, list the stresses that you probably cannot change and that are difficult to accept:

_____

_____

_____

_____

Discuss with your physician or counselor your feelings about these stresses. Why are they so difficult to accept? Write down some of the reasons you identify:

_____

_____

_____

_____

Worry, Positive Anticipation, Procrastination

In order to illustrate the importance of the practice of acceptance of external stresses that are not within your control at this moment in your life, let's review the major negative consequences of a lack of acceptance:

- **Worry**: If you tend to worry, keep in mind that this feeling state (by its very nature!) has no solution, since it is characterized by ongoing ruminations about potential negative future outcomes, while the future is simply unknown to you at this moment of your life. Many have found that using Jon Kabat-Zinn's mindfulness-based stress-reduction program or similar approaches increases the mind's ability to focus on the present, rather than being occupied with worrisome speculations about the future, thereby enhancing health. Learning to accept negative areas in your life where you cannot effect a change at a given moment may help you to let go of worry, which is one of the negative feeling states with powerful seizure-triggering potential for many individuals.

- **Positive anticipation**: It comes as a surprise to many people that seizures are not only triggered by negative feeling states but can also be triggered by intense positive states, such as positive anticipation or a state of excitement. The similarity between positive anticipation and worry may seem obscure at first, but on closer examination it becomes obvious that both states are characterized by a clear orientation toward a future event with no ability to control this event in the present. It does not matter if the future event's outcome is known to you or not. Your brain may have a hard time handling the mental overload caused by being forced to think about something that is not yet real and therefore cannot be controlled in the present moment.

Procrastination can be very incapacitating due to hesitation or inability to make a decision. The tendency to procrastinate can therefore turn activities that can and need to be addressed in one's present life into major stressors that serve as seizure triggers, similar to the effect of worry. If you tend to procrastinate, it helps to first acknowledge the need to make a decision. Many decisions can be boiled down to a simple choice: you either agree or you disagree about doing something. Interestingly, your decision may lead you to the realization that you want to leave everything as it is and not do anything. The important part is that you do not delay the decision unnecessarily; that is, do not confuse an informed decision for procrastination, where you put off deciding until you have collected *all* facts that you need to make your decision. (You will never have "all" the facts.) Also, do not confuse a healthy passage of time to reflect with some unknown passage of time to avoid a decision. Sometimes you may decide "to sleep on it," that is, to be free to let more time pass. The process of "sleeping on it" can be a type of decision that shows that you are being thoughtful and in control. Any decision-making process can be regarded as a learning opportunity that not only improves your decision-making skills in the present but also helps you to make better decisions in the future.

The stress-reduction process you have begun has two more steps, which you will be addressing in later sessions. They are listed here now for the sake of completeness, so that you can come back to this section at a later date and go through the entire process as a whole. Do not try to complete these steps today; you have already accomplished a lot with your work on steps 1–4 in the Stress Reduction Chart!

5. Get Help With Major Stresses and Inner Conflicts That You Are Unable to Cope With by Yourself

These major stresses and internal conflicts might include serious marital problems, personal feelings of inadequacy, or addiction to alcohol or drugs. Asking for help from your doctor or counselor is often the first step in resolving a major life conflict. Identifying internal issues and knowing when to get help will be discussed next week in Session 9.

6. Take Daily Action to Reduce Tensions

Because a certain amount of stress is unavoidable, most people need some tension-reducing measures to help them cope more effectively with the stress they are unable to eliminate. Specific methods will be discussed in Session 10, "Enhancing Personal Wellness."

CASE STUDY

Oscar started having complex partial seizures when he was a teenager. Now 38 years old, he had a more than full-time job in a busy hardware/electrical supply business. He had been married for 9 years, and he and his wife had two young kids. Even though Oscar had been going to his doctor regularly and was taking his anticonvulsants as prescribed, he was still having seizures.

After Oscar had been seeing his seizure counselor for a few weeks, he experienced a radical change in his attitude. Session 3, which dealt with medications, proved to be a turning point because he had an appointment with his doctor and learned how carefully his physician had adjusted his medications over the years. Up until then, he had believed that his poor seizure control was a result of his doctor being somewhat hit-or-miss with his use of medications; he had thought that his doctor simply had not hit on the right combination yet. But after Session 3, he understood that his medication really was adjusted as well as it could be. If he was going to improve his seizure control, he was going to have to change something other than dosages or drugs.

This realization made Oscar particularly open to the new information provided in Sessions 4–8. Although the concepts of triggers and target symptoms seemed pretty far-fetched, he started to notice how many triggers and external stresses were affecting his life. He began to see his job like an outsider might see it: phone rings off the hook, customers crowd the counter demanding attention, and no one gets lunch or breaks.

Not only that, but Oscar never got the chance to take it easy when he got home. Every unexpected bill came as a blow, and he and his wife would argue about how they were going to pay it. He never had enough time to spend with his wife and kids, or to talk through problems with her. He also realized that he rarely sat down in his easy chair or went for a walk—he spent every spare minute trying to fix the car or work on projects around the house.

The other two major stresses that came to mind as he talked about Session 8 with his seizure counselor were his seizures and his father's death. Although his seizures were

---

brief and he could get back to work promptly, he always felt embarrassed when he had a seizure at work. Sometimes just worrying that he might have one on the job made it harder to function. He was also bothered by the fact that his wife had to drive him to and from his job. He secretly hoped his seizures would just disappear.

It was hard for Oscar to sit down and write about these things in his Workbook, especially to organize his thoughts in brief phrases. When he did fill out the Stress Reduction Chart (below), he found the process helpful. You may want to refer to Oscar's example below in this Case Study when filling out your own Chart.

1. Identify major stresses in your life (Oscar's responses)
   - *Job pressure—too many demands at work, no breaks.*
   - *Money is tight; job is low-paying.*
   - *My father died 6 months ago. I miss him and feel bad.*
   - *I have seizures. My seizures are a source of stress, especially at work.*
   - *Too busy. No time to relax, see friends, exercise.*
   - *Arguments and poor communication with wife.*

2. List stresses that you can realistically modify or reduce: now, later, or probably never:

NOW	LATER	PROBABLY NEVER
Too busy, no time to relax, see friends, exercise.	*Job pressure—long work hours, too many demands.*	*Having seizures.*
Poor communication with wife and kids.	*Money problems, low-paying job.*	*Recent death of father (will be easier to cope in 3–5 years).*

3. Set a few realistic short- and long-term goals to reduce those stresses that can be modified.

SHORT-TERM GOALS	LONG-TERM GOALS
1. Eliminate non-essential activities: *a) At home—no more remodeling projects.* *b) At work—discuss with boss: limit phone calls and other interruptions, take lunch and coffee breaks.* *2. Plan some time alone with my wife so we can talk.* *3. Take 20 minutes to walk, 3 x/week. Invite my kids and/or my wife to join me.*	*1. Plan for job change: improved working conditions, salary, and job satisfaction.* *2. Limit spending until I get a pay raise.* *3. Work with seizure counselor regarding feelings about having seizures; the death of my father.*

4. Try to accept what you cannot change.

   ▪ *I don't want to accept that I have seizures, but I do. I have to accept that I can try to improve my seizure control but I can't get rid of seizures altogether.*

   ▪ *My father's death.*

Now that he had written this information down, Oscar was impatient to begin working on all of the short-term goals he listed under section 3. He thought that if he could accomplish all those goals, it was likely that his seizures would occur less frequently. But his seizure counselor urged him to take one goal at a time, instead of tackling them all at once. She said that trying to do too many goals was stressful, a setup for failure. She reminded him that the idea was to plan for success—to set one goal at a time and get the good feeling from accomplishing one positive change before going on to the next.

Oscar agreed to go along with her suggestion. He had noticed that one of his triggers was having pressured days at work, without any breaks. He chose to start with the goal of talking to his boss about taking lunch and other breaks, along with his ideas about how to make the busy times go more smoothly. In talking with his seizure counselor, he realized that the reason he hadn't done anything about this before was because he thought he should work harder to make up for sometimes having seizures on the job. He found it helpful to talk over this obstacle with his seizure counselor. He tried out some "I messages," role-playing with her as his boss. Then he practiced what he would say if Mr. P. brought up his seizures as a reason that Oscar didn't deserve breaks. Their work together gave him the support he needed to set up a meeting with his boss before he met with his seizure counselor again for Session 9.

In-Office Discussion

Read these sections and make notes in your *Workbook* prior to your appointment, as preparation for the in-office discussion with your seizure counselor.

Review of Assignments

Seizure Log/Thought Records

How often were you able to observe your aura? Discuss Thought Records.

Journal-Keeping

Read any relevant parts of the descriptions you wrote of your aura. Discuss and clarify your aura in detail with your seizure counselor.

Self-Observation Exercise

Did you practice self-observation? Discuss any relevant observations or experiences.

Relaxation Exercise

How are you doing with daily practice of relaxation at home? Which exercise are you practicing? Any problems or experiences to report? Do you enjoy your relaxation process?

Goal Review From Prior Session

Were you able to meet your goal for this week? How are you doing with the overall process of goal-setting as a tool for personal change?

Review of Obstacles

What obstacles do you notice in yourself when you think about reducing external stresses in your life?

Tool

In-Office Stress Reduction Meeting

1. Show your seizure counselor your Stress Reduction Chart where you have listed your stresses. Go through steps 1–4, discussing what you have written and adding or modifying as needed.
2. Select how stress affects you on Figure 9.1 (the body and stress diagram).
3. The focus of the session is on helping you choose one goal toward reducing external stress in your life. Remember that it may not be realistic to complete your stress-reduction process in one week. You and your seizure counselor may want to designate a future time to discuss Session 8 in more detail. The important thing is to begin—by picking one goal that you can accomplish successfully.

Seizure Log/Thought Records

Continue keeping your Seizure Log and doing Thought Records.

Journal-Keeping

What is your experience of trying to identify and reduce external life stressors? Record your reactions to trying to meet your chosen goal for lowering your stress level this week. What were the difficulties in trying to meet this goal? Were there any satisfactions or rewards in making the effort to meet your goal? Was this a realistic goal for you? If not, how might you modify it so that it would be possible for you to meet a goal that would reduce one of the stresses in your life?

Stress Reduction Chart

Over the coming week, observe any sources of stress that are affecting you that day and add them to the Stress Reduction Chart in your *Workbook*. Underline any that have a particularly strong effect or that seem to trigger seizures. In addition, add any new information or ideas to sections 3 and 4 of your Chart.

Goal-Setting for Session 8

Worksheet: Short-Term Goal

After reviewing possible goals from Step 3 in the Stress Reduction Chart select one short-term goal for reducing one source of external life stress:

_____

_____

_____

_____

_____

I plan to accomplish this goal by _____ (give date).

On (give date[s]) _____, I tried to meet this goal with the following results:

_____

_____

Relaxation Exercise

Practice the relaxation exercise you utilized in this week's relaxation session for 10 minutes or more each day. Remember to allow yourself uninterrupted time for this, with your door closed and phone turned off. These home practice sessions are essential for making progress in your relaxation training. For your personal record, you may wish to make a note of the sessions you do on your Seizure Log forms. As you begin to be able to accomplish relaxation, discuss with your seizure counselor how to apply this skill to other life situations, such as when you experience negative states or your pre-seizure aura.

Preparing for Your Next Appointment

After completing this session and discussing it with your seizure counselor, you will read and complete "Session 9: Dealing With Internal Issues and Conflicts."

Resources for Further Reading

Devinsky, O., Schachter, S., & Pacia, S. *Complementary and Alternative Therapies for Epilepsy.* New York: Demos, 2005.

Holmes, T. H., Rahe, R. H. The social readjustment rating scale. *Journal of Psychosomatic Research*, 1967; 11(2):213–218 (adapted by multiple authors since initial publication).

McEwen, Bruce S. Protective and damaging effects of stress mediators. *New England Journal of Medicine*, 1998;338(3):171–179.

Nakken, K., Solaas, M., Kjeldsan, M., Friis, M., Pellock, J., & Corey, L. Which seizure-precipitating factors do patients with epilepsy most frequently report? *Epilepsy and Behavior*, 2005;6:1, 85–89.

Pelletier, Kenneth. Stress/Unstress, *Medical Self-Care*, Number Five. Inverness, CA: 1978.

Selye, Hans. *The Stress of Life.* New York: McGraw-Hill, 1978.

Swenson, Richard A. *Margin: Restoring Emotional, Physical, Financial, and Time Reserves to Overloaded Lives*, Colorado Springs, CO: NavPress, 1992.

<u>SEIZURE LOG</u>   **For the Week of** ____/____/____ **to** ____/____/____

Instructions: Please fill in the diary at the end of each day to record the number and descriptions listed. This information will be reviewed with your physician at each appointment.

Init:_____
ID:_____
Week: _____
Type:_____

SUNDAY ___/___/___ (day 1)
Number of Seizures:_____
Time(s) of day:_____
Duration (sec or min):_____
Description:_____
Location(s):_____
Severity (1: mild, 2: mod, 3: severe):_____
Trigger(s):_____
Precursor(s):_____
Improved with:_____
Impact on your day:_____
Impact on others:_____

MONDAY ___/___/___ (day 2)
Number of Seizures:_____
Time(s) of day:_____
Duration:_____
Description:_____
Location(s):_____
Severity (1: mild, 2: mod, 3: severe):_____
Trigger(s):_____
Precursor(s):_____
Improved with:_____
Impact on your day:_____
Impact on others:_____

TUESDAY ___/___/___ (day 3)
Number of Seizures:_____
Time(s) of day:_____
Duration:_____
Description:_____
Location(s):_____
Severity (1: mild, 2: mod, 3: severe):_____
Trigger(s):_____
Precursor(s):_____
Improved with:_____
Impact on your day:_____
Impact on others:_____

WEDNESDAY ___/___/___ (day 4)
Number of Seizures:_____
Time(s) of day:_____
Duration:_____
Description:_____
Location(s):_____
Severity (1: mild, 2: mod, 3: severe):_____
Trigger(s):_____
Precursor(s):_____
Improved with:_____
Impact on your day:_____
Impact on others:_____

Total: _____   **Rater:** _____

THURSDAY ___/___/___ (day 5)
Number of Seizures:_____
Time(s) of day:_____
Duration:_____
Description:_____
Location(s):_____
Severity (1: mild, 2: mod, 3: severe):_____
Trigger(s):_____
Precursor(s):_____
Improved with:_____
Impact on your day:_____
Impact on others:_____

FRIDAY ___/___/___ (day 6)
Number of Seizures:_____
Time(s) of day:_____
Duration:_____
Description:_____
Location(s):_____
Severity (1: mild, 2: mod, 3: severe):_____
Trigger(s):_____
Precursor(s):_____
Improved with:_____
Impact on your day:_____
Impact on others:_____

SATURDAY ___/___/___ (day 7)
Number of Seizures:_____
Time(s) of day:_____
Duration:_____
Description:_____
Location(s):_____
Severity (1: mild, 2: mod, 3: severe):_____
Trigger(s):_____
Precursor(s):_____
Improved with:_____
Impact on your day:_____
Impact on others:_____

Use **the space below or on back** to describe any <u>significant information not covered in this record:</u>

_____
_____
_____
_____
_____

Were you successful in stopping any seizures this week:
yes ☐   no ☐

Please mark which seizures you stopped with an asterisk (*).

SEIZURE LOG   For the Week of ____/____/____ to ____/____/____

Instructions: Please fill in the diary at the end of each day to record the number and descriptions listed. This information will be reviewed with your physician at each appointment.

Init:_____
ID:_____
Week: _____
Type:_____

SUNDAY ___/___/___ (day 1)
Number of Seizures:_____
Time(s) of day:_____
Duration (sec or min):_____
Description:_____
Location(s):_____
Severity (1: mild, 2: mod, 3: severe):_____
Trigger(s):_____
Precursor(s):_____
Improved with:_____
Impact on your day:_____
Impact on others:_____

MONDAY ___/___/___ (day 2)
Number of Seizures:_____
Time(s) of day:_____
Duration:_____
Description:_____
Location(s):_____
Severity (1: mild, 2: mod, 3: severe):_____
Trigger(s):_____
Precursor(s):_____
Improved with:_____
Impact on your day:_____
Impact on others:_____

TUESDAY ___/___/___ (day 3)
Number of Seizures:_____
Time(s) of day:_____
Duration:_____
Description:_____
Location(s):_____
Severity (1: mild, 2: mod, 3: severe):_____
Trigger(s):_____
Precursor(s):_____
Improved with:_____
Impact on your day:_____
Impact on others:_____

WEDNESDAY ___/___/___ (day 4)
Number of Seizures:_____
Time(s) of day:_____
Duration:_____
Description:_____
Location(s):_____
Severity (1: mild, 2: mod, 3: severe):_____
Trigger(s):_____
Precursor(s):_____
Improved with:_____
Impact on your day:_____
Impact on others:_____

THURSDAY ___/___/___ (day 5)
Number of Seizures:_____
Time(s) of day:_____
Duration:_____
Description:_____
Location(s):_____
Severity (1: mild, 2: mod, 3: severe):_____
Trigger(s):_____
Precursor(s):_____
Improved with:_____
Impact on your day:_____
Impact on others:_____

FRIDAY ___/___/___ (day 6)
Number of Seizures:_____
Time(s) of day:_____
Duration:_____
Description:_____
Location(s):_____
Severity (1: mild, 2: mod, 3: severe):_____
Trigger(s):_____
Precursor(s):_____
Improved with:_____
Impact on your day:_____
Impact on others:_____

SATURDAY ___/___/___ (day 7)
Number of Seizures:_____
Time(s) of day:_____
Duration:_____
Description:_____
Location(s):_____
Severity (1: mild, 2: mod, 3: severe):_____
Trigger(s):_____
Precursor(s):_____
Improved with:_____
Impact on your day:_____
Impact on others:_____

Use **the space below or on back** to describe any significant information not covered in this record:

_____
_____
_____
_____
_____
_____

Were you successful in stopping any seizures this week:
yes ☐   no ☐

Please mark which seizures you stopped with an asterisk (*).

Total: _____   **Rater:** _____

CHAPTER 10

Session 9: Dealing With Internal Issues and Conflicts

In Session 8, you explored the subject of external life stresses and how they affect health. You began the stress-reduction process with a list of stresses and a plan to begin reducing the external life stresses that you felt were modifiable. In Session 9, you will address another source of stress—internal conflicts and issues. The term "internal conflicts" is used to refer to the inner stresses within each individual—the feelings, conflicts, and issues that are part of a person's inner being and that affect overall health and well-being as much or more than external stresses do.

The most difficult part about coping with internal conflicts is that it is *normal* not to be aware of one's internal conflicts. While external life stress and its connection to health are recognized in the media as well as in the practice of healthcare, most people pay scant attention to the idea that inner conflicts and feelings affect health. It is not surprising that for many people, identifying external life stresses is easier and more familiar than looking inward at the personal issues that affect how we feel about ourselves.

Keep in mind that dealing with internal issues and conflicts is a long-term process. No one is expected to undertake this process in one week! On the contrary, many people who choose to work in depth on internal issues do so over a period of months or years with an experienced counselor. The purpose of Session 9 is to introduce you to these concepts and to encourage those who are interested to pursue this aspect of self-awareness and self-acceptance.

When first introduced to these ideas, many people wonder what the point is of trying to uncover these unconscious issues and conflicts. The most compelling reason is that they often interfere with getting full satisfaction out of our relationships and our lives. You may find that internal issues get in the way of getting what you want—including taking control of your seizures—time and time again. For this reason, it is worthwhile to consider putting some effort into recognizing your own personal conflicts and issues, which is the focus of Session 9. Session 9 offers you yet another way to move toward the goal of taking control of your seizures.

What Kinds of Inner Conflicts and Issues Affect Health?

The inner conflicts and issues that affect personal health often involve deep-seated thoughts and feelings about oneself. Other issues center on the relationships we form with other people.

Sometimes these thoughts and feelings are completely unconscious—which means we do not even know that they exist in our psyches. But usually there are inner voices that express these unrecognized issues and conflicts that affect us so deeply. Some examples of inner conflicts and issues, expressed as inner voices, are listed below:

Personal Conflicts and Issues

Select any statements below that apply to you.

- "I act superior, but I feel inferior."
- "It's his/her fault that I'm having problems."
- "I feel at fault, guilty—and I blame other people for everything."
- "Everyone else is a jerk. I'm the only one who knows anything about this!"
- "It's my fault when anything goes wrong, so I have to keep trying to do everything right."
- "I'm always telling my spouse or coworker what to do, so I can feel better."
- "Inside I feel like a bad person so I'm always trying to be perfectly good."

- "I feel inadequate, so I just don't try."
- "I feel inadequate so I constantly try to prove that I'm better."
- "All those people are out to get me, just because I have seizures."
- "It's always someone else's fault when things aren't going well.. . . "
- "No matter what I do, other people just want me to feel bad."

Issues That Center Around Relationships

Some conflicts and issues seem to be centered on important relationships in our lives. For anyone who may have listed marital conflicts, family, or friendship problems as a source of external stress in Session 8, it may be particularly fruitful to listen to the inner voices that speak about how we feel relating to the people we love. Some examples are listed below:

- "I want you to take care of me and my needs without having to tell you what my needs are."
- "It's your fault when I don't feel okay about myself."
- "I'm just a helpless person so it's your responsibility to take care of me. When you try to make me take responsibility for myself, I get angry with you."
- "I'm miserable because so and so won't change. The only thing I can do is try harder to make this other person be different. If it doesn't work, he or she is a jerk and I'm a failure."

Chronic Feeling States

Another group of internal issues involve negative feeling (or emotional) states that a person experiences so often that they can be called "chronic." Sometimes these feeling states themselves are issues that can be explored and understood. At other times, they are the tip of the iceberg of deeper issues that may need to be uncovered, often with the help of a professional counselor.

- Anxiety
- Depression
- Hostility/Blame
- Anger
- Fear
- Shame

Health is affected by three aspects of human experience: bodily sensation, emotion, and thought. Many people would include the addition of another aspect—the spiritual. In any case, the human mind and body clearly interact so closely that it is impossible to separate physical well-being from psychological well-being.

It is easy to see that physical symptoms such as headaches, a sore throat, or back pain affect health. It is less commonly accepted that psychological symptoms have just as much impact on health. For example, if your body feels fine but you are going around feeling constantly anxious or depressed, these feelings have just as much effect on your health as a headache. In fact, sometimes headaches or other physical symptoms such as seizures actually result from these kinds of chronic feeling states.

This same interaction between mind and body occurs with various kinds of personal conflicts and issues discussed above. For example, an inner feeling that "I'm inadequate" may pervade a person's experience to the point where it's impossible to take positive steps to improve a health problem, such as a seizure disorder, without dealing openly with these feelings of inadequacy.

In summary, inner issues and conflicts affect health as much as physical injuries and illnesses do, and sometimes have a greater influence on well-being than external stresses discussed in Session 8. In working through this section, you will have the opportunity to decide how deeply you want to explore your inner issues at this time. According to your decision, you will be able to take steps to begin this long-term process of dealing with inner conflicts and issues.

While reading the following sections, bear in mind that it is normal to not be aware of most of your inner issues. When you do become aware of them, *it can be extremely difficult to get rid of them*—and that is why this section is called "dealing with major life issues." Rather than seeking to completely *eliminate* conflicts and negative feeling states, the goal is to know oneself and to learn to accept and take care of the parts of oneself that have such a profound effect on health and self-esteem.

How Do I Begin to Work on the Process of Dealing With Inner Issues?

This process begins with self-awareness and self-observation, in order to get to know the hidden, uncomfortable parts of oneself. Often people are not aware of many of the most powerful issues that affect how they feel about themselves because it feels dangerous and painful to explore these issues. On the other hand, getting to know these raw, difficult parts offers the possibility of learning to feel more at peace with oneself—more whole.

If you choose to begin this process now, start by noticing when you are particularly uncomfortable. Ask yourself: "What am I actually feeling inside at this moment that I feel so uncomfortable, confused, or conflicted?" Observe yourself at times when you find yourself feeling one thing, but doing something else—that is, when your feelings and actions are at odds with each other. These moments often provide clues to the inner issues that are unconscious. By *unconscious* we mean that something is not part of your conscious awareness but nonetheless affects much of your experience, decisions, feelings, and thoughts.

Learning to observe yourself will be more rewarding if you approach it with a slow, gentle attitude. One or two observations in a day is a real achievement; no one can expect to make this kind of effort all day long. Sometimes these insights come in spurts, while at other times you may not notice anything for weeks. It is therefore essential to cultivate an attitude of acceptance toward yourself. First of all, try to accept that this process is slow and cannot be accomplished quickly. And second, remind yourself to take a compassionate, nonjudgmental outlook toward the parts of yourself you do observe and get to know.

The following examples illustrate the kind of inner dialogue that may be necessary in learning to self-observe without blame. The different voices that "speak" are all within one person.

Self-Observation Without Blame: Example #1

- *"I'm feeling really uncomfortable; what do I notice at this moment?"*
- *"I'm saying nice words to my spouse, but I'm really feeling very angry. I know what I'm angry about, but I'm afraid to say anything or do anything about it."*
- *"I shouldn't be this way—I should just learn how to say what I really feel!"*
- *"Wait a minute; I'm starting to judge myself, to tell myself that I 'should' be different. I want to go back to seeing that it's so hard for me to express my angry feelings, and to try not to judge myself for it."*

Self-Observation With Blame: Example #2

- *"I just told her off. What a jerk."*
- *"Hey, I just told her off when she actually tried to help me."*
- *"It's her fault that I feel miserable. She deserves to feel miserable too!"*
- *"There I go trying to blame someone for my own problems. I'm the jerk—not her."*
- *"But maybe I could try to stop blaming myself, too. It's not her fault, and it's not my fault either."*

After Compassionate Self-Observation, What Comes Next?

Frequent self-observation helps you begin to identify the inner issues that come up often. As with external stresses, there is a lot of benefit to being able to identify and list these issues. The reason is that you can deal with—that is, learn to take care of—feelings and conflicts that are conscious, or known to you.

When issues, conflicts, and feelings are unconscious and unknown, you have no control over how you take care of them. With the help of a counselor, you may learn to make some of your issues conscious and learn to deal with them in ways that help you feel happier and more accepting of yourself.

Worksheet: Inner Issues

The following space is provided for recording inner issues that you observe. You may want to list one or two that you are aware of now. Gradually add to the list over the next weeks or months, discussing the issues with your physician, seizure counselor, or therapist as they come up. Review the descriptions and examples given above as you begin to work on the following lists:

Personal issues and conflicts:

_____

_____

_____

_____

_____

_____

Issues that center around relationships:

_____

_____

_____

_____

_____

Chronic negative feeling states:

_____

_____

_____

_____

_____

Once You Begin to Identify Your Inner Issues, What Happens Next?

Once you have identified one or more inner issues, it is important to validate these issues and get to know how they affect your feeling states, actions, and thoughts. There are two major ways that you can validate an inner issue and learn how it affects your psyche. You can continue self-observation when this issue arises, reminding yourself to refrain from judging and simply to observe what is going on. Another way involves getting help from another person for validation and clarification; by discussing your observations with your seizure counselor or other professional therapist, you may gain valuable insight and understanding beyond what you are able to obtain by yourself. This approach allows you to get the support you need to explore important internal issues and to learn to manage them in productive ways.

What Is the Benefit of Continuing Validation and Self-Observation?

The benefit of continuing to validate the issues that you uncover, and to observe their impact on your inner and outer life, is that this is the way to gradually *make the unconscious become conscious.* Seeing something once rarely makes it known, accepted, and understood; whereas seeing something a hundred times in many different situations may allow a person to become conscious of issues that have remained unconscious for a lifetime.

"Making the Unconscious Become Conscious" Sounds Hard and Very Time-Consuming. How Can It Help You?

When an issue is unconscious, you have no control over it. On the contrary, often it controls you—by influencing life decisions, feeling states, relationships, symptoms such as seizure frequency—in ways that may not be beneficial to you. As a person becomes aware of an issue (such as a feeling of inadequacy or a tendency to blame others), often the first thought is to ask, "How can I get rid of this issue, now that I see how it interferes with my well-being?" But you cannot get rid of the unpleasant issues or conflicts that you uncover. They are your baggage, your personal albatrosses, as illustrated in Figure 10.1.

What you can do is learn ways to take care of these parts of yourself. Once you know about your own issues and conflicts, you can make choices so that you are in control—rather than being controlled by these unconscious parts of yourself. This is what is meant by learning to "deal" with major life issues. Often, compassionate acceptance of these "unacceptable" parts of oneself becomes a great source of relief, because one no longer has to expend a lot of psychological energy trying to prove to oneself that "I'm not like that."

Making the unconscious become conscious allows you to know who you really are and to be able to say that it is OK to be who you are. This allows you to take control at a whole different level—to decide how you want to take care of those vulnerable parts of yourself. Many people cover the painful parts of their past by diving into another relationship, or hobby, or distraction, or addiction. They may seek validation in something or someone else. In that case, the other person or activity is merely placing a band-aid on a deeper wound. Getting to know yourself sets you on the path to more loving and supportive relationships. The effects of this kind

Figure 10.1

of taking control can be surprisingly positive, giving you the power to make positive choices for yourself, to improve relationships, to limit the effects of seizures or other symptoms, and to find meaning and enjoyment in the experience of living.

Summary of Session 9: Dealing With Internal Conflicts and Issues

1. Self-observe at uncomfortable moments. Do a Thought Record.
2. Cultivate an attitude of self-acceptance and compassion.
3. Identify your major internal issues:
    a. Personal conflicts and issues
    b. Issues that center around relationships
    c. Chronic negative feeling states
4. Validate your issues and observe how they affect your life and experience.
5. Persevere in making the unconscious become conscious and trying to accept yourself as you are.
6. Learn to take care of your issues by conscious choice.

When Does a Person Need Help With This Process of Dealing With Major Life Issues?

Because this process involves uncovering blind spots (in the psyche), which are often protected by layers of defenses to protect these vulnerable places, most people need some help from another person in order to learn to deal effectively with internal issues. Many people find that a trained counselor can provide valuable insight, reassurance, and support during this process, which could not otherwise be obtained from oneself, family members, or friends.

A trained counselor might be

- A psychologist (PhD)
- A marriage and family therapist (MFT)
- A psychiatrist (MD)
- A social worker (LCSW or MSW)
- A psychiatric nurse (RN)
- A pastor or pastoral counselor (MDiv, CpastC or equivalent)

Your seizure counselor may have training to do long-term counseling on internal issues—or he or she may not. You may wish to discuss with your physician and seizure counselor which of the following courses of action you would like to take with regard to "Session 9: Dealing With Internal Issues and Conflicts." Working through issues over time is a process. This work can be done with a counselor or a trusted support person who can listen to difficult things that you may have experienced. Items that may be addressed can include past hurts, memories, experiences, and emotions. It may be helpful to examine past hurts and how they impact you in the present. Memories may crop up at the least expected times, without any apparent reason. Forgiveness can be an important part of the healing process, a gift that comes from accepting that all of us are flawed and make mistakes. Dan Allender, suggests that we do not forgive others for their sake; we do it for our own sake, so that we can be free.[1]

---

[1]Allender, D. B., *The Wounded Heart Book and Workbook* (Colorado Springs, CO: NavPress, 1995).

Four Choices: How I Might Proceed With Session 9

(Select your choice)

1. I choose to work on this process in depth with my physician, therapist, or seizure counselor. (Discuss with him or her whether he or she is licensed and trained to do this kind of counseling.)

2. I choose to work on this process in depth with another trained therapist. (Ask your physician or seizure counselor to recommend some names for referral.)

3. I prefer not to work on this process at this particular time.

4. I prefer not to work in depth on this process at this time, but would like the option of discussing any issues that come up with my seizure counselor.

You are now three-quarters of the way through this process of taking control. Choosing one of the above four options will help prepare for the next steps in the process of taking control of your seizures. Later in this session, you will be given additional options from which to choose.

When Is Referral for Ongoing Counseling Recommended?

Referral for ongoing counseling is recommended when a motivated person, whose physician and counselor think has the potential for making significant progress, tries hard at everything but is simply not getting anywhere. If you think you are in this situation, the question of whether ongoing counseling will help should be discussed with both your physician and seizure counselor. The reason is that it is often one or more powerful internal issues that are blocking the road toward improved seizure control and quality of life. In-depth counseling may be your main recourse for learning to deal effectively with these issues so that you can go on to take control of your seizures and your life.

The Work

Goal

The goal for this session is to deal effectively with internal issues by identifying conflicts, negative feelings, and issues, and learning to take care of them by conscious choice.

Obstacles

Select the statements below that may apply to you, or write in your own.

- Not wanting to know about these issues—it can be painful and difficult to explore this.
- Judgmental attitude toward yourself—the tendency to dislike or even hate the parts of yourself that you uncover in this process.
- Judgmental attitude toward others—the tendency to feel OK about yourself while disliking or hating certain aspects of other people. (For instance, feeling better when blaming or judging others, or feeling that "I always have to be right.")
- Hopelessness and frustration at how difficult it is to change. (Yes, it is difficult or impossible to change the psyche or eliminate an issue, but it is definitely possible to make an issue conscious and to learn to accept it. Then everything changes, because the unconscious issue no longer controls you.)
- Too many other overriding concerns in your life. (This process takes time, energy, and drive. You may not want to undertake it when you are dealing with many other demands, interests, stresses, or life changes.)

CASE STUDY

Oscar was nervous about meeting with his boss, but the discussion he'd had with his seizure counselor in Session 8 gave him the courage to go through with it. At first, Mr. P. was angry that Oscar was taking up valuable time to "complain." Mr. P. contended that Oscar owed the company something because they tolerated his time out for seizures. Luckily, Oscar had prepared an answer to this: he reminded his boss that workers were entitled to one 15-minute break per 4-hour period. He also told Mr. P. that he wanted to start taking a regular lunch break. He suggested that his "time outs" for seizures, which didn't happen that frequently, be counted as sick leave. But he still wanted to have regular breaks and lunch every day.

One positive result was that his boss was responsive to his idea of marking off a line for customer service. This would eliminate crowding at the counter. Another clerk would be designated to answer the phone during busy times. Mr. P. agreed to let Oscar take his scheduled breaks. Oscar had been successful in meeting his goal of talking with his boss and asking for some changes to make his workday less pressured.

Despite this success, Oscar felt discouraged when he began working on Session 9. He was very worried about the problems he was having with his wife. He did not under-stand why there was so much bad feeling between them. He was not sure if he wanted to go on trying to reduce stress and deal with issues if it was only going to make things worse.

In their appointment to talk about Session 9, Oscar told his seizure counselor how he felt. He was angry that his wife was not helping him more, that his life was not a lot better, and that he still had too many seizures. At one point, Oscar accused his counselor of messing things up and said he thought she didn't know what she was doing. His seizure counselor said she understood that he was angry that progress was not faster and that his life was not getting easier. She said she was glad he could express his feelings.

In discussing his marital issues, they noted that arguing with his wife was one of Oscar's seizure triggers. They concluded that it would take more than one Workbook session to work on his relationship. His counselor suggested he might want to schedule additional appointments to work in depth on dealing with this issue, separate from the "taking control" sessions. He could do this either with her or with a different therapist. Because he felt a trusting connection with her, he decided to see her for additional appointments while continuing the taking control process.

After some weeks, Oscar realized something important. He told his seizure counselor that he had noticed his tendency to blame his wife whenever things got bad—especially with money. He justified this blaming by thinking she must be overspending, when he knew that they just didn't have enough money to handle unexpected bills.

At his next therapy appointment, he told his counselor that he had a new insight: he got angry and blamed his wife when he felt like a failure. Money was a sore point because he felt it was his fault that he didn't earn enough money—that because he had seizures he would never be able to get a promotion that would provide more support for his family. Right when he felt inadequate and blamed himself, he would get angry and blame his wife. He was ashamed of this, but decided to bring it up anyway. Oscar's counselor said it was brave of him to see this and to tell her about it. He discovered that blaming was a familiar pattern; as a boy, he had witnessed his father blaming his mother whenever anything went wrong.

The following week, Oscar reported that tensions had eased a little with his wife. Money was tight, but the insight that he started to feel inadequate and then blamed her helped to prevent arguments. He felt far from great, but at least he and his wife could talk about how to pay for a new water heater without getting furious at each other.

Oscar realized that his feelings of inadequacy had started when he was a child, long before he developed seizures. The seizures had merely confirmed his suspicion that something was wrong with him, "that I was broken." He also came to understand that when he blamed others, he no longer blamed himself, so it was a way to make himself feel better.

Oscar also noticed that he felt bad and unworthy whenever he was not doing something productive. This explained his overworking at home—always doing house projects or car repair. He never allowed himself any leisure because he felt he did not deserve it, that he had to earn his way. This contributed to his tension and fatigue, because he never let himself relax.

Although it was rough going, Oscar was eventually able to establish a more positive relationship with his wife. In his opinion, a lot of his success had to do with admitting to himself that he blamed her in order to avoid blaming himself. When the two of them talked about this, his wife acknowledged that she too tended to hold him responsible for their problems. Together they made a plan regarding how they might jointly earn more in the future, spend less now, and talk about money issues. They started going out more and seeing friends. Having good times together did a lot to make their relationship more positive.

While working on these issues, he returned to Session 9 in his Workbook several times to record his insights:

Personal issues and conflicts

Feel inadequate, incompetent, something is wrong with me.

See seizures as confirming this view of myself, that I'll never be worthy and okay.

I overwork myself to try to compensate for feeling incompetent and unworthy.

I blame others when I feel like a failure.

Issues that center around relationships

Blaming my wife in order to avoid blaming myself, especially about lack of money.

I tend to avoid close communication, especially when something is bothering me.

Chronic negative feeling states

I feel that I'm not good enough unless I earn my way—this leads to constant chores and projects at home and no breaks at work!

I feel exhausted and irritable a lot when I overwork.

Note: Remember that it may take some time to reach these kinds of insights about yourself. Don't expect to be clear about your own issues and conflicts after a few appointments with your seizure counselor. If you want to do this kind of work, allow yourself plenty of time to go through the process of in-depth counseling with a trained therapist.

In-Office Discussion

Please read these sections and make notes in your *Workbook* prior to your appointment, as preparation for the in-office discussion with your seizure counselor.

Review of Assignments

Seizure Log/Thought Records

Show your Seizure Logs and Thought Records to your seizure counselor at the beginning of the appointment.

Journal-Keeping

Read any sections you wish to discuss with your seizure counselor about your experience of trying to reduce external life stresses.

Stress Reduction Chart

Show your counselor any additions or changes you made this week on your Stress Reduction Chart from Session 8.

Goal Review from Prior Session

Last week you chose one goal toward reducing external stresses in your life. Were you able to meet his goal? If so, how did it go for you? Were the results helpful or disappointing? If not, why do you think you were unable to meet your goal? Did you learn anything from your efforts?

Relaxation Exercise

Are you working on your relaxation exercises on a regular basis? How is it going for you?

If you are now able to use relaxation to prevent seizures or to stop a seizure once it has started, discuss with your seizure counselor how to apply this skill to other life situations, such as when you experience your pre-seizure aura or a negative state.

Review of Obstacles

What obstacles do you foresee, or have you already experienced, in trying to identify internal issues and conflicts?

Tool

Learning to Deal With Inner Issues

Because the concepts discussed in this section of the *Workbook* are complex, take some time to *answer the following questions before your next appointment.* You can use the space provided or your journal. You and your seizure counselor may want to spend some time discussing and clarifying the following questions:

1. What is your understanding of the terms "issue," "conflict," and "chronic negative feeling state?"

   _____

   _____

2. What issues/conflicts have you already listed in your *Workbook*? Give examples of recent self-observations of these issues.

   _____

   _____

3. How exactly would you go about self-observing and validating these and other inner issues?

   _____

   _____

4. What are some of the issues that you may have discussed in previous sessions but perhaps did not identify as an "issue?" Add them to your list if appropriate.

   _____

   _____

5. Have you had experiences of making an unconscious issue conscious, and learning to take care of that issue by conscious choice? If so, please describe. If not, discuss with your seizure counselor your picture of what this process might be like, taking one of the issues you have identified as an example. (Perhaps your support person or friend has had this experience and would be willing to tell you about it.)

_____

_____

_____

6. What do your critical thoughts tell you about internal issues and conflicts? Critical thoughts, which you may frown upon as somewhat dishonorable feelings, can instead be used as valuable indicators of your own internal issues and conflicts. If you decide to observe the criticism that you have toward other people, you might discover that your critical thoughts result from fears about yourself. If you are afraid of being lazy, it may make it hard for you to take appropriate breaks and rest periods. As a result, you might hold a grudge against people who have a more easy-going attitude toward fulfilling their duties. Realize that sometimes identifying issues in others' lives comes easy because we have some of the traits within ourselves. It can also be easier to point the finger at another person than to reflect on how the same issue may be operating in our own life.
Can you remember a time you chose to criticize rather than look at your own feelings?

_____

_____

_____

7. What do jealous feelings tell you? Jealousy is an obvious sign of a wish to be or to have a certain thing, trait, or skill that you observe in another person. If comparing yourself with others makes you feel inferior, it is important for you to notice this in order to develop realistic expectations of yourself. If you constantly strive to be like someone else and think you will be happy once you become this other person, you have created a concept of happiness that is a setup for failure. This condition for happiness is far from realistic. At times, jealous feelings can be like a gift or inspirational wake-up call to practice self-acceptance.
Can you write about an example that affected you?

_____

_____

_____

Seizure Log/Thought Records

Continue doing Thought Records with your symptoms.

Journal-Keeping

Try to observe yourself at one uncomfortable moment this week. (Plan ahead if you are anticipating any difficult situations.) As soon as possible after the time of self-observation, record your observations in your journal. If possible, include some of the internal dialogue that you notice accompanying the observation. Refer to the examples in the text of Session 9 entitled "Self-Observation Without Blame."

Goal Selection for Session 9

Talk with your seizure counselor about choosing an option from the above section "Four Choices," so that you can deal with your own major life issues. You may want to discuss the option of outside referrals for ongoing counseling. Clarify the choices for your particular situation, and put these choices in writing so that you can make your decision over the next week.

I choose one of the following options for working on the process of dealing with major life issues:

__work with my physician or seizure counselor
__work with another trained therapist
__not to work on this process at this particular time
__not to work on this process at this time—but would like the option to
  discuss any issues that come up with my seizure counselor
__other option: _____

_____

Stress Reduction Chart

Continue to add any new sources of stress that you observe to the Stress Reduction Chart in Session 8 in your workbook. In addition, add any new information or ideas to sections 2, 3, and 4 of your chart.

Relaxation Exercise

Practice the relaxation exercise for 10 minutes or more each day.

Preparing for Your Next Appointment

After completing this session and discussing it with your seizure counselor, please read and complete "Session 10: Enhancing Personal Wellness."

Resources for Further Reading

Adams, S., & Orgel, R. *Through the Mental Health Maze*. Washington, DC: Health Research Group, 2003.

Allender, D. B. *The Wounded Heart Book and Workbook*. Colorado Springs, CO: NavPress, 2008.

Anderson, N. T. *The Bondage Breaker*. Eugene, OR: Harvest House, 2000.

Bloomfield, H., with Felder, L. *Making Peace With Your Parents*. New York: Ballantine Books, 1996.

Curtis, B., & Eldredge, J. *The Sacred Romance*. Nashville, TN: T. Nelson, 1997.

Carter, L., & Minirth, F. *The Anger Workbook*. Nashville, TN: T. Nelson, 2012.

Carter, L. *The Anger Trap: Free Yourself From the Frustrations That Sabotage Your Life*. San Francisco, CA: Jossey-Bass, 2004.

Guthrie, N. *Holding on to Hope: A Pathway Through Suffering to the Heart of God*. Wheaton, IL: Tyndale House, 2006.

McKay, M., Davis, M., & Fanning, P. *Messages: The Communication Book*, 3rd ed. Oakland, CA: New Harbinger Publications, 2009.

Rubin, T. *Compassion and Self-Hate*. New York: Touchstone, 1998.

Yancey, P., & Brand, Paul W. *The Gift of Pain: Why We Hurt and What We Can Do About It*. Grand Rapids, MI: Zondervan, 1997.

Abuse and Neglect Contact Information

- **National Domestic Violence Hotline**, 1-800-799-SAFE (7233) or TTY 1-800-787-3224; www.ndvh.org .
- **National Sexual Assault Hotline**, 1-800-656-4673; www.rainn.org
- **Family Violence Prevention Fund/Health Resource Center**, 1-800-313-1310
- **National Clearinghouse on Child Abuse and Neglect Information**, 1-800-394-3366
- **National Clearinghouse on Abuse in Later Life**, 608-255-0539
- **National Organization for Victim Assistance (NOVA)**, 1-800-879-6682
- **National Resource Center on Domestic Violence**, 1-800-537-2238
- **Rape, Abuse, and Incest National Network (RAINN)**, 1-800-656-4673 www.rainn.org
- **The National Health Resource Center on Domestic Violence**, 1-800-595-4889; www.futureswithoutviolence.org
- **Manweb** (a website with information for battered men), www.batteredmen.com

SEIZURE LOG   **For the Week of** ____/____/____**to** ____/____/____

Instructions: Please fill in the diary at the end of each day to record the number and descriptions listed. This information will be reviewed with your physician at each appointment.

Init:_____
ID:_____
Week: _____
Type:_____

SUNDAY ___/___/___ (day 1)
Number of Seizures:_____
Time(s) of day:_____
Duration (sec or min):_____
Description:_____
Location(s):_____
Severity (1: mild, 2: mod, 3: severe):_____
Trigger(s):_____
Precursor(s):_____
Improved with:_____
Impact on your day:_____
Impact on others:_____

MONDAY ___/___/___ (day 2)
Number of Seizures:_____
Time(s) of day:_____
Duration:_____
Description:_____
Location(s):_____
Severity (1: mild, 2: mod, 3: severe):_____
Trigger(s):_____
Precursor(s):_____
Improved with:_____
Impact on your day:_____
Impact on others:_____

TUESDAY ___/___/___ (day 3)
Number of Seizures:_____
Time(s) of day:_____
Duration:_____
Description:_____
Location(s):_____
Severity (1: mild, 2: mod, 3: severe):_____
Trigger(s):_____
Precursor(s):_____
Improved with:_____
Impact on your day:_____
Impact on others:_____

WEDNESDAY ___/___/___ (day 4)
Number of Seizures:_____
Time(s) of day:_____
Duration:_____
Description:_____
Location(s):_____
Severity (1: mild, 2: mod, 3: severe):_____
Trigger(s):_____
Precursor(s):_____
Improved with:_____
Impact on your day:_____
Impact on others:_____

Total: _____   Rater: _____

THURSDAY ___/___/___ (day 5)
Number of Seizures:_____
Time(s) of day:_____
Duration:_____
Description:_____
Location(s):_____
Severity (1: mild, 2: mod, 3: severe):_____
Trigger(s):_____
Precursor(s):_____
Improved with:_____
Impact on your day:_____
Impact on others:_____

FRIDAY ___/___/___ (day 6)
Number of Seizures:_____
Time(s) of day:_____
Duration:_____
Description:_____
Location(s):_____
Severity (1: mild, 2: mod, 3: severe):_____
Trigger(s):_____
Precursor(s):_____
Improved with:_____
Impact on your day:_____
Impact on others:_____

SATURDAY ___/___/___ (day 7)
Number of Seizures:_____
Time(s) of day:_____
Duration:_____
Description:_____
Location(s):_____
Severity (1: mild, 2: mod, 3: severe):_____
Trigger(s):_____
Precursor(s):_____
Improved with:_____
Impact on your day:_____
Impact on others:_____

Use **the space below or on back** to describe any significant information not covered in this record:

_____
_____
_____
_____
_____
_____
_____

Were you successful in stopping any seizures this week:
yes ☐   no ☐

Please mark which seizures you stopped with an asterisk (*).

SEIZURE LOG   For the Week of ____/____/____ to ____/____/____

Instructions: Please fill in the diary at the end of each day to record the number and descriptions listed. This information will be reviewed with your physician at each appointment.

Init:_____
ID:_____
Week: _____
Type:_____

SUNDAY ___/___/___ (day 1)
Number of Seizures:_____
Time(s) of day:_____
Duration (sec or min):_____
Description:_____
Location(s):_____
Severity (1: mild, 2: mod, 3: severe):_____
Trigger(s):_____
Precursor(s):_____
Improved with:_____
Impact on your day:_____
Impact on others:_____

MONDAY ___/___/___ (day 2)
Number of Seizures:_____
Time(s) of day:_____
Duration:_____
Description:_____
Location(s):_____
Severity (1: mild, 2: mod, 3: severe):_____
Trigger(s):_____
Precursor(s):_____
Improved with:_____
Impact on your day:_____
Impact on others:_____

TUESDAY ___/___/___ (day 3)
Number of Seizures:_____
Time(s) of day:_____
Duration:_____
Description:_____
Location(s):_____
Severity (1: mild, 2: mod, 3: severe):_____
Trigger(s):_____
Precursor(s):_____
Improved with:_____
Impact on your day:_____
Impact on others:_____

WEDNESDAY ___/___/___ (day 4)
Number of Seizures:_____
Time(s) of day:_____
Duration:_____
Description:_____
Location(s):_____
Severity (1: mild, 2: mod, 3: severe):_____
Trigger(s):_____
Precursor(s):_____
Improved with:_____
Impact on your day:_____
Impact on others:_____

Total: _____   **Rater:** _____

THURSDAY ___/___/___ (day 5)
Number of Seizures:_____
Time(s) of day:_____
Duration:_____
Description:_____
Location(s):_____
Severity (1: mild, 2: mod, 3: severe):_____
Trigger(s):_____
Precursor(s):_____
Improved with:_____
Impact on your day:_____
Impact on others:_____

FRIDAY ___/___/___ (day 6)
Number of Seizures:_____
Time(s) of day:_____
Duration:_____
Description:_____
Location(s):_____
Severity (1: mild, 2: mod, 3: severe):_____
Trigger(s):_____
Precursor(s):_____
Improved with:_____
Impact on your day:_____
Impact on others:_____

SATURDAY ___/___/___ (day 7)
Number of Seizures:_____
Time(s) of day:_____
Duration:_____
Description:_____
Location(s):_____
Severity (1: mild, 2: mod, 3: severe):_____
Trigger(s):_____
Precursor(s):_____
Improved with:_____
Impact on your day:_____
Impact on others:_____

Use **the space below or on back** to describe any significant information not covered in this record:

_____
_____
_____
_____
_____
_____

Were you successful in stopping any seizures this week:
yes ☐   no ☐

Please mark which seizures you stopped with an asterisk (*).

CHAPTER 11 — Session 10: Enhancing Personal Wellness

Everyone has an optimal level of wellness that he or she can reach, and we all can benefit greatly from making choices that enhance our wellness. The term "enhancing personal wellness" refers to the process of taking care of all aspects of the self—body, feelings, thoughts, and spirit. These choices are a crucial part of taking control of a chronic condition or target symptom, as well as being vital for overall health and well-being.

Wellness extends beyond physical health into the realm of emotion, spirit, and meaning. Being well means that you feel connected with who you really are, with your most powerful feelings, your deepest needs, and your own vitality and capacity for creativity and love. So much of illness and disease is a result of disconnection from ourselves and other people. In contrast, wellness entails connection with oneself and others—it involves self-awareness, compassion, and acceptance. Ultimately, wellness involves integrating oneself as a whole, healthy person.

To prepare for your upcoming appointment, make sure to allow enough time for this week's reading. Also take the time to consider any feelings and concerns you may have about your regular appointments drawing to a close and the prospect of continuing this process on your own.

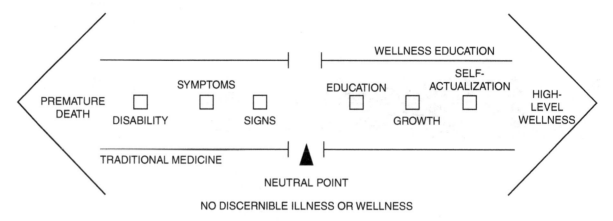

Figure 11.1

Moving Toward High Level Wellness

Adaped from Dr. John W. Travis

How Has the Concept of Wellness Developed?

Health professionals and lay people alike have traditionally viewed health as the absence of illness. It was assumed that if a person did not have any disease or symptom, that person was healthy. But what exactly does it *mean* to be healthy, and how do we improve our chances of feeling well?

Dr. John W. Travis developed a model that defines wellness as different from the absence of illness. Figure 11.1 illustrates the Travis Model, showing a neutral point where there is no discernible illness or wellness.[1] From there, a person can move toward high-level wellness through a process of education, growth, and self-actualization. This model is important because it suggests that there is more to medicine than just curing disease. The Travis Model empowers people to extend their focus beyond healing their illness to the larger aim of reaching optimal levels of health and well-being.

In their book *Self-Care Nursing: Theory and Practice,* Nancy Steiger and Juliene Lipson cite an alternative model, illustrated in Figure 11.2.[2] Their model suggests that health and illness can coexist within the same individual. It conveys the idea that having an illness or recurrent target symptom does not exclude you from reaching a high level of wellness.

While looking at Figure 11.2, think about the idea that your level of health is separate from whether or not you have a chronic condition

[1]Travis, J. W., *Wellness Workbook and Wellness Inventory* (Berkeley, CA: Celestial Arts, 2004).

[2]Steiger, N.J., & Lipson, J. G., *Self-Care Nursing: Theory and Practice* (Bowie, MD: Brady Communications, 1985), p. 58.

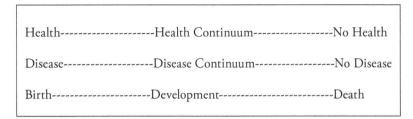

```
Health--------------------Health Continuum-----------------No Health

Disease-------------------Disease Continuum----------------No Disease

Birth--------------------Development-----------------------Death
```

Figure 11.2

Reducing Symptoms While Enhancing Wellness

such as seizures. For example, a person with no evidence of disease can still be tense, lonely, overweight, and overtired—not sick but also not healthy—whereas another person with a chronic condition like seizures or high blood pressure may have learned how to relax, exercise regularly, eat well, and take care of emotional needs—all demonstrating a high level of wellness.

The approach for taking control of your seizures presented in this *Workbook* is based on this alternative model. We believe that having seizures does not exclude you from the possibility of being healthy and fulfilled. On the contrary, often having a troublesome target symptom such as seizures will motivate people to make the efforts necessary to achieve a high level of wellness. Those of you who use your seizures as a motivator to take care of your body, emotions, mind, and spirit may reap a bountiful reward: an enhanced sense of vitality and well-being.

In this session, we explore aspects of wellness that will help you minimize your symptoms and reach your own optimal level of wellness. Some of the work will be familiar to you, and some of it will be new. You will perform a self-care tune-up, appreciating the areas where you are already taking good care of yourself and identifying areas where you want to make some changes. This tune-up will help you to solidify your gains and to set goals for the future—both to control your seizures and to enhance your health and sense of fulfillment.

The Work

Goal

The goal for this session is to learn ways to achieve your optimum level of wellness. To accomplish this, you will review your past successes in coping with seizures, then identify current goals for ongoing self-care and incorporate them into your personal wellness program.

Obstacles

Many people have resistance to taking good care of themselves. It is certainly not easy to make lifestyle changes, even if you have decided they are important for your health. Read through the following feelings that others have expressed.

*(Select the statements that apply to you and write your own in the space marked **Personal Obstacles** below.)*

- "I can't imagine regulating my life so that I get enough sleep every night. It would be too boring and rigid."
- "I want the benefits of exercise but I just can't seem to get started on a regular program. I try jogging every once in a while and it always seems unpleasant and exhausting."
- "I've been smoking all my life. If I try to quit, I'm afraid I'll just fail and feel worse about myself."
- "There are so many stresses and pressures in my life that I can't even think about taking care of myself right now."
- "Nothing I like to eat is good for me. Give me ribs, chips, donuts, and coffee all day long, and I'll die young but happy!"
- "Whenever I do the relaxation exercise, my mind wanders off—to plans, worries, bills, you name it. Why bother if I can't begin to relax?"
- "Sex is the scariest part of my life. I just don't want to deal with it."
- "Some of these methods look like they'd be helpful, but I just don't have time to _____." (Fill in the blank with "exercise," "have fun", "get enough rest," "make friends," "take breaks," "talk out my problems," etc.)

My personal obstacles to wellness:

_____

_____

_____

_____

_____

_____

_____

_____

_____

_____

_____

Ways to Enhance Personal Wellness

Tension Reduction and Relaxation

The following section describes some different tension-reducing methods. These methods help both to reduce stress-related symptoms (including seizures) and to promote good health. Some of these measures can also be used at the particular moment when you experience your aura, as a way to prevent the onset of a seizure.

After reading each section, answer the relevant questions and indicate in your *Workbook* which methods you are most interested in working on now. Learning skills to reduce tension can be tremendously rewarding—both for taking control of seizures and for fostering a sense of well-being.

Method #1: Talk About Your Worries

When tensions build up, discuss the problem with a close friend, family member, or whoever is involved. Keeping your problems to yourself, or bottling up your tension, often leads to emotional and physical symptoms of stress. Talking about your concerns is a healthy release that frequently results in new insights or plans for reducing tensions.

With whom do you feel comfortable talking about your true feelings and concerns?

_____

_____

Do you tend to (*Place a check mark beside whichever statements apply to you.*)

___ Keep your worries to yourself, not discussing them with anyone.

___ Talk sometimes, with one or two trusted people.

___ Talk out your problems often, with several different people.

___ Talk out your problems often, mostly by shouting or making angry statements to other people.

___ Feel that other people care about you when you talk about your concerns.

Method #2: Plan Constructive Outlets for Your Feelings

Finding outlets for your feelings will help prevent the symptoms of chronic stress. You may find it useful to plan in advance so that the next time you feel upset, you have a list of tension-reducing outlets, such as cleaning out the garage, taking a brisk walk, writing in your journal, hitting a punching bag, or working in the yard.

What outlets do you find effective when you are upset? (*list*)

_____

_____

_____

What other constructive outlets for your feelings might be helpful?
(*Remind yourself to look at this list the next time you are angry or upset.*)

_____

_____

_____

_____

_____

_____

Method #3: Take Daily Relaxation Breaks

Set aside time every day to do something relaxing and enjoyable for you. This form of healthy escape truly helps your body and mind cope effectively with stress. Consider taking a daily walk, listening to music, or taking time out for a hobby that allows you to unwind. Other examples of relaxation breaks include reading a book or magazine, watching a favorite TV show, or socializing with a friend. Anything that allows you to experience laughter and a sense of play—from comedies to joking with friends and playing with kids—can provide a needed relaxation break.

List the breaks that you already take for relaxation:

_____

_____

_____

_____

Out of seven days a week, how many days do you usually take at least one 15-minute break for the sole purpose of relaxing and enjoying yourself? _____

What other ideas do you have for your relaxation breaks?

_____

_____

_____

_____

_____

Method #4: Balance Work and Play

Many people who suffer from stress-related symptoms are trying to do too much too fast. If you are one of these people who are always on the go, an important tension-reducing measure is to *slow down your pace.* Slowing down your pace may mean postponing a major new activity or life change, or simply eliminating some of the tasks you expect yourself to accomplish. Learning to balance work (including the work you do at home—housework, childcare, repairs, and so on) and recreation is vital for stress reduction.

On the other hand, some people may have a lifestyle where they don't have enough to do. If you find yourself with empty time on your hands, you probably need to add new activities and tasks to your life. Take on new activities gradually until you strike a balance between time spent working (at home, on the job, and/or going to school) and time spent relaxing.

How would you rate yourself on the following scale? (*Check the pace that you think best describes you.*)

___ Pace "Hyper"—Too many tasks and activities. No relaxation time.

___ Pace Fast—Almost always on the go. Relaxation time rare.

___ Pace Moderate—Good balance between work time and relaxation time.

___ Pace Slow—Not enough to do. Too much free time.

___ Pace Dull—Nothing to do.

If you do not consider the pace of your life to be moderate, what might you do to pace yourself to move toward a more optimum balance between work and play? Increase or decrease activities and responsibilities?

_____

_____

_____

_____

_____

Method #5: Utilize Time Management Skills

Time management, a popular topic in stress-reduction programs, refers to the skill of planning realistically and using time wisely. Dr. Richard Swenson writes about how busy our lives are today, noting, "The conditions of modern-day living devour margin."[3] Margin is the difference between our load and our limit. *Living marginless lives may contribute to our frenzy, fatigue, forgetfulness, and feeling like a failure.* One aspect of time management involves learning how much time to allow for different parts of your life, so that you can avoid the feeling of always being in a hurry. Some people find they can relieve a lot of tension by planning their time a week in advance. Each week they try to learn from the experience of seeing whether their schedule was realistic and comfortable for them.

---

[3]Swenson, R.A., Margin: Restoring Emotional, Physical, Financial, and Time Reserves to Overloaded Lives (Colorado Springs, CO: NavPress, 1992), p. 13.

Another aspect of time management involves setting priorities. Whenever you find yourself feeling overwhelmed by too many responsibilities, establish priorities by asking yourself: What is the most important and urgent for me to do? Make sure your list of priorities includes *taking care of yourself*. For instance, taking care of yourself might include a regular exercise program, relaxation breaks, and time with your children, spouse, and friends.

Once you know your own priorities, sit down with yourself to plan how you will use your time—by the day, week, or month. Eliminate low priority items, telling yourself you'll get to them when more important ones have been accomplished. Break down large tasks into smaller ones that you can accomplish one at a time, giving yourself some credit for each step along the way. Managing your time wisely—by choosing your priorities and planning your time accordingly—will greatly help you to reduce tension.

For the next week, I consider my priorities to be the following:

_____

_____

_____

_____

I currently plan my time by doing the following:

_____

_____

_____

_____

I think I might be more effective at managing my time if I learn to do the following:

_____

_____

_____

_____

Method #6: Practice Assertiveness Whenever Possible

Assertiveness is a method of communicating one's needs and feelings clearly and acceptably to other people. This method, introduced in "Session 2: Getting Support," is included in this chapter because so much tension and stress are due to communication problems with other people.

Passive and aggressive communication styles tend to increase interpersonal stress, whereas assertive communication can help lower stress. First, identify your communication patterns from the explanations and examples given below. Then learn to practice assertiveness, asking for what you want while respecting the needs of others.

- **Passive Communication**: The communicator avoids expressing personal needs directly. This often leads to situations where the person feels resentful that others are taking advantage of him or her.
- **Aggressive Communication**: The communicator verbally attacks and blames others, or threatens them in order to get what is wanted, typically resulting in anger, fear, and rejection from other people.
- **Assertive Communication**: The communicator expresses his or her own needs and feelings clearly, and stands up for self over important issues. The result is often greater understanding and improved communication.

Examples
- **Passive**: Doing the chore by yourself, silently pouting and responding to conversation in resentful monosyllables.
- **Aggressive**: "You 'so-and-so,' you never help me do things when you say you will! If you don't get up and help right this minute, I'll . . . "
- **Assertive**: "I feel angry and hurt that you're not helping with this chore. Yesterday you said you would share responsibility for it when we discussed my busy schedule."

Think of recent examples in which you used each of these three communication patterns. Write down as closely as possible what you said or did, what your need was, and what result you got. Did each result in more or less interpersonal stress?

Personal example of passive communication:

_____

_____

_____

_____

_____

Personal example of aggressive communication:

_____

_____

_____

_____

_____

Personal example of assertive communication:

_____

_____

_____

_____

_____

(If you cannot think of one or more of the examples, observe yourself for these patterns and write in your example later in the week, before your next session.)

Which form of communication do you use most often?

_____

Choose a situation (for example, something that you've been waiting to tell someone, about a need or issue that is important to you) where you would like to try out assertive communication. **Write down the words you might use in the space provided below.** Use "I messages," telling the other person what you want and how his or her behavior makes you feel. Let him or her know the consequences of this behavior, and/or your need, without accusation or blame.

_____

_____

_____

_____

_____

_____

_____

Method #7: Continue Daily Relaxation Practice

In Session 6, you began to learn to relax, both mentally and physically, using progressive relaxation, a vital part of the process of taking control of your seizures. Interestingly, a common medical situation where relaxation exercises are taught is in preparation for childbirth. Pregnant women and their partners attend weekly classes and practice daily relaxation to prepare themselves for labor and delivery—in order to be able to stay in control during this experience. Similarly, if you wish to be more in control of your seizures, you'll need to practice progressive relaxation daily.

The benefits of becoming proficient in this technique are many. Once you learn to relax during practice sessions, you can learn to relax at any point in the process leading to seizures. You may find that you can prevent your triggers from leading to negative states, and that you can prevent negative states from leading to your target symptom—seizures—by using relaxation at these critical times. If you are able to identify your aura, you can remind yourself to breathe mindfully or to go into a relaxed state just for that moment, and you may then prevent many of your seizures. Knowing that others have learned to prevent seizures in this way can be highly motivating and can inspire you to practice progressive relaxation on a daily basis.

Relaxation Exercise

Practice the relaxation exercise on your own, using the relaxation script from Session 6 (on pp. 162–166) that starts with these words:

Begin by getting into a comfortable position, preferably sitting in a chair with your legs uncrossed and your hands resting on your thighs or armrests. . . .

Meditation

Meditation is another highly beneficial method of relaxation that is described at the end of Session 6 and in Appendix III. If you are not doing any meditation at home, you may choose to practice meditation in the office with your seizure counselor.

Tips for Relaxation and Meditation

Rather than blissful tranquility, most people experience a commotion of distracting thoughts, sensations, and feelings throughout their relaxation or meditation practice. If this is true for you, you are not doing it wrong—you may be doing it right! Simply note that your mind has wandered and direct it back to your relaxation script, your breathing, or other meditation focus. Cultivate an attitude of affectionate acceptance, like you would have toward a puppy you are trying to train. Each mindful moment—of being wholly present as you draw your attention back—is of great benefit in helping you take control of your seizures.

Good Nutrition: Feeding Your Brain

Your brain needs a stable blood glucose (sugar) level to function optimally, which means you need to eat a well-balanced diet. If your blood sugar level fluctuates—with high ups and low downs—your brain will rebel by having its own ups and downs, such as mood swings, periods of low energy, and intense negative emotions. When you eat white or sugary foods such as candy, donuts, white bread, sodas, and processed foods, your glucose suddenly increases, creating a demand for your body to produce more insulin to bring the glucose down. This results in sugar highs and lows, exactly what you need to avoid. These same high-sugar and refined foods also contribute to weight gain and obesity, whereas avoiding them will help you reach or maintain a healthy weight. There are four key principles that will allow you to maintain stable blood glucose levels:

Eat Breakfast

After you go through the night without eating, your brain needs glucose. By eating breakfast, you are giving your brain the glucose it needs to get going for the day. When you skip breakfast, the only way for your brain to get sugar is to put out adrenaline (epinephrine) to mobilize sugar from stores in your liver. But adrenaline is the hormone you produce when you are under stress. This means that *by not eating breakfast you are creating nervous energy that stresses your brain.* So it is important to eat breakfast every day, selecting foods that allow your body to maintain even glucose levels, such as whole grain bread, oatmeal or whole grain (low sugar) cereal with milk or yogurt, eggs, and similar foods. If you start your day with a donut and coffee or just coffee, the donut will give you a sugar high and the caffeine in your coffee will push your blood sugar down.

Eat Regular Meals

For most people, this means three meals a day. The brain needs a steady energy supply to function properly. The brain is very sensitive to blood sugar fluctuations. When you consume complex carbohydrates like whole grains, glucose is slowly released through the body's digestive processes and metabolism, thereby ensuring a much steadier supply of sugar to the brain. High-fiber foods, including vegetables, fruits, legumes (beans, lentils, peas), and whole grains, are considered good carbohydrates because they are nutritious, filling, and relatively low in calories. Furthermore, high-fiber foods help maintain a steadier blood glucose level by slowing the absorption of carbohydrates and reducing insulin production. Combining small portions of protein sources such as meat, fish, whole grains, nuts, and legumes in your diet with complex carbohydrates creates a metabolic interaction that maintains optimum glucose levels for your brain.

Include Foods Rich in Vitamins and Minerals in Your Diet

Vitamins like thiamine (B_1), pyridoxine (B_6), B_{12}, and folic acid work with enzymes to help your body's cells metabolize food. These enzymes cannot function properly without vitamins. Fresh produce is the best source of vitamins and minerals. For example, folic acid is found in raw and slightly cooked vegetables and fruits; vitamin B_{12} in dairy, meat, fish, and poultry; and vitamin B_1 in nuts, beans, and fish. Vitamin K is found in green leafy vegetables and grains. Vitamin D, important for bones, is found in fortified milk, fish, and fish oils and is synthesized in the body in response to sunlight. Calcium and magnesium—minerals important for the function of brain chemicals—are present in dairy products.

Anticonvulsant medications (AEDs) make it challenging to absorb adequate levels of vitamins and minerals. A general rule is that combining two or more anticonvulsant drugs reduces the availability of critical vitamins and minerals. For example, AEDs reduce the body's ability to utilize vitamins D, K, and folic acid, as well as the minerals calcium, magnesium, and manganese. Many people on AEDs do not experience deficiencies of these vitamins and minerals. However, people on large doses or multiple AEDs, elderly people, pregnant women, and alcohol abusers require medical advice about diet and vitamin/mineral supplements. Many people taking AEDs require vitamin D and calcium supplements to prevent osteoporosis. Pregnant women taking AEDs should take 5 mg of folic acid per day in addition to a prenatal vitamin/mineral supplement.

Fats used to get a bad rap in causing weight gain and cardiovascular disease. The absorption of fat-soluble vitamins such as vitamins A, D, E, and K is facilitated by fats in the diet. Current research indicates that what matters most to health is eating the *right fats*. Fats from animal sources, such as fatty meat, dark poultry meat and skin, and whole milk dairy products, are high in saturated fatty acids that may contribute to heart disease and stroke. On the other hand, plant and fish sources are high in unsaturated fatty acids that improve serum cholesterol levels and reduce the incidence of cardiovascular diseases. Research has shown that the Mediterranean diet, rich in plant-based foods such as vegetables, fruits, beans, whole grains, nuts, and olive oil, along with moderate amounts of cheese, yogurt, fish, poultry, eggs, and wine, provides good nutrition as well as thousands of micronutrients, antioxidants, vitamins, minerals, and fiber that work together to protect against chronic disease. Including healthy fats in your diet will help you absorb necessary vitamins and minerals and keep your body and brain's cell membranes healthy while minimizing the risk of cardiovascular disease.

Even With the Best Dietary Practices, a Small Percentage of Highly Sensitive People Experience Fluctuations in Blood Sugar Levels That Aggravate Their Tendency to Have Seizures

Here it is necessary for you to be your own detective in order to relate the occurrence of seizures or seizure auras to specific times of the day. Noting changes in your mood, energy level, and negative feeling states in your journal may indicate a time-based pattern related to your mealtimes. If you experience seizure symptoms in the early morning, eat a small snack like nuts before going to bed. If you have periods of low energy later in the mornings or afternoons, you might eat similar small snacks in the middle of the morning or afternoon as well as at bedtime. Or, if you notice marked low energy several hours after most meals, discuss with your doctor whether eating more frequent small meals might help you. The hard part is keeping a detailed journal and making the correlations; supplementing meals with appropriate small snacks is easy.

Note: The ketogenic diet, ongoing hunger, and prolonged fasting change the body's metabolism and require specialized medical advice.

Refer to Resources for Further Reading at the end of this chapter and consult your counselor for more information about nutrition and weight loss.

Sleep and Rest

Grandmother is right—it *is* important to get enough sleep and rest if you want to stay healthy. During sleep, your body can devote its energies to resisting illness, repairing damage, and resting overworked organs. Sleep is also necessary to give your psyche a chance to deal with stresses and upsets by dreaming and taking a hard-earned rest from the awake, conscious state. This explains why people experience more target symptoms, exacerbations of chronic illnesses, emotional crises, as well as injuries, colds, and flu during periods when they aren't getting enough sleep.

Most people with seizures report that their seizure frequency increases during periods of inadequate sleep and rest. If you are fatigued, you may not only experience more seizures but also may find it harder to employ relaxation, recognition of triggers, and other self-care methods that require conscious effort. You simply do not have the energy to employ these methods effectively if you are overtired. Planning your life to include adequate time for sleep and rest is important if you want to take control of your seizures and reach an optimum level of health. If you have trouble sleeping, try increasing your daily exercise, and decreasing your caffeine intake. Since lack of sleep is known to increase seizure frequency, difficulty falling asleep may be worrisome for some people with seizures. Unfortunately, the worry itself may contribute to the inability to fall asleep. Accepting a sleepless resting mode may help to avoid the worry that can directly interfere with sleep.

Discuss persistent symptoms of insomnia with your physician or counselor. **To help with the discussion, answer the following questions:**

How many hours of sleep do you usually get each night? _____

What time do you usually go to bed? _____

What time do you usually wake up? _____

How would you rate yourself on the following scale:

___ 0: Never get enough sleep. Always tired.

___ 1: Hardly ever get enough sleep. Usually tired.

___ 2: Sometimes get enough sleep, sometimes not. Frequently tired.

___ 3: Usually get enough sleep. Mostly energetic; occasional fatigue.

___ 4: Always get enough sleep. Almost always energetic.

Physical Fitness

Regular exercise has long been recognized as essential for maintaining a healthy heart and lungs. But with the recent trend toward physical fitness, health professionals have identified a host of other benefits. Vigorous physical exercise is the most effective stress reducer known—diminishing the fight-and-flight stress response and enhancing relaxation of the body and spirit. Regular aerobic exercise also improves sleep, regulates the appetite, helps to reduce and normalize weight, eliminates fatigue, increases overall energy level, elevates mood, and enhances self-esteem. (Sound too good to be true? Try it for 2 months and see how it works for you.)

Aerobic exercises increase your heart rate (and make you work up a sweat!) for a sustained period of time, without stopping and starting again. Aerobic exercises include brisk walking, jogging, bicycling, aerobic dance, and racquetball. To get the full benefit of a regular exercise program, exercise aerobically 3–5 times per week for 20–30 minutes. If you are not used to exercising, begin with 5 minutes of walking or pedaling an exercise bike once or twice a day. Each week, increase your exercise sessions by increments of 3 to 5 minutes until you reach the target of 20–30 minutes.

To avoid injury and fatigue, always listen to your body. Stop if anything hurts, and avoid overdoing it. You have months, years, a lifetime to become physically fit. If you can get over the hump of maintaining this program for the first 6–8 weeks, you will find that the many benefits described above will help to keep you exercising for the rest of your life. A particular boon is the lowered stress and tension level, which often helps to minimize seizures and other target symptoms.

Avoidance of Harmful Habits and Self-medication

Cigarette smoking is the number one preventable cause of illness and death in the United States. While nicotine is the habit-forming component of tobacco smoke that keeps smokers addicted, cigarette smoke also contains tars, carbon monoxide, and other toxins that contribute toward producing lung and other cancers, chronic bronchitis and emphysema, heart and other blood vessel disease (heart attack, stroke, etc.), and dangers to the babies and children of mothers who smoke. If you're a smoker and decide to quit, this decision may not have a direct impact on your seizures, but it will profoundly improve your overall health and longevity.

Alcoholism is another common addiction that severely impacts health. Excessive alcohol consumption increases seizure frequency directly, and if this practice continues, will eventually damage the stomach, liver, and brain. Alcoholism also has a detrimental effect on relationships, family life, employment, and self-esteem. A person is considered to be an alcoholic if he or she can't cope without drinking daily; if the person binges on alcohol periodically; or if alcohol is responsible for problems such as serious family arguments, poor job performance, or auto accidents. Both alcohol overconsumption and withdrawal can produce seizures, so getting help to prevent or overcome an alcohol problem is particularly important for anyone with seizures. Alcoholics Anonymous and other treatment programs are available at little or no cost in every community.

In addition to alcohol, *overuse of any habit-forming drug* is a serious health risk for anyone, especially for people with seizures. Many drugs increase excitation and seizure frequency, while almost all of them interfere with efforts to take control. Habit-forming drugs that cause health problems include benzodiazepines, like Valium, barbiturates, amphetamines (Dexedrine or speed) and other uppers, PCP, cocaine, codeine, hydrocodone, Percodan, morphine, and heroin. Other drugs that cause problems if taken often or in large amounts include marijuana, caffeine (in coffee, black tea, colas, etc.), and sleeping pills. Often the first step in getting off a habit-forming drug is to ask for help—so do not hesitate to discuss your concerns with your physician or seizure counselor.

It is important to avoid reliance on alcohol or drugs when you are tense or under pressure. Substances such as tranquilizers and alcohol can mask both the causes and symptoms of stress. Medicating yourself with these substances does not help you cope with your stresses. On the contrary, self-medication often compounds stress by leading to alcohol addiction or drug dependence. Try not to compensate for feelings of fatigue by increasing your caffeine intake; rather, respect your body's signal that you need more rest and sleep. Adequate sleep each night and rest periods during the day will help you cope better with stresses that arise and may be a more sustainable way to decrease feelings of stress and fatigue.

Discuss your answers to the following questions with your counselor to help decide if alcohol or drugs are a problem for you:

How many alcoholic drinks (including beer and wine) do you typically consume in one day, week, or month? _____

Do you tend to increase your consumption of alcohol (or other drugs) when you're more tense than usual? Yes __ No __ Sometimes __

Do you ever feel that you cannot get through the day without using drugs or having a drink? Yes ___No ___Sometimes ___

Social Support (from Session 2)

All people have a need for social support, for people to talk with and to share experiences with—people you care about, who in turn care about you. Mental health professionals have made a somewhat obvious discovery—that friends are good medicine. This means that one way all of us can maintain emotional and physical health is by talking out our worries and getting support from other people when we are under stress. We were made to be in community. Connecting with other people is essential for our emotional *and* physical well-being.

What is not so obvious is that each person can have an active role in developing friendships and family relationships that are loving and supportive. If your life is lacking close family members, friends, and/or a love relationship, you may want to actively seek out the kind of relationship you need. How you do this is a personal choice, but it might involve inviting people for social events or participating in activities where you will get to know other people. You could consider taking a class, becoming involved in church activities, or joining (or starting) a support group for people who have seizures.

On the other hand, if you have enough close relationships but find them marred by anger, distrust, or misunderstanding, you can take an active role in working out problems and improving communication. If you find that your family members, friends, and coworkers are so reactive or agitated that their tension is contagious, you might consider talking with them about your situation, inviting them to join you in relaxing and support your efforts to reduce tension. Some people are able to steer their important relationships toward becoming mutually supportive on their own, whereas others require help from a marriage and family therapist, clergyman, or other counselor.

Sometimes the most difficult part of getting adequate social support is admitting to yourself or others that you need other people at all. With a few exceptions, human beings are social animals. We congregate together because we have deep-seated needs for support from other people—needs that include love, respect, understanding, caring, sexuality, conversation, stimulation, attention, appreciation, and companionship. It may be helpful for you to know that you're not alone if you have many of these needs but have a difficult time expressing them to yourself or others. The important thing is to put some effort into gradually developing some positive, close relationships that provide you with social support.

Sexuality

Another aspect of human life is that we are sexual beings, with basic urges shared by all living things for procreation and continued survival of our species. But human sexuality is complicated by the fact that our sexual needs exist before, during, and after our reproductive years—and we often need them to be met in order to feel healthy and fulfilled. Another complex factor in human sexuality is its connection with our emotions and need for love. Sex outside a long-term monogamous commitment can be mistaken for true relationship and may result in many interpersonal difficulties.

It is only in recent years that sex has been a subject of open discussion. For centuries the main discussion about sex has centered on how to control (or repress) sexual urges. This means that for hundreds of years, most people have felt inhibited both about discussing and expressing their sexuality. People with seizures share this awkwardness about dealing with their sexual needs. For some it is complicated by increased feelings of loneliness, alienation, or feelings of discomfort in close relationships.

Anything that causes difficulty in communicating with others will get in the way of close personal relationships and meeting sexual needs with others. For many, if the sexual needs are denied and repressed (that is, controlled to the degree that a person does not even know he or she has sexual urges, or never does anything to fulfill sexual needs), it may increase the general level of tension in the body. In individuals with seizures, this increased level of body tension can aggravate the seizure problem by increasing seizure frequency.

Sexually transmitted diseases (STDs) have caused a new awareness about safe sex. The ABC approach has dramatically decreased STDs and HIV/AIDS in other countries. ABC stands for "Abstinence, Be Faithful, Condoms." Lower infection rates occur when people take care of their sexual needs with a monogamous partner with whom they have a committed, satisfying sexual and emotional relationship. Sometimes life circumstances make this difficult, such as when people are without partners or when marriage does not include fulfillment of sexual needs. It may then be necessary for you to take an active role in seeking help to work out sexual problems with your spouse, perhaps with the assistance of a therapist. Or you may choose masturbation as a safe alternative.

If you are without a sexual partner, you may wish to find another outlet for your sexual drives, such as exercise. The challenge is to find a healthy way of expressing your sexuality and meeting your sexual needs that you are comfortable with—and this may help you to minimize your target symptoms (such as seizures) and to experience a more optimum level of health and well-being.

Coping with Negative Emotions, Stress, and Internal Issues (from Sessions 5, 8, and 9)

How you deal with negative emotional states such as anger and fear, external life stresses, and internal issues and conflicts affects all aspects of your life, health, and feelings of self-esteem. While this part of the taking control program is probably the most difficult and long-term, it is also one of the most rewarding. Why is this process potentially so worthwhile? *It offers you the possibility of participating in your own healing through self-understanding and self-acceptance.* External situations and inner states that seem unmanageable now can become less distressing over time, as you gain skills and cultivate compassion for yourself. Out of this process may come a deep appreciation of your own strength and ability to cope with setbacks and difficulties.

Many people can master new methods of relaxing, getting support, observing triggers and auras, and so on, in a relatively short period of time, whereas most people need years to reach a point where they feel they are dealing well with the major issues in their life. As you approach the end of this *Workbook*, ask yourself whether coping with major life issues is one of your high priorities. Do you sense that inner issues and conflicts might be sabotaging your efforts to reduce tension and take control of your seizures? Persistent agitation and hair-trigger reactivity—getting deeply upset or offended in response to recurrent situations or people—can be signs that the self is grappling with important inner issues that you might wish to address in long-term counseling.

Some people do tackle these issues on their own, through journal-keeping, dream work, and artistic expression, but many find that they require outside help from a therapist or group. If you decide that working on coping with negative emotional states, life stresses, and/or internal conflicts is important to you, talk with your seizure counselor about how you might continue this work. Options to consider include continuing regular appointments with your seizure counselor with these particular goals in mind; enrolling in a stress-reduction group program (if external life stress is the major factor for you); and/or seeing a different therapist on a regular basis to explore these issues.

If you choose not to continue working in this area at this time, give yourself credit for the work you have done, and permission to lighten up for a while. You can always decide to work on coping with major life issues in the future.

Environmental Awareness and Safety

Just as the body and mind are closely interconnected, all of us are connected with the society as well as the environment within which we live. Although there are many healthy aspects of our society, and of our greater environment that is planet Earth, there are many environmental hazards that affect the present and future health of every individual alive today. These include such different environmental threats as violent crime, motor vehicle accidents, problems in the world economy, pollution, depletion of natural resources, and climate change.

Given the global scale of many of these problems, what can an individual do to stay healthy in a threatened environment? There are a number of options that you may choose to adopt as part of your personal wellness plan. The following lists include a number of suggestions to take care of yourself and your family in a challenging world.

- Do not drive if your seizures are uncontrolled. Follow your physician's instructions regarding driving. State laws determine driving privileges for people with seizures.

- Wear seatbelts, and insist that all passengers, especially children, wear seatbelts every time you drive. (Seatbelts significantly lower the risk of injury or death due to a motor vehicle accident.)

- Do not drive with anyone who has been drinking or taking drugs (including yourself!).

- Do not swim alone. Discuss safety measures for swimming and bathing with your physician or seizure counselor.

- Live in a low-crime area.

- Do not keep guns in your house, car, or on your person. If you have firearms, never leave them loaded. Anyone with guns in the household is at greater risk of death from homicide, suicide, or accident.

- Be aware of potential pollution of your air and water. Check out potential toxins at home, in your neighborhood, and at your workplace. Contact the Environmental Protection Agency or other appropriate agency when indicated.

- Minimize chemical pollution of the food you eat:
  - Wash fruits and vegetables carefully to remove sprays.
  - Read all food labels to reduce the amount of preservatives, monosodium glutamate (MSG), artificial flavors, colors, and sweeteners you consume. (Many people think that some food chemicals may prove to be harmful after prolonged use, despite clearance from the Food and Drug Administration.)
  - Eating natural foods that are not canned, frozen, processed, or refined will give you more food value and fewer chemicals.
  - Because meat and poultry are usually raised with many chemicals in their feed, whenever possible remove skin and fat (because this is where chemicals are concentrated).
  - Grow some of your own fruits and vegetables in containers, in your yard, or in a neighborhood garden. Purchase organic or unsprayed produce when affordable.

- If you are pregnant or possibly pregnant, do not take medications or drugs without your physician's approval. Some drugs are harmful to the fetus, especially in the early weeks of pregnancy. (See Session 3 for more information about medications and pregnancy.)

- Avoid highly polluted areas and environments, when possible. Wear protective clothing and a facemask if you must work around hazardous fumes or volatile substances, such as paints, solvents, and glues.
- Some individuals with seizures need to reduce environmental sensory stress because they experience so-called reflex seizures. This can occur when they encounter certain physical stimuli such as flickering lights, high frequency sounds, certain odors, and so on. Even if you do not have reflex seizures, you may have noticed that an excess of sensory stimuli overwhelms you. Strategies for dealing with such sensory overload include this calming technique: Sit down, close your eyes for a moment, take a deep breath, focus on your palms, and simply observe to what extent you can tune in with the inside while you fade out the outside. If that does not do the trick, try making an emergency plan; for instance, to carry a small emergency bag with you at all times. If you are sensitive to light, noise, and heat, your emergency bag might contain a hat, sunglasses, earplugs, and a handkerchief that you can dampen and place on your neck. Sometimes it can be a good idea to leave or go to the restroom for a couple of minutes, preferably with a trusted person accompanying you.

Meaning

An aspect of wellness that is often overlooked is the need that all of us have for meaning in our lives. Different people might describe the idea of meaning with different words, including sense of purpose, connectedness, spirituality, creativity, contact with God or with a Higher Power, and/or a sense of having found one's place in the world.

Some people find meaning in the work they do for a living, while others find it in creative hobbies, artistic expression, or in efforts to solve societal problems. Other people find a sense of meaning principally through their relationships with people—through love of children, spouse, and other family members, through taking care of others in their work, in church or temple or mosque activities, or in other areas of their lives. For some, meaning is religious or spiritual; for others, meaning is derived from fulfillment of down-to-earth personal goals. Many people derive meaning from many parts of their lives—from being a spouse, a parent, a worker, a friend, a musician or artist, as well as a faith-community member and participant in community affairs.

One way to find out how you personally derive meaning in your life is to ask yourself: What would I spend my time doing if I found out I had only one more year to live? What about if I had only five more years? Perhaps your answer would be—"Exactly the same things I'm doing now." If so, ask yourself further: What in particular about my life now is meaningful? What is not meaningful? The answers to these questions will help you clarify the parts of your life that give you a sense of purpose and meaning, thus enhancing your health and sense of well-being.

Perhaps in answering the question about what you would do if you had only one year to live, you would change many things about your life. If this is true, now is your chance to make some changes before there really is only one more year left! What parts of your life do give you a sense of meaning, and how can you increase the amount of time you spend doing them? What is missing from your life? Of the things that are missing, how can you add one or two of them to your life right now or in the not-too-distant future? Are there some aspects of your life that may have more meaning if you let yourself acknowledge and appreciate them?

For some individuals, finding meaning is the key step that transforms their lives. How this happens can be very personal and, sometimes, unexpected. One person might derive meaning from making art, or writing songs. For another, meaning comes from volunteering to assist children with special needs. A third individual finds meaning in Alcoholics Anonymous meetings that provide a connection with other people and a Higher Power. Another finds it with the birth of a child; another with going back to school to train for a new job. Open yourself to your own rich possibilities for finding meaning in *your* life—since this may be what energizes your efforts toward taking control.

Cultivate a Sense of Gratitude, Caring, and Connectedness

Many people derive a sense of meaning from the sense that they are connected with something bigger than themselves. Whether or not you actively engage in a spiritual practice, you can derive great benefit from cultivating a sense of gratitude, compassion, and loving acceptance of yourself and others. This can help to relieve your feelings of negativity, which might include a sense that something is wrong with you, that you're overwhelmed with difficulties, or surrounded by people who disappoint and aggravate you. Life-changing healing, as well as religious and humanist traditions, share the aim of connecting people with their own inborn capacity for generosity and gratitude. One fulfilling practice you can do anytime during the day is to breathe in acceptance of the suffering associated with having seizures and to breathe out your gratitude for life and its blessings, along with compassion for others all over the world who suffer with seizures and other challenges. It's amazing how one breath can allow us to experience connectedness to our deeper selves and to our larger community.

CASE STUDY

After looking over Session 10, Oscar requested an extra appointment with his counselor to work on the wellness material. He told her he'd already decided that he wanted to work on exercise as one of his relaxation goals. Back in Session 8, when he realized how pressured his job was, he thought that taking a walk during his lunch hour would be a good idea. Since then, he tried walking a few times and discovered that it left him more relaxed and able to handle his day. But it was hard to get himself to do it, He was also beginning to realize how hard he worked, both at home and on the job, as well as trying to deal with his inner issues as part of his efforts to take control of his seizures. He was looking forward to putting some energy into relaxation for a change.

At the end of his first Session 10 appointment, Oscar wrote down on his Lifestyle Goal Chart (see below) that he would take a brisk 20-minute walk at least 3 times a week. He planned to do this twice during his lunch break at work and once on the weekend, when he could invite his wife and kids to join him. His seizure counselor was supportive of his choice of exercise, and they discussed some of the benefits. Oscar said that walking left him feeling calmer. His counselor mentioned that her personal exercise program—bicycling and jogging—eased the tension in her neck (her target symptom), kept her weight down, and improved her mood.

Oscar also decided to work on taking daily relaxation breaks. He wrote down this second goal as follows: "To relax in my easy chair for 5–10 minutes, reading a newspaper, book or magazine, 5 days a week." Oscar explained that this was important because he had recently become aware of how he constantly worked around the house instead of relaxing. He knew this was because of an inner feeling that he had to earn his way, but he wanted to give himself the chance to forget about work and read a good book instead.

After his second week of working on Session 10, Oscar told his counselor that the walks were going well. He found that he had to do a lot of explaining to his coworkers, who seemed a little miffed that he was leaving them at lunch to take a walk. But he felt well-equipped to explain his reasons, which they accepted with a few teasing comments like "getting healthy on us, are you?" One man who was recently hired, and

---

whom Oscar liked, expressed an interest in joining him because he wanted to get rid of his beer belly. They walked together once and Oscar hoped this would continue. After his walks, Oscar felt refreshed.

But reading in his easy chair was a different story. Sometimes he felt so tense that he couldn't focus on his reading. He'd get caught up in angry thoughts about his wife, who was always harping on the fact that they never went on vacation. He daydreamed entire arguments with her, in which he soundly put down all her points. By the end of the week, he no longer wanted to sit down to read.

How in the world was he going to learn to relax? After talking it over with his counselor, Oscar decided to try a third tension-reduction method: planning constructive outlets for his feelings. He came up with two ideas. One was to get himself a professional punching bag and install it in the garage. He'd seen a used one advertised in the newspaper and had always wanted to practice boxing, especially when he felt angry and revved up. His second idea was to utilize something he was already doing—writing in his journal. Perhaps if he wrote down his negative thoughts, including those fantasy arguments with his wife, and then went out to the garage to work out with his punching bag, he might be able to read. But what a lot of effort!

At his counselor's suggestion, Oscar chose two lifestyle goals for the following week. He would continue with his 20 minutes of walking, 4 days a week. And he would try one of three constructive outlets for his feelings: punching bag, brisk walk, or journal writing. He decided to wait to make relaxation breaks in his easy chair one of his goals; he wanted to make it enjoyable first. But, as the Workbook suggested, he would add a relaxation practice to his list of goals, practicing progressive relaxation with the script his counselor recorded for him 4–5 times a week.

At his next appointment, Oscar reported that he liked working on constructive outlets for his feelings. He was also becoming more accepting of his own need to work all the time, realizing that this had always been his outlet for his feelings. Just because he didn't like overworking didn't mean he could stop overnight. As for the progressive relaxation, he didn't feel like doing it so he didn't.

With the benefit of insights that he gained from his in-depth therapy, Oscar continued to find ways to talk things out with his wife, even their disagreement about vacations. There were fewer angry feelings, and eventually he could sit down without being preoccupied with his marital problems. During this time, he finally began to work on progressive relaxation on a regular basis. He had the sense that he was teaching himself to relax on every level: physically (by practicing progressive relaxation, going for walks, punching his bag), and emotionally (by expressing his feelings to himself, his journal, his counselor, his wife and family.)

Four years later, he was walking 5 days a week and riding his bicycle in the summer. He enjoyed both reading alone (in his easy chair!) and with his kids, who loved to hear his funny renditions of Dr. Seuss and Fantastic Mr. Fox. In a follow-up visit with his counselor, he reported that he was still doing the relaxation exercise and had started some workouts at a gym. He understood that being well includes paying attention to his triggers, and using his relaxation method when he notices his aura. He had integrated many tension-reduction methods into his life and was pleased to have reached a pretty good work/play balance. He found meaning in an unforeseen way—by taking photographs for a local food bank that posted his pictures on its website. He had interludes of contentment and gratitude—states that had once seemed unattainable.

In-Office Discussion

Read these sections and make notes in your *Workbook* prior to your appointment, in preparation for the in-office discussion with your seizure counselor.

Review of Assignments

Seizure Log/Thought Records

Discuss your Thought Record(s) that you did for your symptoms.

Journal-Keeping

If you wish, read one or more excerpts from your journal describing your self-observations to your seizure counselor.

Goal Review from Prior Session

How did work go with the choice that you made for dealing with major life issues?

Stress Reduction Chart

Did you add any new sources of stress to your chart?

Relaxation Exercise

If you are practicing your relaxation exercise on a regular basis, have you noticed any change in your tension level? What problems have you encountered in learning to relax and reduce tension?

Tools

Establishing Your Priorities

Review the ways to enhance wellness described above and indicate on the chart below whether each one is a low, moderate, or high priority for you.

Then rank them according to their importance to your health and sense of well-being. In the Rank column, list your highest priority as 1, your second priority as 2, then 3, 4, 5 and so on, until you have ranked all of the areas that apply to you. Discuss with your seizure counselor.

Worksheet: Establishing Your Priorities

	Low	Moderate	High	*Rank*
1. **Nutrition**	___	___	___	___
1a. **Weight Control**	___	___	___	___
2. **Sleep and Rest**	___	___	___	___
3. **Physical Fitness**	___	___	___	___
4. **Avoid Harmful Habits**	___	___	___	___
List habits separately:				
4a. _____	___	___	___	___
4b. _____	___	___	___	___
4c. _____	___	___	___	___
5. **Social Support**	___	___	___	___
6. **Sexuality**	___	___	___	___
7. **Relax and Reduce Tension**	___	___	___	___
8a. **Negative Emotions**	___	___	___	___
8b. **External Life Stresses**	___	___	___	___
8c. **Internal Issues**	___	___	___	___
9. **Environmental Safety**	___	___	___	___
10. **Meaning**	___	___	___	___

Write Down Your Ideas for Attainable Goals

Rather than providing you with a list of possible goals, this session asks you to formulate your own goals based on your assessment of your personal needs.

Worksheet: Lifestyle Goals Schedule

Using the Establishing Your Priorities worksheet, brainstorm some potential goals that address your highest ranking needs. Some examples are: take a 20-minute walk 4–5 times per week; talk to (*specific person*) when upset; and replace high-sugar breakfast cereal and muffins with low-sugar, whole-grain cereal or oatmeal.) **Write down your ideas in the space provided below**. Select **three lifestyle goals** and **one relaxation method** to work on during the week and discuss with your seizure counselor at your appointment.

_____

_____

_____

_____

_____

Assignments *(to Complete Prior to Your Next Appointment)*

Seizure Log/Thought Records

Continue your Seizure Log and Thought Records.

Journal-Keeping

How do you feel about your taking control program coming to an end? Describe any positive and negative feelings that you have; anxieties about finishing this program; which aspects have given you a sense of accomplishment.

Goal Selections for Session 10

Choose Your Own Lifestyle Goals

Discuss your three wellness goals that you selected for your assignment for the week. In the coming week, make an effort to meet these three goals and to check off each day that you accomplish your goal in the space provided. (This will help you to be sure that these are the goals you want to work on during the next month when you are on your own.)

Record your three goals with times per week here, and check off each day that you accomplish them:

Goal	Times/Wk	M	T	W	Th	F	S	S
1._____								
_____	____	__	__	__	__	__	__	__
2._____								
_____	____	__	__	__	__	__	__	__
3._____								
_____	____	__	__	__	__	__	__	__

Choose Your Tension-Reduction Practice

In addition to these three lifestyle goals, plan to practice a method of relaxation regularly at home. Refer to pages 162 & 165–166, where you reviewed the progressive relaxation exercise on your own. Decide which relaxation practice you want to do on a daily basis: relaxation or meditation. If your chosen method is meditation, please do a 10-minute session with your seizure counselor at your next appointment.

Fill in the grid below, indicating your chosen method, how often and for how long.

Frequency and Duration

		S	M	T	W	T	F	S
___ **Meditation** _____	WEEK 1							
___ **Relaxation** _____	WEEK 2							
	WEEK 3							

Preparing for Your Next Appointment

- After completing this session and discussing it with your seizure counselor, please read and complete "Session 11: Other Symptoms Associated with Seizures."
- Review any sections in the *Workbook* that you think are important for continuing your self-care program. Your next appointment is your last regular session using this *Workbook*, and is an important time for you to clarify areas about which you have questions. It

will also be your time to evaluate your progress and to plan for the future.

- As you do your reading, write down your list of questions and concerns to bring with you to your last session. **Use the space below or write in your journal.**

_____

_____

_____

_____

_____

Resources for Further Reading

Nutrition, Weight Control, and Physical Fitness

Estruch, R., Ros, E., Salas-Salvado, J., et al. Primary prevention of cardiovascular disease with a mediterranean diet. *New England Journal of Medicine*, 2013;368:1279–1290.

Katz, D. L., & Colino, S. *Disease Proof: The Remarkable Truth About What Makes Us Well.* New York: Hudson Street Press, 2013.

Iknolan, T. *Fitness Walking,* 2nd ed. Champaign, IL: Human Kinetics, 2005.

McDougall, J., & McDougall, M. *The Starch Solution.* Emmaus, PA: Rodale, 2012.

Nash, J., & Ormiston, L. *Lose Weight, Live Healthy: A Complete Guide to Designing Your Own Weight Loss Program.* Palo Alto, CA: Bull Publishing, 2011.

Ornish, D. *The Spectrum: A Scientifically Proven Program to Feel Better, Live Longer, Lose Weight, and Gain Health.* New York: Ballantine Books, 2008.

Pollan, M. *The Omnivore's Dilemma.* New York: Penguin, 2007.

Shamblin, G. *The Weigh Down Diet,* 1st ed. New York: Doubleday, 1997.

Harmful Habits, Social Support, and Sexuality

Alcoholics Anonymous and Narcotics Anonymous (Check online for AA and NA meeting information in your local area.)

American Lung Association, Freedom From Smoking, Online www.ffsonline.org or group programs available at 800-LUNG-USA.

Arterburn, S. *Every Man's Battle.* Colorado Springs, CO: WaterBrook Press, 2000.

Bartosch, B., & Bartosch, P. *A Bridge to Recovery: Overcomers Outreach.* Enumclaw, WA: Pleasant Word, 2009.

Berkman, L. F., & Syme, S. L. Social networks, host resistance and mortality: A nine year follow-up of Alameda County residents. *American Journal of Epidemiology,* 1979;109(2):86–205.

Carr, A. *Easy Way to Stop Smoking*. New York: Clarity Marketing, 2011.

Chapman, G. *The Five Love Languages: How to Express Heartfelt Commitment to Your Mate*. Moody Publishers. Chicago, IL: 2009.

Daley, D., & Marlatt, G. A. *Overcoming Your Alcohol or Drug Problem*. New York: Oxford University Press, 2006.

Harley, W. F., Jr. *His Needs, Her Needs*. Grand Rapids, MI: Revell, 2011.

Orloff, Judith. *Dr. Judith Orloff's Guide to Intuitive Healing: 5 Steps to Physical, Emotional and Sexual Wellness*. New York: Harmony Books, 2001.

Relaxation, Stress Reduction, Meditation, and Internal Issues

Benson, Herbert. *The Relaxation Response*. New York: HarperTorch, 2000.

Brach, T. *Radical Acceptance: Embracing Your Life With the Heart of a Buddha*. New York: Bantam, 2004.

Emmons, R. A., & McCullough, M. E. Counting blessings versus burdens: an experimental investigation of gratitude and subjective well-being in daily life. *Journal of Personality and Social Psychology* 2003;84(2):377–389.

Emmons, R. A., & McCullough, M. E. *The Psychology of Gratitude*. New York: Oxford University Press, 2004.

Foster, R. J. *Celebration of Discipline*. San Francisco, CA: Harper San Francisco, 1998.

Puddicombe, A. Learn how to meditate and receive daily guided meditations (10–20 minutes) via the Headspace mobile app, www.getsomeheadspace.com

Rohr, R. *Men and Women: The Journey of Spiritual Transformation*. Cincinnati, OH: St. Anthony Messenger Press; 2006.

General References on Wellness and Models of Health

Ardell, D. B. *High-Level Wellness*. New York: Ten Speed Press, 1986.

McGee, R. S. *The Search for Significance: Book and Workbook*, revised and expanded. Nashville, TN: W Publishing Group, 2003.

Steiger, N. J., & Lipson, J. G. *Self-Care Nursing: Theory and Practice*. Bowie, MD: Brady Communications, 1985.

Swenson, R. A. *Margin: Restoring Emotional, Physical, Financial, and Time Reserves to Overloaded Lives*. Colorado Springs, CO: NavPress, 1992.

Travis, J. W. *Wellness Workbook and Wellness Inventory*. Berkeley, CA: Celestial Arts, 2004.

SEIZURE LOG   **For the Week of** ___/___/___ **to** ___/___/___

Instructions: Please fill in the diary at the end of each day to record the number and descriptions listed. This information will be reviewed with your physician at each appointment.

Init:_____
ID:_____
Week: _____
Type:_____

SUNDAY ___/___/___ (day 1)
Number of Seizures:_____
Time(s) of day:_____
Duration (sec or min):_____
Description:_____
Location(s):_____
Severity (1: mild, 2: mod, 3: severe):_____
Trigger(s):_____
Precursor(s):_____
Improved with:_____
Impact on your day:_____
Impact on others:_____

MONDAY ___/___/___ (day 2)
Number of Seizures:_____
Time(s) of day:_____
Duration:_____
Description:_____
Location(s):_____
Severity (1: mild, 2: mod, 3: severe):_____
Trigger(s):_____
Precursor(s):_____
Improved with:_____
Impact on your day:_____
Impact on others:_____

TUESDAY ___/___/___ (day 3)
Number of Seizures:_____
Time(s) of day:_____
Duration:_____
Description:_____
Location(s):_____
Severity (1: mild, 2: mod, 3: severe):_____
Trigger(s):_____
Precursor(s):_____
Improved with:_____
Impact on your day:_____
Impact on others:_____

WEDNESDAY ___/___/___ (day 4)
Number of Seizures:_____
Time(s) of day:_____
Duration:_____
Description:_____
Location(s):_____
Severity (1: mild, 2: mod, 3: severe):_____
Trigger(s):_____
Precursor(s):_____
Improved with:_____
Impact on your day:_____
Impact on others:_____

Total: _____   **Rater:** _____

THURSDAY ___/___/___ (day 5)
Number of Seizures:_____
Time(s) of day:_____
Duration:_____
Description:_____
Location(s):_____
Severity (1: mild, 2: mod, 3: severe):_____
Trigger(s):_____
Precursor(s):_____
Improved with:_____
Impact on your day:_____
Impact on others:_____

FRIDAY ___/___/___ (day 6)
Number of Seizures:_____
Time(s) of day:_____
Duration:_____
Description:_____
Location(s):_____
Severity (1: mild, 2: mod, 3: severe):_____
Trigger(s):_____
Precursor(s):_____
Improved with:_____
Impact on your day:_____
Impact on others:_____

SATURDAY ___/___/___ (day 7)
Number of Seizures:_____
Time(s) of day:_____
Duration:_____
Description:_____
Location(s):_____
Severity (1: mild, 2: mod, 3: severe):_____
Trigger(s):_____
Precursor(s):_____
Improved with:_____
Impact on your day:_____
Impact on others:_____

Use **the space below or on back** to describe any significant information not covered in this record:

_____
_____
_____
_____
_____
_____
_____

Were you successful in stopping any seizures this week:
yes ☐   no ☐

Please mark which seizures you stopped with an asterisk (*).

SEIZURE LOG   For the Week of ____/____/____ to ____/____/____   Init:_____
Instructions: Please fill in the diary at the end of each day to record the number and descriptions   ID:_____
listed. This information will be reviewed with your physician at each appointment.   Week: _____
  Type:_____

SUNDAY __/__/__ (day 1)
Number of Seizures:_____
Time(s) of day:_____
Duration (sec or min):_____
Description:_____
Location(s):_____
Severity (1: mild, 2: mod, 3: severe):_____
Trigger(s):_____
Precursor(s):_____
Improved with:_____
Impact on your day:_____
Impact on others:_____

MONDAY __/__/__ (day 2)
Number of Seizures:_____
Time(s) of day:_____
Duration:_____
Description:_____
Location(s):_____
Severity (1: mild, 2: mod, 3: severe):_____
Trigger(s):_____
Precursor(s):_____
Improved with:_____
Impact on your day:_____
Impact on others:_____

TUESDAY __/__/__ (day 3)
Number of Seizures:_____
Time(s) of day:_____
Duration:_____
Description:_____
Location(s):_____
Severity (1: mild, 2: mod, 3: severe):_____
Trigger(s):_____
Precursor(s):_____
Improved with:_____
Impact on your day:_____
Impact on others:_____

WEDNESDAY __/__/__ (day 4)
Number of Seizures:_____
Time(s) of day:_____
Duration:_____
Description:_____
Location(s):_____
Severity (1: mild, 2: mod, 3: severe):_____
Trigger(s):_____
Precursor(s):_____
Improved with:_____
Impact on your day:_____
Impact on others:_____

THURSDAY __/__/__ (day 5)
Number of Seizures:_____
Time(s) of day:_____
Duration:_____
Description:_____
Location(s):_____
Severity (1: mild, 2: mod, 3: severe):_____
Trigger(s):_____
Precursor(s):_____
Improved with:_____
Impact on your day:_____
Impact on others:_____

FRIDAY __/__/__ (day 6)
Number of Seizures:_____
Time(s) of day:_____
Duration:_____
Description:_____
Location(s):_____
Severity (1: mild, 2: mod, 3: severe):_____
Trigger(s):_____
Precursor(s):_____
Improved with:_____
Impact on your day:_____
Impact on others:_____

SATURDAY __/__/__ (day 7)
Number of Seizures:_____
Time(s) of day:_____
Duration:_____
Description:_____
Location(s):_____
Severity (1: mild, 2: mod, 3: severe):_____
Trigger(s):_____
Precursor(s):_____
Improved with:_____
Impact on your day:_____
Impact on others:_____

Use **the space below or on back** to describe any significant
information not covered in this record:
_____
_____
_____
_____
_____
_____
_____

Were you successful in stopping any seizures this week:
yes ☐   no ☐

Please mark which seizures you stopped with an
asterisk (*).

Total: _____   **Rater:** _____

CHAPTER 12 | Session 11: Other Symptoms Associated With Seizures

There are times when the condition of having seizures seems to take on a mind of its own. Seizures come on suddenly, often with little or no warning. Moods change just as suddenly, sometimes with no apparent cause. Individuals with seizures experience all of the variations of inner state, feelings, and behavior that people without seizures experience. Additionally, there are some states, such as *déjà vu* or scattered thinking, which people with seizures experience more often than most individuals who don't have seizures. We call these states "other symptoms associated with seizures" because anyone who experiences them needs to be able to understand and deal with them.

Why devote a chapter of this *Workbook* to understanding other symptoms associated with seizures? Because these other symptoms are part of the secret inner life of many people with seizures: thoughts and sensations that are interesting but sometimes disturbing and hard to understand. Often these inner states or outer behaviors lead a person with seizures to feel more alone and out of control, cut off from others, with sensations that are more intense and worrisome than those that others experience. It may be reassuring to know that these experiences are common among people with seizures.

Session 11 will help you become familiar with the different states of consciousness and types of behavior that constitute your "other symptoms." By recognizing these "other symptoms," you have the possibility of becoming more comfortable with yourself and more at home with the condition of seizures. In keeping with this *Workbook*'s focus on wellness, the purpose of Session 11 is to allow you to become more accepting of yourself and to see yourself as a whole, healthy person. Understanding and accepting these "other symptoms" constitutes another important step in taking control of your seizures.

The content of this chapter is divided into two major categories of "other symptoms": (1) inner states or sensations, and (2) types of behavior. Anyone may have these symptoms occasionally, but individuals with seizures tend to experience these symptoms frequently and more powerfully As you read the descriptions of these different states, note whether any of them are familiar to you. In addition, some people find that they have other unique states and sensations that do not fit the descriptions in this *Workbook*. Bear in mind that it is normal for people with seizures to have a variety of unusual inner experiences, and for that reason, space is provided for you to describe your own personal states and sensations. Later you will have the opportunity to discuss all of your "other symptoms" with your seizure counselor as you proceed with the In-Office Discussion later in Session 11.

What Are the Common Altered States Experienced More Often by People With Seizures?

Déjà vu is the feeling of "having been there before," of having experienced something before. With *déjà vu*, even though you've never been in a particular place or talked with a particular individual before, it seems like you have. This phenomenon is common in children and decreases as people get older. Some hallucinogenic drugs accentuate this feeling. *Déjà vu* can precede a seizure as an aura, or it can occur by itself.

Jamais vu is the opposite of *déjà vu*. It is the experience of *not* recognizing a situation you've been in before. This state is much less common than *déjà vu*. An example would be going into a room filled with furniture and people that you've seen before and not recognizing any of it. In French, *jamais vu* means "never seen," and the feeling an individual experiences is one of lack of recognition despite past exposure. This feeling state can be frightening if a person does not understand what is going on.

Dissociation is often experienced as a floating sensation, such as lifting up out of a chair, or floating in the air. At other times a person will look at his arm or leg and it will seem like it doesn't belong and is strangely separate from his body. Or, while engaged in some activity, a person might perceive herself as if she were an observer watching a different person doing that activity. All of these experiences have in common a sense of being dissociated and separate from oneself, one's body, or parts of one's own body.

Nonlinear thinking is an intuitive thought process that is often based on the *gestalt* or whole, rather than on parts of the whole. Many people with seizures have the ability to think in a nonlinear, intuitive fashion, and may lack the ability to think in a logical, linear mode. Since Western society generally values logic and linear thinking more than gestalt or holistic thinking, individuals with seizures sometimes feel at a disadvantage. They may have a clear picture of a situation and feel certain that their understanding is right, but they find themselves unable to explain the reasons for their viewpoint to others.

For example, sometimes while journal-keeping, you may feel that your writing is not good enough or you have more trouble expressing yourself than you should. Those feelings may be magnified if you compare your writing to published work. It is important to remember that your thoughts and feelings are of vital importance to the process of taking control, and whatever you write in your journal is a true and valuable reflection of your inner experience.

Individuals who have the ability to think in a nonlinear way can learn to value this capacity and to use it creatively. Nonlinear thinking is often the basis for creative works of art, music, or literature, as well as the basis for insights into oneself and other people. People who are strong in nonlinear thinking can also benefit from recognizing, and letting others know, that their ideas are intuitive and lack a logical basis. In this way, they can avoid frustrating attempts to explain something that other people can easily refute with logic.

Scattered thinking is a very common experience among individuals with seizures. They may find that they are sometimes unable to organize their thoughts. At times they may notice that they can't concentrate on something they are reading or make sense out of what someone is saying. They may have trouble keeping their mind on a problem or remembering things that that they recently learned. At other times, individuals with seizures may have the feeling that their thoughts have sped up, or at the other extreme, that their thinking has slowed down.

Random sequences of unrelated thoughts will sometimes occur, interrupting a particular train of thought and creating the feeling of being out of control.

Note: The important thing is to recognize these different patterns of thinking and to learn to cope with them. Most people can learn to wait for periods of scattered thinking to pass, or find ways to minimize distraction and fatigue so that they can concentrate and think clearly when they need to. Some people find that disorganized thoughts are just a fact of life that they can learn to live with. Whatever your personal experience with scattered thinking, it is useful to know that this is probably the most universal of "other symptoms" associated with seizures. Because it can have a big impact on your self-image, particularly regarding whether you view yourself as being able to function competently, it can be of great benefit to discuss your experiences and concerns regarding scattered thinking with your seizure counselor.

Memory problems are extremely common in people with seizures. Many people report lapses of memory, difficulty with recent memory, and/or memory fluctuations, where sometimes they remember things clearly and sometimes memory is poor.

There are three major reasons for memory problems in individuals with seizures, and you will need help from your doctor and counselor to determine the most likely cause of your particular memory problems.

- The first reason is that memory problems can be part of the seizures. The seizures may occur frequently enough or in a way that interferes with thinking and memory.
- A second reason for memory problems is over-medication, where too much CNS active medicine causes sedation, slowed mental functioning, and poor memory. In this situation, your doctor will suggest lowering your dosage of medication to improve the symptoms.
- The third cause of memory problems can be a past brain injury, especially when there was damage to the temporal lobe—the part of the brain most responsible for memory. Sometimes this kind of memory problem can be improved by decreasing your overall level of tension and arousal through practicing techniques such as relaxation. But it may be necessary to learn to cope with some degree of difficulty with memory, by accepting the situation and learning to live with it.

Out-of-body experiences are characterized by the sensation of leaving one's body. Some people report that they leave their body, travel to another place, and later can recollect what occurred in a place distant from where their physical body actually was. A great deal of controversy surrounds this phenomenon. Some researchers have reported this phenomenon among individuals who have had a near-death experience, such as cardiac arrest followed by successful resuscitation. Severe physical or psychic shocks seem to increase the experience of this phenomenon. Individuals with seizures report out-of-body experiences more frequently as well.

Vertigo is the sensation of spinning or of momentary dizziness and loss of balance. This sensation may occur by itself or as an aura prior to seizures.

Crawling sensations might feel like ants are crawling up a person's leg or chest, when in fact there is nothing there. These sensations can occur independently or may precede a seizure as an aura.

Unpleasant stinging or jabbing sensations in the head or other parts of the body that feel like needles or hot pokers. These sensations occur sporadically in people with seizures, and can occur as an aura. They are also experienced by people who don't have seizures.

A **premonition** is a sense of knowing that something is going to happen in the future. Many individuals with seizures experience premonitions, especially associated with their dreams. For example, a person with seizures might report that she had a dream at night and the next day experienced the events that occurred in the dream. Or, a man might remember having a dream in which someone tells him something important and soon after that same person tells him the exact same message in person. Less often, an individual with seizures might experience a premonition before or during a seizure and later report that the event does actually happen.

It is difficult to assess objectively whether premonitions are true indicators of future occurrences, or simply "flukes"—that is, they happen by chance. Obviously, there are many possible explanations for these phenomena. For example, an individual might be unconsciously aware that something is likely to happen and might then be surprised by a dream that predicts this occurrence. A full discussion of whether people might have psychic powers to predict the future is beyond the scope of this *Workbook*. But it is important for you to know that individuals with seizures report states like this more frequently than do people who do not have seizures.

In addition to noting these phenomena among modern-day people with seizures, this experience is mentioned in historical documents about people with epilepsy, such as Alexander the Great and Julius Caesar. There is also some speculation that the people who were consulted about the future at the Oracle at Delphi in ancient Greece may have had seizures.

Telepathy is the phenomenon of extrasensory perception of thoughts, feelings, or events. Some people report that they can read another person's mind at a distance, as far as the opposite side of the country. For example, a person might relate that she was thinking the same thing at the same time as a relative many miles away. Some individuals claim to perceive events occurring thousands of miles away with no prior knowledge. For example, a common telepathic claim is to feel the death of a loved one who is far away at the exact time that it occurs. As with other altered states, some individuals with seizures relate frequent telepathic experiences.

Perceptual changes are more common in people with seizures, who may experience altered perceptions of time and space. Past, present, and future might seem to occur simultaneously, or time might otherwise seem distorted. For example, a second of time might feel like hours, or an entire day might seem like minutes. Some people with seizures feel as though they are melting into space. For others, stationary objects might seem to become larger or smaller, close or far away. Some individuals experience an awareness of infinity or eternity.

Religious and mystical experiences seem to be reported more often among people with seizures. Examples include the experience of death, reliving past incarnations, union with God, physical rebirth, cellular consciousness, communication with the dead, and many others. Some people report a feeling of being overpowered or overwhelmed by these experiences. While these experiences can be positive and compelling, they can also be frightening and may increase feelings of being out of control. For some people with seizures, they may accentuate the sense of being different from others, resulting in loneliness, alienation, and isolation. For others, they may become the basis for cherished beliefs and a source of connection and meaning.

What if I Have "Other Symptoms" That Do not Correspond to Any of the Descriptions in This Chapter?

You may find that you do indeed experience "other symptoms" of seizures, such as different states or sensations, but they do not correspond to the descriptions in this chapter. Bear in mind that many other sensations occur in people with seizures—in addition to those described in this *Workbook*. It would be a good idea to discuss any feelings or sensations that you consider unusual with your physician or seizure counselor to get a better understanding of them. *The main thing to know is that unusual feelings and sensations occur more frequently in people with seizures, and they do not mean that you are out of control, or that you are losing your mind.*

Sometimes feeling afraid or worried about these different states can be more of a problem than the actual experiences. The purpose of Session 11 is to familiarize you with the many variations of "other symptoms" and to encourage you to discuss your own experiences with your physician and/ or seizure counselor.

In order to facilitate this discussion, the following space is provided in your *Workbook* for you to describe any states or experiences that have not been included in the text thus far.

My personal altered states, sensations, or experiences, which do not fit any of the descriptions in the text, are the following:

_____

_____

_____

_____

_____

What Is the Significance of These Various Altered States That Have Just Been Described?

It is not possible for us to know if the altered states described above are purely subjective experiences (that is, only felt by the person experiencing them), or whether there is any objective truth to these phenomena. This question is complex and falls outside the scope of this *Workbook*. What we do know is that these states occur normally in individuals with seizures and do not constitute a form of insanity or mental disorder. It is helpful for each person to recognize these altered states as common and to learn to feel at home with the particular phenomena that he or she experiences. This understanding can be extremely helpful to people who are fearful, or who feel "different" and therefore socially isolated, as a result of these experiences. Simply acknowledging to oneself and others that altered states are normal and expected for people with seizures can have a major impact in relieving anxiety about this subject.

Altered states of consciousness, such as those described above, are not limited to individuals with seizures. Scientists studying the effects of hallucinogenic drugs have reported similar experiences. Also as mentioned above, other investigators have reported increased incidences of these phenomena among individuals who have almost died. This leads us to believe that it is important for researchers to learn more about such experiences. Until more is known about altered states, we have found that talking about these experiences with an understanding doctor, therapist, or friend helps people to deal constructively with them.

Common Behavioral and Emotional Symptoms Experienced by People With Seizures

There are a wide variety of behavioral and emotional changes that may be experienced by individuals with seizures. (These are summarized in Table 12.1.) In contrast to altered states that are apparent only to the individual who experiences them, some behavioral changes are more obvious to others than to the individual who is having them. For example, behavioral and emotional symptoms can be dramatically overt, such as anger expressed in fighting or yelling. On the other hand, you might have emotional changes that are both personal and subtle, such as mild mood swings, or feelings of anxiety or hurt.

Some behavioral and emotional symptoms represent the ways individuals have learned to cope with their lives and their seizures, while others are

Table 12.1 Summary of Behavioral and Emotional Symptoms

Behavioral State	Some Other Possible Cause	Causes Related to Seizures
Slowing of activity or lethargy	Psychological (depression, loss), lack of sleep, other medical conditions (anemia, hypothyroidism)	Frequent seizures or subclinical seizures, overmedication, psychomotor slowing
Agitation or outbursts of rage	Psychological (poorly expressed anger, hostility, anxiety), substance abuse (alcohol, stimulant drugs)	Manifestation of seizures, effect of being restrained during or after seizures, side effect of medication, psychomotor excitability

a direct result of anticonvulsant medications or seizures themselves. The benefit of understanding your own behavioral and emotional changes is that you can learn to observe and understand them, to minimize any negative impact on yourself and others, and to feel more comfortable with these "other symptoms" of seizures. After you read the following descriptions of common behavioral and emotional symptoms, you may wish to use the space provided for noting any additional symptoms that have not been mentioned in the text.

Depression is a psychiatric disorder that is characterized by extended periods of decreased appetite, difficulty sleeping, problems concentrating, lack of interest or enjoyment, feelings of guilt or worthlessness, and sometimes, thoughts of wanting to die. Depression is commonly seen in people with nonepileptic seizures, occurring in 50%–80% of patients. If you are not currently being treated for depression but feel you may have these symptoms, talk to your prescribing physician or your counselor about getting treatment.

A slowing of activity, or psychomotor slowing, is a behavioral symptom sometimes experienced by individuals with seizures, particularly among those with complex partial (focal dyscognitive) seizures. Individuals with this symptom appear slow in speech and action, withdraw from others, and often seem depressed. This is called "psychomotor slowing" because it consists of a decrease in the normal rate of thinking, speech, and physical activity. Anticonvulsant medications can cause psychomotor slowing. Frequent but unrecognized (subclinical) seizures can also appear as a decrease in activity.

If the tendency to psychomotor slowing is intermittent or has recently increased, it is important to consult your physician to be sure that an adjustment of medication would not improve the symptom. Of course, situational depression caused by disappointment in a relationship or job can also cause social withdrawal, so it is important to know whether the decrease in activity is primarily physical or psychological in cause.

The opposite of psychomotor slowing is an **increase in activity**, or "psychomotor excitability." This, too, is common in individuals with seizures, particularly those with complex partial seizures. At times, seizures are preceded by unexplained agitation, such as pacing about, talking continuously, or even yelling or lashing out at others. Infrequently, a complex partial seizure may actually consist of a sudden outburst of randomly directed anger. Or, if an individual is interrupted or physically restrained during a complex partial seizure, he or she may become uncontrollably violent. Other people become agitated after a seizure, and may actually fight if approached.

Anxiety is associated with increased worry or distress and may be accompanied by a number of physical symptoms. Panic attacks present with discrete periods of intense fear or discomfort, along with trouble breathing, chest pain, tingling/numbness, blurred vision, dizziness, sweating and shaking, feelings of unreality, and fears of death. Generalized anxiety is more pervasive and may lead to difficulties with sleep, concentration, and muscle tension. Post-traumatic stress disorder (PTSD) is a type of anxiety disorder that sometimes occurs after an individual experiences a traumatic event or a history of abuse. Individuals with PTSD may have nightmares, startle easily, avoid people or places that remind them of the event, experience flashbacks, or have feelings of numbness or lack of connectedness to their surroundings. Anxiety disorders commonly occur in individuals with seizures.

Anger and Physical Violence

In contrast to the outbursts of anger discussed below, anger and physical violence associated with psychomotor excitability is not due to poor impulse control. It may, in fact, have nothing to do with actual feelings of anger, but occurs as a result of the brain excitability associated with seizures. However, knowing that this behavior is a symptom of your seizures does not mean that there is nothing you can do about it. If you know that you sometimes become violent when you have seizures, you have the responsibility to protect yourself and others from possible harm.

The way to deal with this kind of symptom is to know your own behavioral pattern and to use your knowledge to avoid difficulties. For example, if you have been told that you hit others if they restrain you during a seizure, it is your responsibility to inform people about this. You might want to be sure that family and friends understand the importance of leaving you alone at these times, explaining that it is a symptom associated with your seizure disorder. In addition, it is critical that you wear an Identi-bracelet that states something like: "I have seizures. May become violent after seizures. Do not physically restrain." Identi-bracelets, necklaces, and wallet cards are the only way to inform strangers of your condition and your own particular needs. By routinely wearing identifying jewelry, you can help to avoid awkward situations with strangers, needless ambulance calls, and possible trouble with the law.

Extreme expressions of anger may also be a psychological response to life pressures, rather than a result of the seizures themselves. With some people, **sudden outbursts** of rage may occur during which a person expresses pent-up anger at a particular person or situation. This can happen because a person carries around a lot of unexpressed anger until it can't be contained, and then suddenly explodes by yelling or, more seriously, by throwing things or hitting others. In these individuals, when anger builds up, an increase in the frequency or severity of seizures may result.

Why is it that this uncontrolled expression of anger unrelated to seizure activity sometimes occurs? It may be that some individuals have not learned to control impulses or to express their emotions in appropriate and productive ways. When their guard is down, they may then express their feelings as uncontrolled laughing, crying, yelling, hitting, or other forms of acting out.

Because these forms of behavior are uncomfortable and unacceptable to others, they may result in troubled relationships with the people who matter the most. This in turn can increase feelings of self-doubt and self-hate, alienation, or unresolved anger toward others, which further erodes feelings of self-esteem. It is important for you to know if you experience this type of behavior so that a counselor can help you cope with it and lessen the negative effects on yourself and others. If you experience this type of behavior, you have a lot to gain if you can find the courage to observe it, understand it, and get help from your counselor in exploring ways to deal positively with this phenomenon. Your counselor can help you determine the probable cause of your behavioral state and discuss ways to cope.

Sometimes I Behave in Unusual Ways That Are Not Described in This Text. Is This Behavior One of My "Other Symptoms" of Seizures?

Most likely, the answer to this question is "yes." As with the altered states and perceptual changes described in the first section of this session, some people with seizures experience other unusual behavioral symptoms that are not described in the text. If you have noticed (or others have commented on) behaviors that you think might be "other symptoms" of seizures, use the following space to make notes about them now. This information will be extremely useful when you discuss this subject with your seizure counselor.

My other behavioral or emotional symptoms that are not described above are the following:

_____

_____

_____

_____

_____

Creative Perception: A Personal Experience

Donna Andrews, one of the authors of this *Workbook*, has kept a continuous journal since the onset of her seizures at age 18, during her first year of college. She used her journal to record her inner experience, obstacles, perceptions, and pursuit of wellness. Many of the insights that she has used to control her seizures, as well as in her work to help patients take control of their seizures, are detailed in this *Workbook* and are presented below, in her own voice, for each session.

- Introduction about talking to the professional—"Can you talk to him [or her]?"
- Session 1: Making the Decision to Begin the Process of Taking Control—"'Yes' and 'no' are the hardest answers you will ever have to give."
- Session 2: Getting Support—"The best mirror is an old friend."
- Session 3: Deciding About Your Drug Therapy—"If they are not helping they may be hurting."
- Session 4: Learning to Observe Your Triggers—"An exercise in self-awareness, you will find your triggers in what you do or is done to you."
- Session 5: Channeling Negative Emotions Into Productive Outlets—"Emotions are a demand for action!"
- Session 6: Relaxation Training: Experiencing the Sensation of the Brain Changing Itself—"Reposed but not in thought you enter the portal of the universal mind, free to walk the corridors of wonder . . . released for a time from the pressures of your life."
- Session 7: Identifying Your Pre-Seizure Aura—"Attack warning! It could be everything you're feeling or something specific, but it will

always be the same, and you will need to listen to it once you find its name."

- Session 8: Dealing With External Life Stresses—"Try to be yourself, quit hiding in the clown face or feeling the truth."
- Session 9: Dealing With Internal Issues and Conflicts—"I wonder if that small clear face would be disappointed to see the you that I replaced?"
- Session 10: Enhancing Personal Wellness—"Optimal health is a gift that you have to work hard to receive."
- Session 11: Other Symptoms Associated With Seizures—"Where is it I go, that I have to look back to see reality?"(adapted from journal of Carrie Ashton)
- Taking Control: An Ongoing Process—"The cycles of illness are vicious . . . while the spirals of health are ongoing."

The Work

Goal

The goal for this session is to recognize, accept, and cope positively with the inner states and sensations, and/or behavioral and emotional symptoms, which constitute your "other symptoms" of seizures.

Obstacles

Select the statements below that may apply to you, or write in your own.

- Difficulty noticing your own unusual sensations or behavior.
- Reluctance to reveal or discuss "weird" experiences—because of fear that others will judge these as crazy or unacceptable.
- Feeling totally alone with these inner experiences—the sense that no one could possibly understand.
- Not wanting to give up the special, meaningful aspects of these experiences. (Note that this *Workbook* is supportive of any positive meaning that you derive from your inner states. In addition, Session 11 seeks to demystify whatever aspects are frightening and to alleviate any feelings of alienation or aloneness that these symptoms might cause you.)
- Feelings of shame and fear about discussing any behavioral/ emotional symptoms, such as rage, yelling, or striking out at others.

- "There's nothing I can do about my behavior when I have a seizure, so why discuss it?"
- Unwillingness to accept that one or more "other symptoms" that you find uncomfortable or unpleasant may be an unavoidable part of having seizures.
- The assumption that one or more "other symptoms" associated with seizures means that I'm totally out of control, or losing my mind.

In-Office Discussion

Read the sections and make notes in your *Workbook* prior to your appointment, as preparation for the in-office discussion with your seizure counselor.

Review of Assignments

Seizure Log/Thought Record

Review your seizure log from the past week and discuss any Thought Records with your counselor.

Stress Reduction Chart

Have you added any new stresses to your chart? How are you handling these stresses?

Relaxation Training

If you have not already done so, proceed now with your relaxation training session as directed in Session 6. Discuss with your seizure counselor how to apply this skill to other life situations, such as when you experience tension, negative feelings such as anger or fear, or your pre-seizure aura.

Journal-Keeping

Did you make any observations of your other symptoms in your journal that you would like to talk about with your seizure counselor?

Goal Review From Prior Session

Discuss your checklist of the three wellness goals that you chose at the end of Session 10 with your counselor. Are these the goals that you want to continue to work on during the next month when you are on your own, or would you like to modify your wellness goal selection?

Review of Obstacles

What are your obstacles to discussing, identifying, and coping with your "other symptoms" associated with seizures? How did you feel about reading Session 11? How do you feel about telling your seizure counselor about these experiences?

Tools

Topics

The following list of "other symptoms" associated with seizures discussed in Session 11 is provided to facilitate discussion with your seizure counselor.

1. *Déjà-vu*
2. *Jamais-vu*
3. Dissociation
4. Nonlinear thinking
5. Scattered thinking
6. Memory problems
7. Out-of-body experiences
8. Vertigo
9. Crawling sensations
10. Unpleasant stinging or jabbing sensations
11. Premonitions
12. Telepathy
13. Perceptual changes
14. Religious or mystical experiences
15. Other altered states, sensations, or experiences not described in the text
16. Sudden outbursts of rage
17. Slowing of activity (psychomotor slowing)
18. Excessive activity (psychomotor excitability)
19. Other behavioral or emotional problems not described in the text.

Suggested Areas of Discussion

- Which of these symptoms do you experience frequently? Occasionally? Not at all?

- Which of these experiences are positive for you? In what ways are they positive? For example, do you find them enjoyable, unusual, or interesting? Do they make you feel special and unique? Do they provide insight and meaning? Are they a source of creativity for you?
- Which of these experiences are negative for you? In what ways are they negative? For example, are they disturbing emotionally or do they disrupt your thinking? Do they make you feel alone, strange, or alienated? Do they cause embarrassment or interfere with relationships with others?
- Do you have experiences that are different from those described in the text that you think might be "other symptoms" associated with seizures? If you choose to bring these up with your seizure counselor, you'll have the opportunity to discuss whether these experiences are most likely connected with seizures.
- Are there any of your "other symptoms" for which you would particularly like to develop a positive coping strategy? If so, how have you coped with this experience in the past? How would you like to cope with it in the future?
- How do you feel about having seizures, and experiencing these "other symptoms?" Does self-acceptance make sense to you, as one of the ways to take control of your seizures? What are the hardest things to accept?

Improving Memory Performance

Remember the last time you misplaced an item or forgot a word? This can be maddening and frustrating. Many people notice that the moment they start thinking about something else—suddenly—the memory will resurface. This common phenomenon illustrates how frustration and impatience can interfere with the normal functioning of the brain's memory retrieval. So, the next time you struggle with your memory, relax, take a deep breath and trust that the memory will return at its own time.

You might observe a similar phenomenon when it comes to learning and memory formation. The brain integrates new information during sleep (meaning that breaks are an important part of the learning process). Therefore, it can be beneficial to decide to take a break if you notice a feeling of frustration while you attempt to study. Upon returning to the desk, you may find that your brain has taken the previously studied material to a new level of understanding.

If you notice a recurrent tendency to forget things, it might help you to carry a little book around in which you can take notes—names, numbers, chores, insights, questions, and so on. This not only provides instant relief of the fear that you might forget something important, it also provides your brain with other learning channels: writing and reading.

Forgetting can also be a defense mechanism in which you protect yourself from a memory. As you learned in Sessions 8 and 9, your sensitivity level and internal conflicts may influence your emotional reactions to external life events. At times, the intensity of negative emotions that are stirred up by seemingly minor life events can be surprising. You may tend to protect yourself from the experience of negative life events by denying yourself access to the memory, leaving that memory on a subconscious level—perhaps because you are afraid that it might trigger a seizure. This process, called repression, may at times lead to a general decline of memory function. If you suspect that repression interferes with your memory function, you can discuss the option of continuing in-depth psychological counseling with your seizure counselor or a therapist in order to address this problem.

Assignments *(to Complete Prior to Your Next Session)*

Seizure Log/Thought Record

Continue your Seizure Log and Thought Records.

Journal-Keeping

As you approach the end of your counseling appointments, continue to write in your journal about anything new that you notice that pertains to your seizures. This includes symptoms that you think are related to your seizures and observations about your triggers and pre-seizure aura. Write about:

- Moving toward wellness, in what ways do you feel well, healthy, and good about yourself?
- What positive changes have you made in your life, in moving toward taking control?
- What aspects of your lifestyle do you feel are not healthy?
- In what ways do you feel that your life or self-image is lacking in wellness?

Tension Reduction Plan

Select another goal for reducing tension this week. You might want to choose the same goal if it was particularly beneficial, or you may want to try something different. Indicate your goal, and how many times you plan to do it (frequency) in the space provided:

Goal   **Frequency**

_____

_____

_____

	S	M	T	W	T	F	S
WEEK 1							
WEEK 2							
WEEK 3							

(During the coming week, check off the days of the week that you meet your goal.)

Relaxation Method

Indicate which method you've decided to practice this week:

Goal   **Frequency**

_____

_____

_____

	S	M	T	W	T	F	S
WEEK 1							
WEEK 2							
WEEK 3							

(During the coming week, check off the days of the week that you meet your goal.)

Self-Observation

Perhaps you and your seizure counselor discussed some aspect of other symptoms that you would like to work on and record in your journal. This might include self-observation of one or more of your "other symptoms," trying out a plan for coping positively with one of your symptoms, or describing some of your feelings and experiences in more detail. Describe below what specifically you plan to do.

_____

_____

_____

Preparing to Continue the "Taking Control" Process on Your Own

After completing this session and discussing it with your counselor, please read "Taking Control: An Ongoing Process."

Resources for Further Reading

Moody, R., & Kubler-Ross, E. *Life After Life*. New York: HarperOne, 2001.

Dostoevski, Fyodor. *The Idiot* (trans. McDuff, D.). London: Penguin Classics, 2004.

Richard, A., & Reiter, J. *Epilepsy: A New Approach*. New York: Walker, 1995.

Tart, C. *Altered States of Consciousness*, 3rd ed. New York: Harper, 2001.

Tempkin, O. *The Falling Sickness*. Baltimore, MD: The Johns Hopkins Press, 1945.

SEIZURE LOG   For the Week of ____/____/____to ____/____/____   Init:_____

Instructions: Please fill in the diary at the end of each day to record the number and descriptions   ID:_____

listed. This information will be reviewed with your physician at each appointment.   Week: _____

                                                           Type:_____

SUNDAY ___/___/___ (day 1)

Number of Seizures:_____

Time(s) of day:_____

Duration (sec or min):_____

Description:_____

Location(s):_____

Severity (1: mild, 2: mod, 3: severe):_____

Trigger(s):_____

Precursor(s):_____

Improved with:_____

Impact on your day:_____

Impact on others:_____

MONDAY ___/___/___ (day 2)

Number of Seizures:_____

Time(s) of day:_____

Duration:_____

Description:_____

Location(s):_____

Severity (1: mild, 2: mod, 3: severe):_____

Trigger(s):_____

Precursor(s):_____

Improved with:_____

Impact on your day:_____

Impact on others:_____

TUESDAY ___/___/___ (day 3)

Number of Seizures:_____

Time(s) of day:_____

Duration:_____

Description:_____

Location(s):_____

Severity (1: mild, 2: mod, 3: severe):_____

Trigger(s):_____

Precursor(s):_____

Improved with:_____

Impact on your day:_____

Impact on others:_____

WEDNESDAY ___/___/___ (day 4)

Number of Seizures:_____

Time(s) of day:_____

Duration:_____

Description:_____

Location(s):_____

Severity (1: mild, 2: mod, 3: severe):_____

Trigger(s):_____

Precursor(s):_____

Improved with:_____

Impact on your day:_____

Impact on others:_____

Total:_____   **Rater: _____**

THURSDAY ___/___/___ (day 5)

Number of Seizures:_____

Time(s) of day:_____

Duration:_____

Description:_____

Location(s):_____

Severity (1: mild, 2: mod, 3: severe):_____

Trigger(s):_____

Precursor(s):_____

Improved with:_____

Impact on your day:_____

Impact on others:_____

FRIDAY ___/___/___ (day 6)

Number of Seizures:_____

Time(s) of day:_____

Duration:_____

Description:_____

Location(s):_____

Severity (1: mild, 2: mod, 3: severe):_____

Trigger(s):_____

Precursor(s):_____

Improved with:_____

Impact on your day:_____

Impact on others:_____

SATURDAY ___/___/___ (day 7)

Number of Seizures:_____

Time(s) of day:_____

Duration:_____

Description:_____

Location(s):_____

Severity (1: mild, 2: mod, 3: severe):_____

Trigger(s):_____

Precursor(s):_____

Improved with:_____

Impact on your day:_____

Impact on others:_____

Use **the space below or on back** to describe any significant information not covered in this record:

_____

_____

_____

_____

_____

_____

_____

Were you successful in stopping any seizures this week:

yes ☐   no ☐

Please mark which seizures you stopped with an asterisk (*).

SEIZURE LOG   **For the Week of** ___/___/___ **to** ___/___/___

Instructions: Please fill in the diary at the end of each day to record the number and descriptions listed. This information will be reviewed with your physician at each appointment.

Init:_____
ID:_____
Week: _____
Type:_____

SUNDAY ___/___/___ (day 1)
Number of Seizures:_____
Time(s) of day:_____
Duration (sec or min):_____
Description:_____
Location(s):_____
Severity (1: mild, 2: mod, 3: severe):_____
Trigger(s):_____
Precursor(s):_____
Improved with:_____
Impact on your day:_____
Impact on others:_____

MONDAY ___/___/___ (day 2)
Number of Seizures:_____
Time(s) of day:_____
Duration:_____
Description:_____
Location(s):_____
Severity (1: mild, 2: mod, 3: severe):_____
Trigger(s):_____
Precursor(s):_____
Improved with:_____
Impact on your day:_____
Impact on others:_____

TUESDAY ___/___/___ (day 3)
Number of Seizures:_____
Time(s) of day:_____
Duration:_____
Description:_____
Location(s):_____
Severity (1: mild, 2: mod, 3: severe):_____
Trigger(s):_____
Precursor(s):_____
Improved with:_____
Impact on your day:_____
Impact on others:_____

WEDNESDAY ___/___/___ (day 4)
Number of Seizures:_____
Time(s) of day:_____
Duration:_____
Description:_____
Location(s):_____
Severity (1: mild, 2: mod, 3: severe):_____
Trigger(s):_____
Precursor(s):_____
Improved with:_____
Impact on your day:_____
Impact on others:_____

Total: _____   **Rater:** _____

THURSDAY ___/___/___ (day 5)
Number of Seizures:_____
Time(s) of day:_____
Duration:_____
Description:_____
Location(s):_____
Severity (1: mild, 2: mod, 3: severe):_____
Trigger(s):_____
Precursor(s):_____
Improved with:_____
Impact on your day:_____
Impact on others:_____

FRIDAY ___/___/___ (day 6)
Number of Seizures:_____
Time(s) of day:_____
Duration:_____
Description:_____
Location(s):_____
Severity (1: mild, 2: mod, 3: severe):_____
Trigger(s):_____
Precursor(s):_____
Improved with:_____
Impact on your day:_____
Impact on others:_____

SATURDAY ___/___/___ (day 7)
Number of Seizures:_____
Time(s) of day:_____
Duration:_____
Description:_____
Location(s):_____
Severity (1: mild, 2: mod, 3: severe):_____
Trigger(s):_____
Precursor(s):_____
Improved with:_____
Impact on your day:_____
Impact on others:_____

Use **the space below or on back** to describe any significant information not covered in this record:

_____
_____
_____
_____
_____
_____

Were you successful in stopping any seizures this week:
yes ☐ no ☐

Please mark which seizures you stopped with an asterisk (*).

CHAPTER 13 ▶ Taking Control: An Ongoing Process

The process outlined in this *Workbook* is paradoxical. With each session, you have been working to understand your seizures and the effects on your life, to accept and embrace this vulnerability—in order to become strong. Your strength, now and in the future, comes out of taking responsibility for this vulnerability. Your hope lies in making your way through the pain, fear, and guilt within you in order to reach the other side of despair—contentment, clarity, and well-being.

In this ongoing process of taking control, the paradox lies in the fact that acceptance of pain, weakness, and lack of control allows you to learn to love and accept yourself and your specialness, which includes your seizures. Self-acceptance allows you to take responsibility for your seizures, to take control of living your life to the fullest, and to find joy, meaning, and self-esteem.

Each person has a vulnerable place, a place of pain and what is often judged as weakness. For some, this place is psychological—depression, raw anger, anxiety, or feelings of inadequacy. For others, it is physical, and manifests as symptoms such as migraine headaches, ulcer pain, backache, or seizures. For many people, vulnerability is both psychological and physical. But most people can hide their vulnerable place from others, whereas people with seizures cannot. When you have a seizure, others can see this weak and vulnerable place. And others may not accept your seizures or may try to protect you by treating you as an invalid.

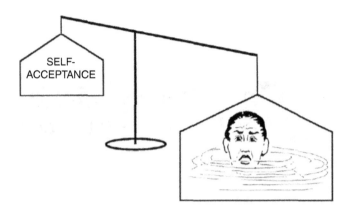

Figure 13.1

Drowning in Responsibility

Considering that other people are so often judgmental and express discomfort about seizures, it is not surprising that many people with seizures come to judge themselves as inadequate. But by blaming yourself and judging yourself harshly, you are not able to take responsibility for accepting yourself. On the other hand, if you blame others for your seizures, or your lack of happiness or success, you are also avoiding responsibility for accepting yourself by becoming a victim. Much of this *Workbook* has been concerned with these basic human dilemmas, in order to help you to come to terms with what it means to take control of your seizures and your life. These dilemmas or pitfalls, which are pictured in Figures 13.1 through 13.3, apply to all people and have particular significance for anyone with seizures.

The person who is drowning in responsibility (Figure 13.1) has a lack of self-acceptance and a tendency to take too much responsibility for his or her own problems. This person might feel something like this: "I have to prove myself because I have seizures—I have to try to do more than anyone else. It's okay if my boss doesn't give me regular breaks, or any vacation; after all, he's given me a job even though I have seizures. If I can't make it under these conditions, it's my own fault."

On the other side of the spectrum, the victim who is stuck in the muck (Figure 13.2) lacks an understanding that he or she has any power or responsibility to take care of personal difficulties. Instead, the victim is over-accepting of his or her own weaknesses and tends to blame others or hold others responsible for problems. Sometimes seen in people with a history of abuse, a victim who is stuck in the muck might see the situation something like this: "I don't work—after all, I have seizures. My wife has

300

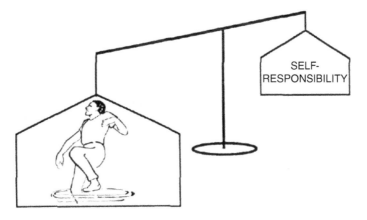

Figure 13.2

The Victim: Stuck in the Muck

to work to support both of us, and she does the housework and shopping, of course not very efficiently. She keeps busy and seems irritable most of the time, which makes my life miserable. I can't do anything about it because I have seizures."

The third alternative, as illustrated in Figure 13.3, is to try to strike a balance between self-acceptance and self-responsibility. This dynamic balance involves liking and accepting yourself and at the same time taking responsibility for making your own life as fulfilling as it can be. A person who balances these two elements might view his or her situation something like this: "Having seizures certainly isn't easy, but I can learn to accept this hassle in my life and get on with things. I can still have a good job and earn the respect of my boss and colleagues. I can have a good relationship with my husband and do my part to work things out when problems come up. When setbacks arise, it's up to me to get through them and make my life what I want it to be."

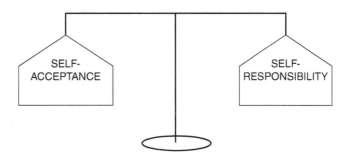

Figure 13.3

Self-Acceptance and Self-Responsibility in Balance

The emphasis of the "taking-control" process outlined in this *Workbook* has been on the emotional insight that is needed to find the dynamic balancing point between self-acceptance and self-responsibility. Gaining psychological insight by connecting with your true feelings has been the focus of many sessions, *including those dealing with social support, triggers, negative states, external life stresses, and internal issues and conflicts.* Your sessions with your seizure counselor and the personal work with your journal have served as a sounding board for your developing awareness of your emotional self.

In order to learn to accept yourself, you have had to encounter many of the painful feelings that lie beneath the surface but affect so much of your life. Somewhere along the way, you have probably encountered the fear that prevents self-understanding, the anger that interferes with support and help from others, and the self-hate and self-pity that stop movement beyond fear and anger to self-acceptance. It has been necessary to learn about these emotions in order to remove the greatest barriers to allowing your spirit to fully embrace life. The ongoing challenge is to find a way to become okay with yourself, to learn to love yourself, and to understand that it is up to you—and only you—to live your life to the fullest.

In addition to emotional insight, going through this process of "taking control of your seizures" has given you information. Throughout this *Workbook*, as well as in your discussions with your physician and seizure counselor, you have had the opportunity to learn a great deal about the condition of seizures and how to live with them. The sessions concerning triggers, relaxation, aura, drug therapy, and other symptoms of seizures all deal with practical knowledge about the nature of having seizures.

Now you have the information you need to know what is true and what is false about all that you've previously been told about your seizures. You now have the knowledge to think for yourself, to dispel myths, to answer questions that your friends or family members might have. Most important, *you have the information you need to make decisions about how you can best live harmoniously with your seizures.*

Besides emotional insight and information about seizures, the third area of emphasis in this process of "taking control" has been on lifestyle: how to have a happy, healthy, meaningful life. The first session, on making the decision to take control, was a critical one because it dealt with the importance of decision-making and goal-setting in making important life choices. Later sessions on getting support and improving relationships, dealing with stresses, learning to relax, and enhancing personal wellness all have given you tools for making your lifestyle compatible with your needs, whether physical, emotional, or spiritual.

Now you have reached the point where you have completed the process outlined in this *Workbook*. Most likely, you feel much more in control of your seizures and your life than you did when you started. And most likely, you do not feel that you have finished this process. You may be trying to understand and accept some parts of yourself. You may be working to become more independent, or you may be trying to improve your seizure control. You may be in the process of making your peace with not being able to drive or needing some help from other people. This is why we call taking control an "ongoing process." No one can expect to feel that this process is completed in a relatively short period of time. The important thing is that you have the tools to continue this process on your own now, to continue to work toward realizing your optimum potential and toward coping with your seizures in a way that's best for you. One insight that will help you with your own ongoing process is the knowledge that life isn't smooth sailing ahead. New situations will arise; new problems will have to be overcome. By now you have had a lot of experience dealing with unforeseen ups and downs. The important thing is to remember that you have the resources to handle whatever comes your way. *You have in your repertoire a whole toolbox*, which provides you with emotional insight, factual information about seizures, and knowledge about how to have a happy, healthy lifestyle. You may sometimes feel that you just cannot cope, but remind yourself that YOU CAN DO IT. You can overcome setbacks. You can deal with problems. You can continue this ongoing process of taking control of your seizures and your life.

If at any time you find that your life feels out of control or your seizure frequency is increasing, this is the time to get all the help you can. Reread your *Workbook*, set new goals, do a Thought Record, work on relaxation. Sit down with your journal and ask yourself what you need to do to get back on track. Avoid self-blame, and remind yourself about the importance of self-acceptance. Remember that everyone needs help from others, so seek support from friends or a support group, and make an appointment to see your physician and seizure counselor. Do the best you can, and be sure to give yourself a lot of credit for coping positively with the obstacles and frustrations that come your way.

At this point, after completing an intensive program such as this one, most people want to ask: "Where do I go from here?" "What now?" The answer lies in you. Up until now, this *Workbook* has given you specific guidelines about what to do each week. But starting this week, you make the decisions. You can choose whatever ongoing activities and goals are most useful for you. You might want to write daily in your journal, join a seizure support group, or follow up with your therapist or counselor. You might continue daily relaxation sessions, join an exercise program, or put your *Workbook* in a drawer and take a well-earned vacation. The choice is yours. Now it is up to you to determine how you want to continue this ongoing process of taking control. This process does not have an end: it is a way of continuing your growth, of living your life to the fullest, of making a path that leads you where you want to go. May you go in peace and in health!

SEIZURE LOG   For the Week of ____/____/____ to ____/____/____

Init:_____
ID:_____
Week: _____
Type:_____

Instructions: Please fill in the diary at the end of each day to record the number and descriptions listed. This information will be reviewed with your physician at each appointment.

SUNDAY __/__/__ (day 1)
Number of Seizures:_____
Time(s) of day:_____
Duration (sec or min):_____
Description:_____
Location(s):_____
Severity (1: mild, 2: mod, 3: severe):_____
Trigger(s):_____
Precursor(s):_____
Improved with:_____
Impact on your day:_____
Impact on others:_____

MONDAY __/__/__ (day 2)
Number of Seizures:_____
Time(s) of day:_____
Duration:_____
Description:_____
Location(s):_____
Severity (1: mild, 2: mod, 3: severe):_____
Trigger(s):_____
Precursor(s):_____
Improved with:_____
Impact on your day:_____
Impact on others:_____

TUESDAY __/__/__ (day 3)
Number of Seizures:_____
Time(s) of day:_____
Duration:_____
Description:_____
Location(s):_____
Severity (1: mild, 2: mod, 3: severe):_____
Trigger(s):_____
Precursor(s):_____
Improved with:_____
Impact on your day:_____
Impact on others:_____

WEDNESDAY __/__/__ (day 4)
Number of Seizures:_____
Time(s) of day:_____
Duration:_____
Description:_____
Location(s):_____
Severity (1: mild, 2: mod, 3: severe):_____
Trigger(s):_____
Precursor(s):_____
Improved with:_____
Impact on your day:_____
Impact on others:_____

THURSDAY __/__/__ (day 5)
Number of Seizures:_____
Time(s) of day:_____
Duration:_____
Description:_____
Location(s):_____
Severity (1: mild, 2: mod, 3: severe):_____
Trigger(s):_____
Precursor(s):_____
Improved with:_____
Impact on your day:_____
Impact on others:_____

FRIDAY __/__/__ (day 6)
Number of Seizures:_____
Time(s) of day:_____
Duration:_____
Description:_____
Location(s):_____
Severity (1: mild, 2: mod, 3: severe):_____
Trigger(s):_____
Precursor(s):_____
Improved with:_____
Impact on your day:_____
Impact on others:_____

SATURDAY __/__/__ (day 7)
Number of Seizures:_____
Time(s) of day:_____
Duration:_____
Description:_____
Location(s):_____
Severity (1: mild, 2: mod, 3: severe):_____
Trigger(s):_____
Precursor(s):_____
Improved with:_____
Impact on your day:_____
Impact on others:_____

Use **the space below or on back** to describe any significant information not covered in this record:

_____
_____
_____
_____
_____
_____
_____

Were you successful in stopping any seizures this week:
yes ☐   no ☐

Please mark which seizures you stopped with an asterisk (*).

Total: _____   Rater: _____

SEIZURE LOG   **For the Week of** ____/____/____ **to** ____/____/____

Instructions: Please fill in the diary at the end of each day to record the number and descriptions listed. This information will be reviewed with your physician at each appointment.

Init:_____
ID:_____
Week: _____
Type:_____

SUNDAY ___/___/___ (day 1)
Number of Seizures:_____
Time(s) of day:_____
Duration (sec or min):_____
Description:_____
Location(s):_____
Severity (1: mild, 2: mod, 3: severe):_____
Trigger(s):_____
Precursor(s):_____
Improved with:_____
Impact on your day:_____
Impact on others:_____

MONDAY ___/___/___ (day 2)
Number of Seizures:_____
Time(s) of day:_____
Duration:_____
Description:_____
Location(s):_____
Severity (1: mild, 2: mod, 3: severe):_____
Trigger(s):_____
Precursor(s):_____
Improved with:_____
Impact on your day:_____
Impact on others:_____

TUESDAY ___/___/___ (day 3)
Number of Seizures:_____
Time(s) of day:_____
Duration:_____
Description:_____
Location(s):_____
Severity (1: mild, 2: mod, 3: severe):_____
Trigger(s):_____
Precursor(s):_____
Improved with:_____
Impact on your day:_____
Impact on others:_____

WEDNESDAY ___/___/___ (day 4)
Number of Seizures:_____
Time(s) of day:_____
Duration:_____
Description:_____
Location(s):_____
Severity (1: mild, 2: mod, 3: severe):_____
Trigger(s):_____
Precursor(s):_____
Improved with:_____
Impact on your day:_____
Impact on others:_____

Total: _____   Rater: _____

THURSDAY ___/___/___ (day 5)
Number of Seizures:_____
Time(s) of day:_____
Duration:_____
Description:_____
Location(s):_____
Severity (1: mild, 2: mod, 3: severe):_____
Trigger(s):_____
Precursor(s):_____
Improved with:_____
Impact on your day:_____
Impact on others:_____

FRIDAY ___/___/___ (day 6)
Number of Seizures:_____
Time(s) of day:_____
Duration:_____
Description:_____
Location(s):_____
Severity (1: mild, 2: mod, 3: severe):_____
Trigger(s):_____
Precursor(s):_____
Improved with:_____
Impact on your day:_____
Impact on others:_____

SATURDAY ___/___/___ (day 7)
Number of Seizures:_____
Time(s) of day:_____
Duration:_____
Description:_____
Location(s):_____
Severity (1: mild, 2: mod, 3: severe):_____
Trigger(s):_____
Precursor(s):_____
Improved with:_____
Impact on your day:_____
Impact on others:_____

Use **the space below or on back** to describe any significant information not covered in this record:

_____
_____
_____
_____
_____
_____
_____

Were you successful in stopping any seizures this week:
yes ☐   no ☐

Please mark which seizures you stopped with an asterisk (*).

Biofeedback: Experiencing the Sensation of the Brain Changing Itself

Some individuals and counselors may choose to use biofeedback training to augment relaxation training. The following biofeedback procedures are guidelines that the Andrews/Reiter Epilepsy Research Program has utilized with biofeedback training.

Most of us are comfortable with machines. From early life we have had positive experiences with automobiles, computers, cell phones, washing machines, refrigerators, and so on, and we believe that machines are helpful in our lives. Suppose a machine could help you learn to take control of your brain—by letting you know each time you had accomplished the task of changing your brain state? Pretty soon you would be able to go from one brain state to another at will. Your brain would have experienced the "sensation of changing itself."

This has been observed on EEG biofeedback machines, helping some individuals learn to change brain wave states at will. EEG machines record the difference in electrical potential between points on the surface of the brain. It is these differences in electrical potential that are recorded as "brain waves." This same kind of machine is used as a diagnostic tool, to check brain wave activity and to look for areas of focal brain wave disturbance over particular areas of the brain. Most people with seizures have had one or more "baseline EEG" tests for diagnostic purposes but have never used such machines for EEG biofeedback.

EEG biofeedback equipment is designed to make a signal, usually a soft noise, when you go into a particular brain wave state and/or provide a visualization of your brain wave state. Brain waves change normally from states described as "awake, relaxed" to "awake, working on a problem" to drowsiness to sleep. These transitions in brain wave states are normal. Most people don't know what brain wave state they are in, or how to change from one state into another. However, anyone can learn to change his or her brain wave state in a particular way, and to recognize how

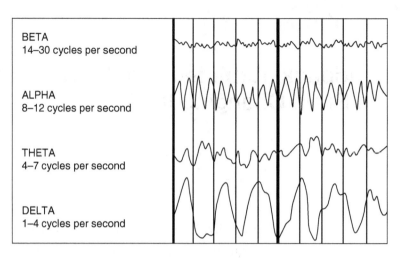

Figure A.1

Normal Brain Wave States

a particular brain state feels, with or without biofeedback equipment. Normal brain wave states are illustrated in Figure A.1.

Definitions of Normal Brain Wave States as They Appear on an EEG Tracing

Frequency: number of waves ("cycles") occurring each second abbreviated as "cps." The term "cps" is the same as the term "hertz," abbreviated "hz," which is the scientific term for the number of waves occurring each second. In this text we use cps, which is more intuitive.

Amplitude: height of each wave, indicated in microvolts (μv).

Awake, active pattern:

Low amplitude 12–30 cps
"Beta pattern"
Experienced as "alert, anxious, energetic and/or tense"
Thinking, problem-solving, worry, decision-making.

Awake, relaxed pattern:

Medium amplitude 8–12 cps
"Alpha pattern"
Experienced as "passive, calm, unfocused, at ease"
May notice heightened body sensations, absence of thought.

Drowsy pattern:

Medium amplitude 5–7 cps
"Theta pattern"
Experienced as "drifting, hazy, dreamy"

Seizures often take place during this state.

Sleep pattern:

High amplitude 1–4 cps
"Delta pattern"
Experienced as sleep.

Are the Brain Waves of People With Seizure Disorders Different From These Normal Patterns?

All individuals, including people with seizures, have a mixture of these normally occurring EEG patterns depending on how alert, concentrated, relaxed, tense, drowsy, or asleep they are. During actual epileptic seizures, "spikes" are seen, which result from the electrical activity in the brain occurring during the epileptic seizure itself. These "spikes" do not appear during nonepileptic seizures. At other times, individuals with seizures may have waking patterns that are the same, slower or faster, or more irregular than individuals who do not have seizures.

Individuals with complex partial epileptic seizures often have temporal region EEG slowing, theta pattern, that is slower than the normal alpha pattern pictured above. For example, they might experience themselves feeling awake and relaxed when their brain waves are at 4–7 cps. It is useful to know that if you have complex partial epileptic seizures, your EEG pattern may be slower than what is average for other people. (Please note: A slow EEG pattern does not correlate with lower intelligence.) Conversely, as noted in earlier sessions, the EEG during nonepileptic seizures is normal.

Can EEG Biofeedback, or the Alpha State Itself, "Cure" Seizures?

No, EEG biofeedback cannot "cure" seizures, epileptic or nonepileptic. Nor is there a specific EEG brain wave state that actually "cures" seizures. Our research has simply shown that training individuals to go into a relaxed, awake brain wave state in the alpha range (8–12 cycles per second) at medium amplitude (50 microvolts or more) will help them reduce seizure frequency and develop a sense of being in control. In the majority of our research subjects, this improvement was a lasting one.

Biofeedback and relaxation are relatively new fields of research, and their medical benefits are still being evaluated. Researchers use two different techniques to reduce seizures. Several researchers, notably Sterman, recommend a more rapid rhythm, called sensorimotor rhythm (12–16 cps) rather than the alpha rhythm (8–12 cps) recommended here. While both of these rhythms serve to suppress the slower theta rhythm (4–7 cps) and can be effective for decreasing seizure frequency, we recommend the alpha rhythm rather than the more rapid sensorimotor rhythm because patients have reported feeling much more at ease in alpha, thereby enhancing seizure control. Other researchers also have reported excellent results from training patients with seizures to go into an awake, relaxed alpha rhythm.

How Does Biofeedback Actually Work to Reduce the Frequency of Seizures?

We simply do not know the answer to this question. In looking at the various research approaches to EEG biofeedback for individuals with seizures, it is interesting to note that different approaches have been found to be effective. All of them teach people to change their brain wave state, all result in decreased seizure frequency, and all seem to give people a greater sense of being in control. It appears that learning to change the state of the brain, on a moment-by-moment basis, has a major effect both on seizure frequency and on how much a person feels "in control." This improvement occurs without changing the baseline EEG pattern of an individual, as it appears on a regular diagnostic EEG.

As previously mentioned in the *Workbook*, it may simply turn out that short sessions of the awake, relaxed alpha state are effective because they relieve stress and produce mind/body relaxation. EEG biofeedback sessions may act like meditation or vigorous exercise to lower a person's level of tension and arousal. This reduction of tension could then act to prevent target symptoms of all kinds, including seizures. Some individuals with seizures use relaxation techniques to prevent seizures, incorporating relaxation in a daily routine. Others use relaxation techniques at the onset of a seizure or in a stressful situation to stop the progression of the symptoms. Either or both can lower the number of seizures one experiences.

It may be that the greatest benefit of relaxation training for people with seizures is that it gives them the sensation of being in control. It is undoubtedly of great value for people to regain a sense of being in control of their own brains, after suffering a loss of self-esteem from a malady that makes them feel helpless and out of control. Additionally, some people have reported that when they sense an aura, or a negative state prior to a seizure, relaxation training has enabled them to go into an awake, relaxed state that can help prevent the seizure. The experience of "the brain changing itself" may make biofeedback with relaxation training such an effective tool for people working to take control of their seizures.

Undertaking EEG Biofeedback Training

Who Will Do the Biofeedback Training?

The most desirable option is to see your own seizure counselor for biofeedback training, because you are already on your way toward building a therapeutic relationship together. If not already trained in the use of EEG biofeedback, counselors can obtain training by attending a seminar offered by the authors of this *Workbook*, or from one of the resources mentioned at the end of this Appendix. If this is not possible, you can consider a referral to a biofeedback specialist for this aspect of your "taking control" program while continuing to see your epilepsy counselor weekly or biweekly to discuss your progress and proceed with Sessions 7–11.

Scheduling

Biofeedback sessions are usually scheduled weekly for 5–6 weeks, then every 2 weeks for 1 or 2 months, and then once a month for 3 months. The total number of sessions required depends on individual progress, interest, and consideration of cost. Biofeedback practice sessions are generally 30 minutes long, but this may vary from 10 to 30 minutes, depending on how long each person can concentrate optimally on the EEG training. Specific scheduling options include the following:

1. Weekly 1½ hour sessions (30 minutes of biofeedback and 60 minutes of counseling, proceeding with Sessions 7–11). Progress will be optimal with this option.
2. Week #1: 1½ hour session (30 minutes of biofeedback and 60 minutes of counseling, proceeding with Sessions 7–11).

    Week #2: ½ hour session (biofeedback only)
    Week #3: 1½ hour session (biofeedback and counseling)
    Week #4: ½ hour session (biofeedback only), and so on

3. Meet every other week for 1½ hours (30 minutes of biofeedback and 60 minutes of counseling, proceeding with Sessions 7–11). Choosing this option will mean that it will take longer to make progress with biofeedback.

4. Weekly 1 hour sessions (30 minutes of biofeedback and 30 minutes of counseling, proceeding with Sessions 7–11). Plan to spend at least two weeks on each session, since you will only have ½ hour for discussion at each session.

Making the decision: Do you want to begin biofeedback training?

___yes ___no

Biofeedback Training

Note

GIVE THE FOLLOWING INFORMATION (WHICH CONTAINS A BIOFEEDBACK TREATMENT PROTOCOL) TO YOUR BIOFEEDBACK THERAPIST. THIS MATERIAL IS NOT INTENDED FOR INDIVIDUALS TO USE ON THEIR OWN.

The following Biofeedback protocol for use in enhancing seizure control is based upon work with patients researched by the Andrews/Reiter Epilepsy Research Program, Inc. It is intended to be utilized by counselors or therapists who have experience with the application of biofeedback instruments.

Biofeedback Session #1: Becoming Familiar With the Basics of EEG Biofeedback

1. Explain what will be done in today's session. Discuss the patient's questions and concerns.
2. Attach electrodes to the patient. Turn on biofeedback machine. Hear alarm, which tells you to avoid a certain brain wave pattern.
3. Set alarm for a theta pattern (4–7 cps). Explain that the first goal is to avoid the sleepy, hazy state of theta—to "wake up." The patient has reached this goal whenever the machine is silent (no feedback), most likely meaning that the patient is thinking in the beta pattern (13–20 cps).
4. Now reset the frequency window for the patient's current brain activity, so that he or she can hear the "auditory feedback" of this instrument. Explain that from now on, this feedback will be reinforcing the desired brain wave states that have been set on the machine.
5. Set open window at alpha: 8–12 cps, amplitude 10–150 μv. If a client shows no brain wave activity above 7 cps, then the window for training should be lowered to the highest level of brainwave activity that is seen naturally. For example, if the highest level seen on resting EEG is 6 cps, set the training window at 6–12 cps.

    Explain that the patient will hear the reinforcing audio feedback whenever he or she goes into the alpha range, which is an awake, relaxed state. The alarm will go off whenever the patient goes into theta, so this state should be avoided.

6. Instruct your patient to lie back and relax in a comfortable lounge chair. Explain that the purpose of this next exercise is to help the brain associate a slow deep breath with going into the awake, relaxed alpha state. After many sessions of practice, a patient may be able to go into this state simply by taking a relaxed deep breath.

To the count of 4, tell the patient to take a slow deep breath through the nose down to the diaphragm and abdomen. Hold breath for 1 second. Slowly release this breath through the mouth to the count of 4. Repeat this slow deep breathing a few times and see if the patient can go into the alpha range, at which point the patient will hear the auditory feedback. (Tell the patient not to be concerned if he or she is not able to do this today. There will be ample opportunity in future to practice this.)

CLINICIAN'S NOTE

In teaching deep diaphragmatic breathing, be sure to watch patients and help them to avoid shallow high chest breathing (hyperventilation). In some instances, hyperventilation can precipitate seizures. On the other hand, deep diaphragmatic breathing is an effective relaxation technique that will often help them avoid or abort seizures.

---

7. To facilitate free interaction with the EEG biofeedback machine, read the following script to the patient: *"Think about different things that make you happy, sad, or worried. See what kind of brain wave state you are in while you are feeling or thinking different things. Ask questions, experiment, and indulge your curiosity. This is your chance to learn to feel comfortable with the EEG biofeedback apparatus, as well as to become more knowledgeable about different brain wave states."*

Biofeedback Session #2: Finding What Works to Produce an Awake, Relaxed Alpha State

1. Explain what will be worked on in this session. Discuss patient's questions and concerns.
2. Set window at 8–12 cps, 10–150 microvolts. Explain that the purpose of this session is to try various autogenic relaxation methods, which may produce an awake, relaxed brain wave state. When this state is reached, the pleasant "auditory feedback" will let the patient know that he or she has been successful.
3. Practice an autogenic technique such as this one, where you lead the patient through the exercise by slowly reading something like this:

Sit in a comfortable position. ... Let your breathing become slow and relaxed. ... Become aware of the palms of your hands ... sense the palms of your hands ... now become aware of the soles of your feet ... sense both soles of your feet at the same time ... good ... Now begin to warm your palms, forearms, and upper arms at the

---

same time. … Keep all your attention on your arms as you make them feel warm and heavy … warming your hands from the palms all the way up to the shoulders … good … Now move your attention to your legs … your legs are becoming warm and heavy … beginning with the soles of your feet and moving up to the ankles, calves, knees, thighs … all your attention is on your legs … your legs feel heavy and warm … good. . . . Now move your attention to your shoulders … your shoulders are becoming warm, heavy, and relaxed … you feel your shoulders melting into the chair . . . good.. . .

4. You may choose to continue this exercise with other parts of the body or to switch to another autogenic relaxation exercise, depending on how the patient is responding. The goal is to try to achieve feedback 40% of the time during this or similar exercises.

Biofeedback Session #3: Finding What Works to Produce an Awake Relaxed State, Part II

1. Explain what will be worked on in this session. Discuss patient's questions and concerns.
2. Set window at 8–12 cps, 10–150 microvolts. (If the patient achieved 10 microvolts or more, 40% of the time in the previous session, then increase lower range of amplitude by 5–10 microvolts; for example, set window at 20–150 μv.) Explain that the purpose of this session is to try various visualization methods, which may produce an awake, relaxed brain wave state. When this state is reached, the pleasant "auditory feedback" will let the patient know that he or she has been successful.
3. Practice a positive visualization, which might include an ocean beach, or walking through the forest along a dirt path. Once you agree on a scene that has peaceful and relaxing associations for the patient, verbalize this visualization for a few minutes. Follow this with a period of silence to allow practice, self-visualization, and listening for the feedback that will signal an awake relaxed state.
4. A second method of reaching an awake, relaxed brain wave state involves positive thoughts. Suggest that your patient pick a positive thought such as peace, love, or well-being, or concentrate on an affirmation such as "I believe in myself." Thoughts have great power and can be useful in teaching oneself to relax and feel at peace. Ask the patient to pick one of these, or another thought or affirmation, and follow through by concentrating on this positive thought for a period of time, trying to produce the auditory signal that indicates an awake and relaxed brain state.
5. Note that much of this session may be conducted with you out of the biofeedback training room. Many people find it easier to concentrate when they are alone, although some patients are not comfortable with this arrangement or feel the need for frequent comments and assistance. Allow 10 minutes or so at the end of the biofeedback session for comments and discussion.

Biofeedback Session #4: Progressive Relaxation

1. Explain what will be worked on in this session. Discuss patient's questions and concerns.

2. In this session, the patient will utilize a progressive relaxation exercise in order to reach an awake, relaxed alpha state. This exercise is the same one that was taught in Session 6. Today the patient will either listen to a digital recording of this exercise or you will read it aloud. As in previous biofeedback sessions, the patient will hear auditory feedback whenever in an awake, relaxed state. Instruct the patient to sustain this state with feedback for as long as possible.

3. Set window for 8–12 cps, 10–150 microvolts (µv). (Increase lower range of amplitude by 5–10 µv per session, if the patient accomplished previous level in last session.)

4. Read the relaxation script (or a recording) from Session 6. If your patient is unable to produce alpha during this relaxation exercise, lower the amplitude setting down to 10 µv. Encourage your patient by telling him or her to "let go" even more, with positive suggestions that "you can do it." If the patient appears sleepy and/or is producing theta brain waves, give him or her a problem to solve to wake up. You may also utilize autogenic techniques, visualization, or positive thoughts if these were useful in biofeedback sessions #2 or #3.

Biofeedback Session #5: Further Practice With Progressive Relaxation

1. Explain what will be worked on in this session. Discuss patient's questions and concerns.

2. In this session, the patient continues to practice progressive relaxation exercise as a method for reaching an awake, relaxed state. This time, the patient will first attempt the exercise without a written script, verbal instructions, or a recording. Later in the session, he or she can utilize the tape again, or you can read aloud the relaxation script. It is important here that the patient not become dependent on your voice or presence (or on the tape or mp3 recording) in order to reach an awake, relaxed alpha state.

3. Set window at 8–12 cps, (10 to 50)–150 microvolts. (Lower amplitude setting depends on the patient's progress in previous sessions. Set it at 5–10 µv above level that was successfully achieved 40% of the time in previous session.)

4. Read the following instruction to the patient: *"Try a progressive relaxation exercise on your own, utilizing slow deep breathing and attention on relaxing different parts of your body. Do as much as you remember of the exercise that was introduced at your last session, but don't worry if you forget parts of it or make up your own variations. The important thing is to learn to relax on your own. Whenever you are in an awake, relaxed alpha state, you will hear the reinforcing auditory feedback of the biofeedback machine."*

5. The patient may now practice with a recording or with verbally guided relaxation, and reinforce the time spent in alpha by taking a deep breath.

6. Instruct the patient in a homework assignment that consists of practicing progressive relaxation approximately 10 minutes a day, with or without the assistance of a digital recording.

Biofeedback Session #6 and Subsequent Training Sessions

1. Explain what will be worked on in this session. Discuss patient's questions and concerns.

2. The purpose of the EEG biofeedback training sessions are to work on spending more time in an awake, relaxed state, and to gradually increase the amplitude of the alpha waves produced. You will gradually raise the amplitude setting on the

feedback machine to help the patient reach the goal of alpha at 50 microvolts or above. Once the patient can reach this goal, he or she should sustain it as long as possible during the biofeedback training session.

3. Set window at 8–12 cps. As training proceeds, gradually raise the lower limit of the amplitude to 50 μv. (i.e., 50–150 μv). The lower amplitude limit is never set above 50 μv unless a client already demonstrates a baseline alpha at 50 μv, at the start of EEG feedback training.

4. Read the following instructions to your patient: *"Practice a progressive relaxation exercise, deep breathing, visualization and/or positive thoughts. Try to maintain longer and longer periods of an awake, relaxed alpha state. Plan to spend most of your session on your own in the training room, leaving a short time at the end for follow-up with me."*

5. Periodically check the patient's progress. This is done by recording what percentage of the practice session he or she spends in alpha, and at what amplitude. This information will help you to chart your patient's progress and keep track of improvements.

6. Once the patient has reached the goal of being able to go into an awake relaxed state at 8–12 cps, 50–150 μv (or less if *very* relaxed), he or she will then spend time in the sessions learning how to use this new skill. The patient can use the ability to change his or her brain wave state when tense or over-aroused, experiencing a powerful emotion such as anger or fear, or when sensing a pre-seizure aura. Between training sessions, ask the patient to begin to work on taking a deep breath and trying to change the brain wave state to awake relaxed, whenever he or she remembers or feels the need to do so. Discuss progress with applying this skill to various life situations at every subsequent biofeedback or counseling session.

Yoga by Rosa Michaelis

What Is Yoga?

When thinking of yoga, most people in the West imagine an incredibly fit and flexible body that bends into positions that far exceed the range of motion of an average person's joints. But those visual images of yoga reflect the Western perspective of yoga, which is often dominated by an external, somewhat superficial measurement of success.

Yoga is not about what a posture looks like from the outside. It is about what it looks like from the inside of the person doing it. It is about finding and accepting the balance between the follow-through of yoga instructions and personal assessment of what seems to be right in the moment. Therein lies one of yoga's most powerful tools: the recognition of the validity of inner guidance, and that sustainable happiness can only be found if you deliberately detach from the motivation to succeed.

The term "yoga" summarizes many different traditions. Each tradition encompasses techniques geared toward integration of the human mind, body, and personality. Depending on the tradition, one will find commonly practiced physical postures intermixed with breathing exercises, contemplative practices, ethical guidelines, and philosophical ideas.

How Can You Decide if Yoga Is for You?

Ultimately, only you will be able to decide if you want to explore whether yoga will be helpful for you in the process of taking control of your seizures. Remember, don't avoid trying yoga because you think that it is only for people who are fit, flexible, or followers of a spiritual path. It is fine if you focus on what is most useful to you and give yourself permission to ignore the rest.

One thing is for certain: neither a review of research nor the sharing of personal experience can answer the question of whether you will benefit from the practice of yoga. The key to understanding the potential benefits of yoga is to establish a regular practice.

From a yogic perspective, setting an intention means formulating a plan of action; for example, you might decide to attend a community yoga class twice a week. Here are some core yogic principles that highlight the benefits of yoga for mind and body:

- **Yoga is action-oriented**: follow-through is the measurement of how real an intention is. Yogis apply this tool just as much to movement as to thoughts. Observing your own follow-through with the intention to commit to a regular practice of physical postures will result in success that will help you build confidence.
- **Yoga is present-oriented**: it allows you to realize that the present moment is the only real opportunity to manifest change. The fact that you might have failed yesterday matters just as little as the hope to succeed tomorrow. Yoga teaches you to accept the past and to let go of worry about the future.
- **Yoga is habit-oriented**: following the previous statement, this might sound paradoxical at first. From the perspective of yoga, good choices in the moment lead to the formation of good habits, which is the safest way to eliminate bad habits. Modern science describes this with the term "neuroplasticity," meaning that the repetition of these newly introduced actions leads to a systematic strengthening of new connections between neurons in the brain.

If You Think You Would Like to Start a Yoga Practice, How Do You Get Started?

Yoga teachers emphasize that good yoga practice combines regular attendance at classes with regular practice at home. A yoga class should be a safe environment in which you can try new poses. You should only practice the poses at home that you have mastered, that is, poses in which you are confident about getting into the pose, staying in it, and getting out of it comfortably by yourself.

If you have never done yoga before, you can look for beginner classes. If you have doubts regarding your level of fitness and flexibility, be sure to speak with the teacher in advance to find out if the classes will be appropriate for you. During class, make sure to use common sense: if you are not sure whether you can get into a certain pose safely, don't do it, or ask the yoga teacher for assistance and more detailed instructions. Good teachers will usually suggest modifications in order to tailor the general idea of a pose to the individual student. If you notice pain or other worrisome symptoms, do not look at others or try to be brave, but come out of the pose and notify your teacher. Keep in mind that it is always better to be safe than to be sorry. Sometimes yoga teachers will go around during class to adjust their students' poses. If an adjustment does not feel comfortable, you always have the right to politely refuse the adjustment. The practice of yoga is very safe if it is done with respectful awareness of your own comfort zone and is undertaken with proper instructions.

Note

If you have an EEG that shows epileptiform changes during hyperventilation, it is necessary to avoid certain techniques that include fast and heavy breathing.

Joining a yoga class not only allows you to practice yoga under the guidance of an experienced teacher, it also has a social component. Going to class allows you to spend time in the company of other participants—each one of whom has his or her own story and strives to get closer to his or her own purpose by attending the class. One of the rewarding features of practicing yoga in a group is a feeling of community, which occurs with little verbal communication among participants. Each student wants to be able to trust that his or her process of balancing the inner comfort zone with the external instructions is met with respect and compassion. No one should feel pushed to achieve the outward form of a posture by worrying about what anyone else might think.

Resources for Further Reading

McCall, T. *Yoga as Medicine*. New York: Bantam Dell, 2007. www.drmccall.com

Meditation

First: Select a focus for concentration during your meditation sessions. Consider using a phrase, prayer, mantra, or scripture verse; you may want to select one that has particular meaning for you, such as, "Lord Have Mercy." Or you might select a visual image, such as a candle flame, a cross, a Buddha, or a different spiritual picture. Some people use breathing as a focus.

Second: Set aside 10–20 minutes of uninterrupted time daily for meditation practice. Sit comfortably in a straight-backed chair or cross-legged on the floor. As with relaxation exercises, meditation begins with allowing your body to relax. Adjust your position and clothing until you feel comfortable; then try to keep your body still throughout the meditation session. Let your breathing become slow and relaxed. Scan your entire body for tension, releasing tension and relaxing deeply as you do so. You may want to do a brief version of the relaxation exercise described in Session 6 of this *Workbook*.

Third: Now that your body feels more relaxed, sit quietly while you think of the words or image you have selected as the focus for your meditation. Concentrate on this focus, allowing other thoughts and feelings to pass without judgment or comment. Cultivate an uncritical, quiet, compassionate attitude toward yourself and your meditation efforts. Whenever you notice other thoughts, simply let them go, refocusing your attention on the object of your meditation.

A Word of Caution Regarding Meditation

It has been our experience that individuals with seizures may show increased seizure activity during initial attempts to meditate simply because our minds tend to become more active when our bodies become still and we decrease distraction through sensual input. We, therefore, recommend that individuals

*who want to establish a meditation practice for relaxation purposes use scrip-
tural meditation, guided meditations (e.g., mindfulness meditation by Jon
Kabat-Zinn, Richard Foster, or similar programs), or seek the guidance of an
experienced teacher. Your seizure counselor may have experience with guided
meditation or, if not, may be able to refer you to a respected meditation
teacher.*

Resources for Further Reading

Chodron, P. *How to Meditate: A Practical Guide for Making Friends With Your Mind*. Louisville, CO: Sounds True, 2013.

Foster, Richard J. "The Inward Disciplines: Meditation." *Celebration of Discipline: The Path to Spiritual Growth*, 3rd ed. San Francisco, CA: Harper, 1998, pp. 13–32.

Kabat-Zinn, J. *Mindfulness for Beginners: reclaiming the present moment-and your life*. Louisville, CO: Sounds True, 2011.

Joel M. Reiter, MD, is Associate Clinical Professor and Director of Neurology training, Emeritus, at UCSF—Santa Rosa Family Practice Residency. He conducted a private practice in Neurology for 35 years, devoting clinical and research time to investigating behavioral interventions that improve seizure control and quality of life for individuals with epilepsy. He is boarded in Neurology and received degrees from Harvard, New York University, and University of California, San Francisco. In 1981, he and Dr. Andrews founded the Andrews/Reiter Epilepsy Research Program. He subsequently published *Epilepsy: A New Approach* and other pioneering work; lectured internationally on neurobehavioral management of epilepsy; and served as the sole neurologist in Bhutan.

Donna Andrews, PhD, is Director of Therapy Research at the Andrews/Reiter Epilepsy Research Program. At age 18, she contracted viral encephalitis, followed by complex partial seizures refractory to multiple antiepileptic medications. Donna had a unique insight that enabled her to achieve complete seizure control. She utilized this experience to develop treatment methods that allow her to work effectively with thousands of patients. She and Dr. Reiter researched these methods and describe them in this workbook. Dr. Andrews has a Master's degree in Rehabilitation Administration from the University of San Francisco, a Ph.D. in psychology from the SFPSP, and she travels the globe to lecture and treat patients.

Charlotte Reiter, NP, earned her BS in Nursing and Family Nurse Practitioner certification from Sonoma State University, where she was the first nursing graduate to be chosen as a commencement speaker. She brought skills honed in developing patient education materials for UCSF's Family Practice residency program to writing and editing *Taking Control of Your Epilepsy: A Workbook for Patients and Professionals*. As a College FNP at Santa Rosa Junior College, she coordinated with the Enabling department to provide services for students with epilepsy and developmental disabilities. She edits publications for the Andrews/Reiter Epilepsy Research Program and writes/edits for the Tarayana Foundation, a Bhutanese nonprofit.

W. Curt LaFrance, Jr., MD, MPH, is Director of Neuropsychiatry and Behavioral Neurology at Rhode Island Hospital (RIH) and Assistant Professor of Psychiatry and Neurology at Alpert Medical School, Brown University. He is the neuropsychiatrist for the RIH Comprehensive Epilepsy Program and a faculty member of the Brown Institute for Brain Science. He studied at Wake Forest University (BA in psychology), Medical College of Georgia (MD), and Brown University (MPH). He trained in Brown's combined residency in Neurology and Psychiatry and is double boarded. His research is in neuropsychiatric aspects of epilepsy, somatoform disorders, and traumatic brain injury. He is co-editor of *Gates and Rowan's Nonepileptic Seizures*.

CPSIA information can be obtained
at www.ICGtesting.com
Printed in the USA
BVHW091734080122
625025BV00005B/17